SUNSHINE UPRISING

by

P. E. FISCHETTI

1846 E Innovation Park Dr STE 100 Oro Valley, AZ 85755
1-855-674-2878 | info@stonehengeliterary.com

Stonehenge Literary and Media is committed to excellence in the publishing Industry.

Published in the United States of America

ISBN: 979-8-8690-0369-0
eISBN: 979-8-8690-0370-6

Part I
Lincoln Street

Chapter 1

Peg's feet dangled in the sand with her toes pointing down sweeping those last grains of warmth for the day just before she stepped up on the wooden bridge and slipped into her sandals. The walk of three blocks to her apartment on Lincoln Street was the saddest part of Sunday evenings, she mused, as she crossed the scarcity of activity on Beachside Avenue in Cape Atlantic. It had only a few cars trembling by at a snail's pace that barely interrupted the last of the beachgoers for the day, which had included families dragging all kinds of sundries back and forth to their apartments on the north side of Lincoln Street with their faces shining various shades of red from the sun's radiation.

On this Sunday in April of 2022, the south side of Lincoln Street was lined with houses full of citizens who never went to the beach to suntan or swim, unlike most humans living next to the beach. Instead, they only went to the beach for walks, bike riding, or watching blastoffs of the *Atlas V, Falcon 9 & Falcon Heavy* rockets into Space recently.

They did their swimming or tanning, if at all, in their backyard pools. Some of them were rich with exclusive homes on quiet streets, but most of them were retirees of state or city jobs or veterans with pensions to supplement their social security and spent most of their time in their favorite darkly lit corner bar, *VFW,* or *American Legion Hall* if they weren't fishing or boating. They all had a common dislike for the north side of Lincoln Street, full of old apartments with a diverse population and lots of activity involving people talking in groups and laughing out loud.

As the sun blasted its last rays of the day from the West directly down Lincoln Street, Peg strode with her head down, eyeing the asphalt, for the last part of her block, trying not to notice the Caribbean teenage drug couriers reporting for work at the poolside of the block-wide and several blocks long Neptune Apartments complex on the north side of Lincoln Street. With various degrees of hyperactivity, the teenagers would smoke cigarettes, vape weed, or drink from bags of hidden bottled beer; and tell Island stories of deals that went down when they were young kids. Most had been recruited by the A1A Pawn Shop owner, Anmar Douglas, on his yacht that traveled the various ocean islands looking for talent. This group of eight lived in two, two-bedroom, hell holes in the complex that bordered Peg's one-bedroom apartment building, a decent stand-alone building of four units.

Peg existed on the top level which gave her some feeling of comfort and distance from the drug activity. Ammar's A1A Pawn Shop was a block away facing the main road, A1A, that ran forty-one miles from the entrance to the Cape Atlantic Air Station, just north of the Port, to *Sebastian Inlet*. This thin strip of land, never more than two miles wide, was better known as the *Space Coast*. The Pawn Shop anchored the corner of the strip mall in front of the local *American Legion Hall* at the end of Lincoln Street.

Anmar appeared to run an honest business in the two and a half square miles of Cape Atlantic, but besides selling pawned goods, that were possibly stolen and illegitimately traded, the store was a front for his local drug services which he ran for a wealthy family and received a substantial cut. As a young teenager, growing up in the Bronx, he learned from some of the scummiest crooks to be a pawn trader and sell to the public what he wanted, after he came to this country with his family just before the 1979 Iranian revolution. He learned the drug

4

business as a college student in the eighties while living in downtown Baltimore. But now a twenty-something-year-old boy, a relative of a Baltimore drug lord taken down by the FBI in 2020, was getting out of a Florida Federal prison in Orlando soon, after doing eighteen months, and Anmar had received word to provide for him.

The Covid crisis was finally receding enough nationwide, except for the South, to bring back the tourists to the Space Coast. Florida State government was determined to mitigate the crises into a battle of natural selection and survival of the fittest, where only the strong withstand death.

Peg Patterson was someone who found the heights of anxiety from the extremes of situations. Covid had tied her hands emotionally and physically for two years. She was ready to break free. But tonight, she was hungry and felt dirty.

It was true there was drug activity in Cape Atlantic on the *Space Coast,* but most of the customers were Europeans looking for pot or cocaine when they came off cruise ships at Port Atlantic for the day. She had seen a few transactions on Lincoln Street and heard about stories from other occupants on the Street, but non-drug citizens of Cape Atlantic had nothing to fear in reality. The teenagers who worked for Anmar had no time or the balls to inflict crime on non-customers. If there was violence in Cape Atlantic, it rarely became a crime statistic. The Cape Atlantic Police along with the Port Atlantic Police were under orders to take care of most assaults, robberies, or drug transactions themselves without reporting them as crimes. The local economy needed the tourist business and crime could not be noticed by the public or reported to the tourists as a problem.

Peg was in the sixth year of finishing her teaching degree at *Eastern Florida State College* in Cocoa, Florida on the mainland. She was a Progressive Democrat and had been in a funk about State politics ever since the last three Florida state elections fearing a fourth in the Fall, State Elections. Her politics were a rarity in *Brevard County* for millenniums, who were either far left-wing progressives or right-wing conservatives, unless they were high school dropouts who tended to stay away from politics and voting or good folks who straddled the middle hoping not to stir up trouble. Peg was more moderate than the far left but wanted women to win out ultimately. However, she did love men, but she was tired of their domination of power in society, especially in this town, even though she loved the Mayor, Jackie Calvanese, and followed him at every town meeting in person hoping to catch a word with him afterward.

She did some Nanny work for a rich family living on Merritt Island, which paralleled Cape Atlantic to the west, but made most of her money selling clothes for *Macy's* at the Merritt Island Mall. It also gave her access to deep discounts that kept her wardrobe updated. She liked fashion but rarely had a chance to dress up other than work. As much as she loved the beach, Peg adored Merritt Island because it had a spectacular Wildlife Sanctuary that masterfully split the Indian and Banana Rivers before slimming to a point of land just south of Satellite Beach.

Her life ambition was to educate fourth graders at Satellite Beach Elementary School where she grew up during the last decade of the Space Shuttle launches. Peg was uncertain about some things in life, but she was specific about not teaching first, second, third, or fifth graders as an elementary school teacher. From her experiences, it was embedded in her brain that a nine-year-old kid, starting fourth grade, was the most important age to teach and the most impressionable. Peg personally felt lost at that age and that it cost her a productive decade of her life. She had studied nine-year-old kids extensively since high school and found them to be the most interesting human beings on the Space Coast – at least the girls. For the most part, she found them to be curious, smart, attentive, polite, and athletic. They were generally under control, interested in fashion but not nuts about it yet, pre-pubescent for the most part, but ready to learn what was going on in their bodies. And unlike when her mom grew up, they were physically active in sports and body development. The boys were half and half in qualifying for the above description; the better half was even more interesting in some ways than the girls, but the lesser half had the Florida disease FBHS – fishing, boating, and hunting syndrome, according to the Peg doctrine. Most of this group were lost causes, Peg hypothesized sadly, but some were retrievable with the help from the Florida Male types that might get their attention – Fish and wildlife officers, Police officers, war Veterans, and Firemen. Another sliver of boys would be swayed by athletic types: coaches, former baseball, and football athletes (which there were plenty of from the Space Coast area) that could mentor kids that age. The rest would have to be treated with respect and taught as well as possible, but she knew in her heart they would end up in the corner bars on the Space Coast at her age causing trouble or drinking themselves to death.

At twenty-eight, she had wasted four years working in retail full-time out of high school and screwing boys her age. Since she started college, she stopped wasting her time with any young men near her age and wanted the calming effect of older men. She liked them generally to be age fifty and above. Currently, her crush on the reigning Mayor of Cape Atlantic, who lived several blocks away and was fifty-two, took up most of her romantic concerns. He seemed to care about the perceived drug problem on Lincoln Street listened very well to her concerns and had high political aspirations in the state. He wanted to build a new development on a mile of the current Azalea Avenue that went by her apartment and make it a southern extension of Cape Atlantic Avenue. It would have wonderful stores, condominiums, bike paths, and all the Cape Atlantic City services in one town center. It would be a perfect destination for some money folks and clean up the apparent drug problem at the same time. In his first six years as mayor, Jackie had used federal and state funds to remake the northern mile of Cape Atlantic Avenue into a gateway to the Port.

Peg was currently in a dry spell and had little time to find romance. Now that almost two years of the COVID-19 virus had forced her mostly inside and lonely, she was hoping this Spring would be a re-awakening of her senses and sexual feelings. A thin summer dress felt like the right thing to throw on after her shower as she decided to drive up to Barry's Chicken Shack, a mile north on Cape Atlantic just across George Royal highway in Port Atlantic. She would order enough fried chicken and sides for the week and drink a cold draft while she waited eighteen minutes for the frying. Frankie, the woman bartender, would entertain her during her wait. She assumed Frankie's other job was being a self-employed hooker or stripper with her aggressive sexual personality. She was brash with her language and usually had an audience of guys at the bar enjoying her presence. Her style was to sexually harass male customers as much as possible and get big tips from the fantasies she created for them.

Peg drained half of the cold draft of Stella down her throat, helping to overrule her anxiety for the coming week. Overall, she poorly managed her disorder with on-again, off-again medication, alcohol, and being one with the ocean. She had not been to the Psychiatrist for six months to update her prescription, which had been very effective for several years. Her medical insurance had forced her to find a psychiatrist that accepted Medicaid (which was impossible) or pay her current one an exorbitant amount of money she did not have. Instead, she settled for the numbing sensation of alcohol and more time with the ocean.

The doors and windows of the shack were wide open which helped funnel a pleasing draft of air through Peg's dress. The cooler wind helped dry off the wetness of her just-showered and uncovered pubic hairs. She loved to not wear underwear after a beach day. It somehow let her feel still connected to the Beach and the Ocean – one with the earth. She called her day at the Beach, her 'Sunday of Sea Level'; where the Earth met the Ocean, the Sun left the Horizon, and the grains of Sand were pounded into submission by the Waves – and like Time were endless in number.

Peg felt she had a talent to write, at least in her fantasies. At times she could gaze at the head of a Stella draft before sucking it down and seeing a poem or the beginning paragraph of a short story. Unfortunately, she would never write it down. When she walked on the beach, battling the incoming and outgoing ocean with her feet, she became overwhelmed by the power of the tides that moved oceans over a hundred yards, in and out, four times a day. *This was nature providing the entertainment*, she thought, *where forces of the universe were the actors for her to witness.* When she wanted to find God or a higher power, that was the place to be.

Getting As in schools was never a problem, it was her parents who seemed worthless to her while growing up. Lester Patterson and Hazel Bannister were older hippies who had survived tripping on LSD, bong hits of pot, snorting cocaine, and breathing in the poison of methamphetamines. Their incessant years of partying, working at service jobs, and following bands all happened while living inland near the city of Cocoa in trailer homes off US Route 1.

Hazel always lost track of her period and her use of birth control; therefore, became pregnant again during a Dead Head tour in June of 1993. She decided this time to forgo a sixth abortion and have a baby at the age of 40. She believed, after watching a late-night recycled evangelist during a meth high, that God was trying to tell her something.

They met in the Fall of 1977 in a bar listening to Steely Dan on the jukebox, they revealed that they both loved the newly released "Aja" album. Later that evening, they ended up in Lester's trailer listening to the phonograph in high fidelity and started having sex somewhere before the first side ended. Lester performed 'coitus interruptus' and rolled over towards the spinning disc and flipped it over to Side B. As the needle dropped on the Vinyl, Lester lowered on Hazel and erupted into climax near the end of the four minutes of the first song 'Peg.' Afterward, he finally felt 'Home at Last' cuddling his new companion Hazel following his perfect climax.

They cared little about parenting or saving money for college. Lester was currently spending half the year on the West Coast cultivating pot, mostly in California and Oregon; and living out of a well-constructed-for-living van in Slab City, California, and playing music. He drove home to Hazel for the end-of-the-year Holidays with hundreds of pounds of pot to sell to finance his next year's exploration. Lester's goods would find their way into Anmar's selling network on the Space Coast.

Hazel now lived locally in a nicely maintained trailer park inland off US Route 1, just south of Titusville. She was a lifelong server, who looked older than her sixty-eight years from constant smoking and sporadic meth use.

Peg was no hippie and could only take Hazel and her smoking friends in small doses. She assumed she had been molested at some point, waking up in the beds of strangers all the time. When she reached puberty, her mother protested her wanting to wear a bra and panties for years. She assumed her anxiety came from the fear of strangers and feeling insecure about her home and future. Worrying was an obsession that she had turned into an art form.

Peg had tied her shoulder-length, damp black hair into a ponytail at the bar and traveled to get her weekly chicken without makeup on. Her constant tan and thinness gave her a hidden attraction if you were looking for a woman full of anxiety. Her posture at times hid her full B-cup breasts and muscular legs. She was a walker but otherwise avoided

10

athletics. Her half-buttoned-up dress showed a good deal of her chest to someone on her left side, which was unintentional, but felt great as the wind continued to spin through the room.

Eyeing her cold Stella, Peg avoided most eye contact while she was parked at the end of the bar away from the main door. The shack had seating behind her for about thirty and a cute outside deck that the owner, Barry, would come around at times and complain that nobody used. A trio of men hovered around Frankie at the other side of the bar as Peg waited patiently for her chicken. She was in no hurry as she worked to finish her first draft and would quickly order a second.

The next week in April would start with classes on Monday and work that she hated. Her internship was the best part of her week as she would go to Satellite Beach three days a week to student-teach. It was a pleasure compared to retail work. On every other Wednesday, she would sit in the back at a Cape Atlantic Council meeting at the dashing new City Hall building and watch the mayor conduct business. He would always check in with her after the meeting for any update on Lincoln Street he should know about. One day she hoped he would take her for a nighttime walk on the beach. It was a dream she obsessed about in her present fantasies.

She checked IG on her phone and looked at posts and pictures by past friends from high school and acquaintances since, quietly she heard a deep voice emanating from her left. Frankie left her posse and greeted a tall older man with her usual excitement, even coming around the bar to hug him and rub his muscular backside. Peg could not immediately see his face but noticed how well his athletic ass filled his shorts and his barrel forearms stretched on the bar. Frankie hung her small breasts which were barely covered by her top, on his well-developed bicep. He quietly ordered a Stella draft and eight pieces of chicken to go.

Well… he must have good taste, Peg thought, *and if Frankie would leave, she might have someone to talk to for 15 minutes.* She checked her hair and decided to take off her Lululemon glow-on, hair tie and shake out her hair. She liked the feel of dampness on her bare shoulders, then took a big gulp to finish her Stella as Frankie returned to her rightful spot behind the bar. Peg caught Frankie's eye and pointed to her empty mug. She nodded without a smile but brightened up as she served her new customer from behind the bar first.

Peg turned her attention to the older male with thinned-out, partially gray hair, two stools away; noticing his dark brown eyes were peaceful and friendly as he boomed out a "thank you" to Frankie for the cold draft of Stella. His massive hands dominated the handle of the draft beer like a teacup and his large shoulders filled out his florescent orange, *Under-Armour* t-shirt while his green running shorts seemed to barely cover his muscular thighs. A well-placed scar ran vertically on the inside of his right knee underneath his kneecap, indicating past misery. He seemed to be in his fifties, but an athlete. Suddenly Peg worried that her breasts would be big enough for such hands, but she calmed herself with a fresh gulp from her newly served draft.

"This cold draft of Stella is great… isn't it?" he directed at her as she finished a hurried swallow.

She looked down her chest to see if she had spilled herself. Finally, her eyes darted towards him and back at her beer before she answered. "I love Stella because it's so smooth. I don't drink a lot of beer," she lied, "usually wine during the week…but I was at the beach all afternoon and I needed a cool beer." She spurted out as she managed a smile.

"You look like it with that tan. I love your dress. You don't see summer dresses much these days."

A smile returned to her face from deep inside, but she then felt nervous to show it, "What brings you to Barry's?" She cleared her voice to calm herself.

"I love to see Frankie and her harem… It's very entertaining." He grinned with confidence, "Actually, I'm dying for the fried chicken. It's been almost four months since I've been here, and I only let myself eat fried chicken twice a year." He started to look at her intently and noticed her cute body and wide-open dress. Her usually hidden breasts and sculpted collarbones atop a perfect chest made her an unobserved beauty to most men, but he noticed; how her hair lay nicely on her shoulders, freshened by the drafts of wind flowing by.

"You live down here?" Peg blurted out after another deep gulp.

"I have a condo on the beach in Atlantic Oceanfront… and get down here 3 or 4 months a year. I live outside of DC."

"That sounds nice." Peg felt a sweet vibe but then was disappointed when she saw him hesitate to disclose further and turn back to his beer, "I live here," she muttered, "I'm finishing my degree in education, and I hope to teach at Satellite Beach Elementary in the Fall." She let her smile finally light up her face for a moment.

"That's so cool… my cousin is the mayor of Satellite Beach, it's a great little town, but I like it better up here... the beach is so grand."

"I live three short blocks from the beach, it's my life ambition to spend time on it."

"What Street?"

"Lincoln Street."

"Neat...that's where the Pawn Shop is. My wife loves that place."

"I know the owner," Peg blurted out, as she now felt more comfortable with this stranger, who was married. Most men who hit on her never mentioned they were married in the first five minutes of conversation. *I like his honesty*, she thought. "What do you do?"

"I've been retired from a real job since 2011. I've written three novels...well four really since then."

Peg stared for a few seconds, wondering who he was and that he must be loaded. *And a writer...Oh My God!* She leaned over after another gulp of her Stella, "I love to write, but I never put it on paper..." She left that idea hanging as she looked deep into his eyes, they were so appealing, she thought.

"Just keep up your interest, don't worry about it. This is a great place to become inspired, especially walking on the beach."

She felt his eyes on her chest with her dress hanging open. Just then her chicken order came out. Slowly she grabbed her order and finished her beer. "Nice chatting with you, I'm

Peg Patterson. I live on the top floor of a four-unit apartment building on the left. It's the first one...if you ever walk along Lincoln Street just past Azalea. I would love to talk to you about your writing sometime." Peg surprised herself with her offer but felt a kindred spirit with the stranger as she offered her hand.

"I'm Phillip...and that sounds like fun, enjoy your chicken, and nice talking with you, Peg."

She walked outside with her heart beating a mile a minute. It was a great way to survive Sunday night. Already an obsession would begin in her head about wondering when he would come by. She should clean up the apartment in case it was soon, she worried.

Chapter 2

On the ride home down Cape Atlantic Avenue to A1A, Peg was suddenly famished as she smelled a chicken leg, already in her fingers, and started munching the steaming hot, crispy crust part of the leg. As she rode home, her heart continued to beat furiously thinking about the writer she had met. Sometimes it would reach one hundred and thirty beats per minute for hours at a time. Tonight, it would calm some as she filled her belly with chicken.

It felt free and breezy to have her dress still half unbuttoned as she turned onto Lincoln Street and rolled into her parking space. All she could think of was making love to the writer as she finished every morsel, including the cartilage, of the chicken leg. Instead of wiping off her hand, she put her fingers through her unbuttoned dress and on her chest, then felt her breathing and slipped her hands between her breasts to her open breastbone area and wiped her fingers up and down her chest. Her eyes closed for a few seconds as she imagined his large hands touching beneath her breasts and up to her nipples. The smile on her face extended from side to side as she opened her eyes and grabbed her bag of chicken to go inside.

As she closed the door and went to wash her hands at the kitchen sink, her heart was still pounding an unending *Ramones* chord. She turned and decided to dart out the door to overcome her nervousness. The daylight was waning, but a walk on the beach would be her antidote to the oncoming anxiety. She ran quickly down the steps and onto the Street with the breeze blowing through her dress as she crossed the beach road in a minute, then hopped onto the crossover bridge and flipped off her shoes. The sun was settled in the west and the dark was minutes away. The ocean met her quickly with the high tide dominating the beach as she breathed in rapidly. She wanted to run into the ocean, but she settled for some swooshing of the water as she walked north, holding up her dress just above her thighs enough to cover her bare ass and pubic hair. Her mind raced with ideas and feelings as the warm water splashed up her legs. She was beginning to feel clarity and contentment:

"I am so alive and young,

So eager to be loved,

Why do I splash the sea and walk so free,

When danger is around the corner,

And make me so sad and displeased,

I want a man to love me and use me when I want,

To be sexual when I feel the urge to flaunt,

But now I can only dream to please me.

Peg felt the darkness as she turned around and headed back to the crossover. The gang would be out, she feared. Again, she ran the three blocks home and saw a new face, older than the teens, moving them out of the street. He nodded and tipped his cap, "Nice dress Ma'am," he called out. She slowed to a walk and turned to notice his nicely cropped beard and dark hair. They seemed similar ages and wondered if he was a recruit for the Pawn Shop man.

She closed the front door, locked up for the night, and shut the blinds. Her dress came off quickly as she grabbed a notebook and a pen. *I should write for Phillip*, she thought, *in case he comes by.* Her poetry came out easily and flowered like love for her body. She found herself between her legs as she wrote. Her pen finally fell out of her right hand as her left hand gave her pleasure. Like a high tide, she kept coming until gravity reversed its course and then receded into the night.

Sleep came naturally after she crawled to her bed like a mountain climber reaching the summit and returning to the base tent. In her dreams, words flowed all night like lava after an eruption. She woke up before sunrise and wrote down what she remembered. It was the beginning of a love story; she decided while thinking of Phillip and his visit. Without breakfast, she put on her sneakers, sports bra, and shorts and ran down to the beach. She made it down to the Cocoa Beach pier and back in thirty minutes. Her energy felt endless. It was time to make a list. What to do for the week? *Work, Walk, Write, and Wonder*, she thought, *this would be her creed for the week and maybe her life,* she hoped.

The following weeks followed a pattern of unusual organization and determination. She had written down her thoughts and ideas every day. It was not a consistent flow, like a storyline, but emotions that needed words or tunes that needed lyrics, but were not ready to be connected to a song.

When she went to the next Cape Atlantic Council meeting, she felt that Mayor Calvanese was losing interest in her. She wondered if he knew of her love for Phillip. It seemed impossible, but something she became concerned about. She decided one afternoon to walk north on the beach towards the top of the Space Coast. She guessed about three miles total, up and back. She hoped to see Phillip. He mentioned that the beach was inspirational, so he might be there…somewhere in the dunes writing away. She was disappointed that he had not come by to see her. *I gave him excellent directions*, she thought.

She reached the rocks at the end of the beach that bordered Port Atlantic and sat for a minute. She looked down the coast south towards the Cocoa Beach pier almost three miles away, seemingly a miniature toy left out in the ocean. More in focus to her eyes were the eight condo buildings (each five stories tall) that littered the last mile of the coastline. Though far back from the beach and ocean, *they housed thousands*, she thought, even though it seemed not to match the lack of humans on the beach any time she walked up this way. She wondered which one of the first eight, was Phillip's. She imagined either the seventh or eighth building. It was about three-quarters of a mile away, just about halfway to Lincoln Street. Every morning she could walk three miles and hope to run into Phillip. *It was worth the exercise*, she surmised.

Her creed for the week turned into a month. Work, Walk, Write, and Wonder became her mantra. Every day she did her three miles, hoping to impress Phillip with her writing, but he was not to be seen. She finished her classes and hectic schedule. Now she would finally graduate and start the whole job-searching thing, but there was only one job she wanted.

May was the beginning of summer in Cape Atlantic. Most of the Northerners had gone home for Canadian Spring and Summer. The crowds were even scarcer on the beach as the sun got hotter. The ocean became warmer and more delicious for Peg. She loved to spend up to an hour at times in the ocean; then setting up an umbrella and a chair, hiding farther back in the dunes, imagining how Phillip wrote farther north.

She noticed the young man, around her age, who called her "ma'am" one night on Lincoln Street, walking into the ocean and swimming. He played, like she did, for a long time in the ocean. Finally, he retreated within fifty yards of her, but unaware of her. He looked maybe, Middle Eastern, but nicely built, surprisingly without tattoos. He sat shirtless on the beach for an hour reading a book. She was impressed.

19

As she lounged under her umbrella, he took the pounding of the Florida sun on his already dark skin. Finally, she gave in to the heat and headed to the ocean to cool off. She did a quick dip and felt refreshed. Her body was feeling toned and tan as she walked wet towards her retreat in the dunes. The bikini she had purchased for the season fit her perfectly as it tied behind her head, revealing her shoulders and arms. Her breasts fit nicely into their cups leaving an open plain between, revealing her ribs up to her symmetrical collarbones. The wetness gave her a feeling of nudity as her suit was cemented to her body. Her nipples pushed through her suit revealing her fullness. The past few weeks and the heat had given her some confidence about her sensuality, missing since her post-high school days.

"Hello Ma'am…how's the water? Still refreshing?"

Peg came within ten yards of him and stared at him. "It's very nice, thank you…" she decided to stop and ask him a question. "What are you reading?"

"Oh, this is my easy-reading pleasure… just a Gresham book. I just can't stop picking them up. I think I've read twenty-five of them." He seemed to like what he saw in front of him, "What's your name?"

"Peg…I live on Lincoln Street, next to the Neptune Apartments. How about you?"

"I got out of prison…a couple of months ago. The Pawn Shop guy knows my family from Baltimore and is helping me get on my feet…I'm Dragmar by the way, nice to meet you."

Peg looked at him and was stunned by his honesty. "Prison huh! That's pretty brutal. Drugs?"

"I was young and pretty stupid. I thought this drug lord in Baltimore was some kind of God. I was a soldier for him. It's a long story. Maybe we can talk sometime. Right now, I'm staying out of trouble and starting classes this summer."

"You know the Pawn Shop guy is a drug and money launderer person."

Dagmar laughed, "Yeah, he's pretty small-time and contained. Nobody cares about what he does around here as long as he stays inside City limits and the Port area."

"So, you are doing some consulting for him?"

"He wants me to keep some of his minions in line, but I'm not interested. I'm hoping to be inland in six months, but I do like this little paradise of an ocean down here."

Something stirred in Peg, maybe a hollowness of waiting for someone who was not coming. She knew meeting Phillip had started an obsession that made her feel something new, but he was older like the mayor. Dagmar was twenty-something, an age she had sworn to stay away from. She blurted out, "Why don't you come over for dinner night? I can make something simple, and we can walk on the beach at sunset." She felt emboldened by her sudden confidence.

Dagmar sat up and took off his sunglasses. His dark eyes pierced her soul, "That would be heaven. Let me know which night works for you."

"How about tonight around seven?" Peg shocked herself with the suggestion, not able to shut down her longing for being close to maleness. The wetness on her body seemed to disappear with the intensity of the sun's rays and her inner body heat. She felt close to naked standing in front of him, wondering if she had stepped out too far. It had been years since she had been so forward. During her post-high school years, alcohol usually freed her inhibitions to go after sex. This was different, she wanted sex, but much, much more. Something that would soothe her anxiety for an evening and maybe an insight into prison life and someone connected to the Lincoln Street gang. That excitement twirled in her stomach as she waited for an answer.

Dagmar felt a stirring in his pants, thinking of a nice lady for the first time in three years. Overall, she was not his type, but it had been so long since he had been with his type, maybe it was all just fantasy. Porn had been his only outlet, not movies but just pictures on the internet. Always a young woman breasted and blonde usually got him going, but it was over six years since his last real relationship, he thought, what did he know?

Maybe he could talk to her, like a college friend. He yearned to be in a learning environment, he was tired of all the machismo pride around him and the mistreatment of women. Before prison, he had been like that too, now he was different. The prison had taught him composure. It was that or insanity. He read books constantly and did meditation. The eighteen months went quickly after the first two weeks. It was nice to miss two northern winters in Florida because he loved the warmth.

He wanted a companion. Someone who loved to learn like he did. What a treat it would be to talk about something other than the wives of LA or NYC or American Idol or the Voice. *He realized she was waiting as he tried to focus on his response*, he screamed to himself, *respond to the woman*!

"I'll be there at 7 pm… I'll bring some wine."

Chapter 3

Peg's body tingled with joy the whole way home. She removed her suit and showered immediately. The fire between her legs could not be extinguished as she turned on the cold water at the end of her cleaning ritual. She hoped to keep from sweating as she cleaned up and cooked. The air-conditioning worked best when she was cooled off in the shower first. The first few seconds were torture, but she screamed a rhythmic verse of obscenities from 'Lil Wayne' that distracted her, and finally, after thirty seconds, she caught her breath counted to sixty, and then turned off the shower. The fire was out but the burning embers remained to ignite her with Dragmar for the night.

As she toweled off, she wondered about attire for the night. Should she go with the Frankie-whore style or the preppy-virgin look? It was a tough choice, so she merged the two and decided against any undergarment (which was her favorite thing after a beach day) with her nicest summer dress that could be buttoned up to her neck. She left three buttons undone for now. Her hair needed some work, so she decided to curl it to give it some bounce. She added some eyeliner and lipstick and there she was, she agreed, styled for love.

She laughed and hinted at a broad smile as she wondered what it might be like to be in love as she lay down on her couch and closed her eyes. Soon a dream occurred with her at a party in the corner of the room watching her parent's friends at her age. People were dancing to a beat that she could feel. She tried to find her mother, but she was swept up by someone with a lot of hair, then she felt a lot of weight on her, she tried to scream but could not. Suddenly she awoke, sweat was on her forehead as she looked at the clock and worried that she had only thirty minutes to cook something.

Dagmar stayed at the beach until six p.m. reading his novel. He was dying to finish, but the priority of dinner with Peg filled his mind instead. Maybe he could find out the mystery tonight, he thought, because he was dying to know the ending. A pretty woman his age asked him to dinner, *how lucky,* he said to himself. As horny as he was, he was determined not to have sex tonight. This could be something special, he decided, and he did not want to blow it on the first date.

As he walked back to his dingy apartment, Dragmar kept thinking about Peg. She seemed to have an edge, and a bit fragile maybe, he surmised from their short conversation. He had noticed her several times on Lincoln Street, keeping her head down to get home. A cautious cloud of worry seemed to be hanging over her personality, like a character in one of the mystery novels he read in prison, but in real life, he was very interested to have a conversation with her and find out more clues about Peg. One thing was for sure, her body was pretty sweet, he decided, nothing perfect but everything to notice.

Luckily, the other boys in the apartment were on the streets doing work. He had the bathroom to himself to make himself presentable. He had little patience for their youthful slander about women. He was already looking for another place. There was some money coming his way.

He took a scorching shower for as long as he could survive the boiling on his skin. He loved the pain of heat. It made him feel reborn. Hot water and cleanliness were something he never got enough of during his experience in prison. His JBL Pulse speaker seeped out some cool jazz that helped him feel calmer. A white linen shirt made him look darker than usual with some beige shorts. He liked looking dark with help from the sun and everything looked good in the mirror. Picking up some wine around the corner and getting to his dinner date on time were his next two priorities. Prison kept him on time, it was a hard habit to make and one that he wanted to keep.

Thank goodness for microwaves, Peg said to herself. To the rescue would be some frozen *Alaskan Salmon*, sautéed in a pan with olive oil and *Old Bay* seasoning with *Uncle Ben's* long-grain rice and *Birds-Eye* frozen broccoli packages cooked in the microwave. She could knock out a decent-looking meal from the freezer through the microwave to the table in fifteen minutes. She loved all kinds of fish, but rarely got her act together to get fresh fish, so frozen was better than fried. She sometimes liked her chicken fried and that was for convenience.

She was putting on the final touches when a knock came on the door. He was early, she noticed, five minutes ahead, now that's a good sign. *Prison keeps you on a schedule*, she guessed to herself. She looked forward to learning more about his experiences, he seemed honest and willing to share them. Surviving a prison experience without becoming a monster seemed something special.

The knock came again as she reached the door and unbolted it without looking through the keyhole and immediately heard, "Hey Peg...nice to see you."

She was frozen in space for a second as she searched for words, "Phillip...my goodness...you came by."

"Yes...I just came back down this month. I was away for six weeks. I was walking the area and I thought I should knock on your door."

Her anxiety returned in full force, but she acted quickly anyway, "This is so awkward, but I have a young man coming over tonight for dinner... maybe we could meet some other time...soon! Could I get your number?" Peg feared a disaster was moments away.

He pulled out his phone, "Sure... what's yours?"

"321-631-2484... I'm so sorry. I would love to talk with you about writing. I walk up to the Port every morning hoping to run into you." She said without thinking.

"No worries. Have fun tonight. Call me sometime or some morning on your walk."

"Will do...Phillip. Thanks for stopping by." She smiled nervously while her chest started panting as she closed the door quickly. Panic suddenly overwhelmed her. She went to the kitchen for some whiskey, swigging a gulp from the bottle before she could find a glass. She prayed that Dragmar would be a few minutes late and not see Phillip leaving the steps to her apartment. What would she say if he did? How could she be sure either way?

"What kind of wine do women like?" He spoke in a whisper as he pondered over the limited selection at the *7-11* around the corner. In Florida, everybody sold beer and wine. He loved the convenience compared to being at college in Baltimore. After growing up during the micro-brewery beer explosion in the last ten years, he had settled on dry red wine for his alcoholic pleasure. It was soothing to his mind and palate. Part of his maturing process, he figured. It's hard to go wrong with a pinot-noir, or maybe she did not like wine at all, he worried. Either way, as he checked the time, he did not want to be late for his date. The line was long but moving with various characters in front of him, all looking like beach bums playing parts as extras in a film about Cape Atlantic.

As he briskly walked around the corner, he eyed the small four-unit structure of Peg's apartment and noticed an older man walking through some cars parked in front. He was interesting looking as he got closer. He was a good-sized older man wearing a *curly-w* hat but seemed to be a little high-class to be a beach bum on Lincoln Street. *Whom was he visiting*, he wondered, knowing there were only four choices and discounting that he lived in one of those apartments. As he started to pass him, the older man looked him over quickly and nodded with a gentle smile. *Wow, he seems familiar…maybe a DC guy with the hat and all…*

Peg was focusing on her breathing as she finished a healthy dose of whiskey in a glass. She swirled the ice in her mouth and started grinding it with her teeth. It was a bad habit for her teeth but helped her nervousness. As she sat for two minutes, she pondered her dilemma if their paths crossed. Her heart was calming as the alcohol worked its magic.

The tap tap on the door was strong and quick, she spit out the ice into her glass and gathered herself, playing with her nicely curled hair as she went to the door. She looked through the keyhole this time and unlocked the bolt, "Please come in Dragmar…welcome to my little abode," she said cheerfully in her best Natalie Wood enthusiastic character. He cautiously smiled as he entered and held the bottle in the bag next to his chest. "There's not much here, but it's nice to have my place on the second floor," she continued to push through her nervousness with colorful conversation as she tried to judge his temperament.

"It's very nice…Peg…Oh, this is for you, I'm sorry I hope you like pinot-noir?"

"Very nice…one of my favorites," she lied as she stumbled to the kitchen to find a bottle opener. "Do you want to open this? While I get some glasses…dinner is ready anytime, but we should enjoy a glass in the living room first."

"Great idea…Peg, you look so nice, and I love your hair." Dragmar tried to make eye contact with her, but her eyes darted towards the kitchen nervously. It added to his feelings of emotion as he looked forward to the wine; he was concerned he might drink the whole bottle before dinner. As he waited for her on the couch, he watched her move through the kitchen. She looked so cute, yet plain and sensual. Something he had not expected. Her summer dress showed great fashion taste, something he loved.

He thought about the man in the *curly-w* cap. *Could he have come from her apartment?* Should he just ask her about him and get it over with or should he live with not knowing? Maybe that's why she didn't meet his eyes. Or maybe she's just a little edgy like he was feeling.

"Here we go, let's drink some wine!" Peg spoke loudly as she handed Dragmar a full glass. "Let's toast to something!" She sat near him on the couch.

"How about your pretty dress and lovely apartment." They clicked glasses. Dagmar drank most of the glass. "I'm so jealous of your place. I live in a shit-hole with three roommates. I hope to get out soon."

"There's plenty of affordable one-bedrooms in Cape Atlantic. Unless you're not planning to stay here."

"It's a great place. I'd be lucky to stay here. I just need a job that pays enough for my place and a car. I've got a lead on some things with Port maintenance. I'm pretty good at fixing things."

"Wow… that's good to know."

"Yeah, engines and machines are my specialty. I learned a lot in Prison. I studied engineering in college a couple of years before I got caught up in the drug stuff."

Peg was feeling some calm for the first time since the beach. The alcohol was working its magic. She was ready to put aside her concerns about Phillip being noticed and zone in on Dragmar. He seemed so nice and calm.

Dagmar filled up his glass again and started to ask Peg about herself. They talked non-stop for thirty minutes and just about finished the wine bottle. He was sure that she wanted to kiss him, but he kept his distance to make her feel safe. The last thing he needed was to make a wrong move.

Peg was shaking with renewed anxiety and dripping with desire as they walked to the beach in the dusk of the evening. The dinner had gone well and was full of lovely conversation. She grabbed a small blanket, hoping to find a quiet spot on the beach to watch the waves and fulfill her fantasies. At the end of high school, she lost her virginity on this blanket on the beach after a summer party. It became a routine for her when she met a new boy. Take a walk on the beach, see the waves, smell the air, feel his touch, wait for the dark, and get on top. She loved to control the sex and find her orgasm. Most of the boys came up short of satisfying her wishes. The first encounter was like an audition, otherwise, she moved on to the next candidate. In her first four years of mating, she found only two boys that met her qualifications, and both flamed out after a couple of months. Then she stopped and reset her feminist priorities. Finally, at age 25, she found an older man, who rocked her world for six months, but then an ex-wife showed up and took him away. She fell into a deep hole of depression and bottled her desires ever since in her head and deep in her soul.

Now Dragmar took her hand as they stepped on the sand in their bare feet. The tide was out, and the only bodies around were folks walking near the ocean. They found an open area of sand in the dunes and threw down the blanket. Her head was spinning from the wine and whiskey and her desires. She stood in front of the blanket and looked through the beckoning darkness to see the energy of the ocean. It was always noticeable even on a moonless night. Low tide was always her favorite. It felt like the coast was holding off gravity for a few hours and the beach became plentiful.

Dragmar stood behind Peg with his hands on her shoulders wanting to kiss her neck and face. As a teenager, he learned about sex from his second favorite sport – baseball. Getting to second base always felt like a big hit in the game. He could hardly forget the vision of her dripping body standing ten yards away from him on the beach with her breasts staring at him through her bikini top. She seemed open and confident about her body even though her anxiety seemed to permeate her personality.

Peg touched his hands on her shoulders and slightly fell back into his chest as she turned her face to the side. She wanted him to unzip her dress and lay back on the blanket, so she could mount him. It was all she could imagine as she felt "Hey Nineteen" in her desires.

Dagmar was battling his penis which wanted to be on Peg from behind as soon as possible. His head wanted no part of easy sex with her, but she was making him hard as a boulder. He slid his hands down her chest and felt no bra and further to her hips and encountered no panties. He felt her breathing hard in his ear as he found her lips and locked them up in a long kiss. His arms felt detached as he slid down his shorts and lifted her dress. His hardness was searching for a spot to slide between her ass cheeks as his hands felt her breasts and pubic areas.

It was not like she imagined as she felt his member on her ass and fingers poking her pussy. She turned to face him and saw his face and then his body. He was muscular and on fire. She thought maybe she should give him a hand job to gain some control because she did not want to be mounted from behind. It made her feel gross and dominated.

30

She wanted to embrace him and touch his hardness, but he grabbed her instead and tried to kiss her again, but she retreated. Her first instinct was to run, but it might make it worse. In one quick move, he threw her face down on the blanket and mounted her in a wrestling mode to control her. All she could do was plead, "Please Dragmar let's slow down…No, No, not like this! Please you're hurting me." He could not hear a thing as he rubbed on her ass while the depths of his desires filled his head with the guilt that always followed. All he remembered was laying on the transgender prison mate that last gave him pleasure almost fifteen months ago. He did it once and felt shame and pain ever since.

Peg gathered all of her strength and gave it one last push to free herself. She managed to turn and face Dragmar and screamed at him as she scooted away. He finally stopped and sat back on the blanket as she gathered herself and stood up to run away. She made it twenty yards and looked back to see a pathetic figure sitting on her blanket. In the middle of the walkover, she leaned back on the railing and put on her sandals, "that little fuck has my blanket." She muttered almost silently.

Her gait was a fast walk as she headed in the dark towards home. "These boys are not worth a shit," she said as a topic in her conversation voice almost detached from herself. She jogged across the beach road, hitting full speed as she passed the Neptune Apartments, she shouted at the darkness around the pool how she felt, "You fucking, worthless, horny dipshits." Finally, she reached her apartment building out of breath and overwhelmed with fear and anxiety. Climbing the stairs, tears started to flow down her face. She locked her door and slid a heavy chair in front of it; then plopped down on the couch and cried herself to sleep.

Chapter 4

Peg woke up to an eerie darkness in her living room. She worked her way to her bedroom and the light in the bathroom. Her pretty dress was littered with sand inside and out as she climbed out of it and backed into the shower. She wanted to feel clean and get back to sleep. Both would be hard to achieve with her present emotions. *What happened?* she asked herself. Maybe this was not the best time for an autopsy of an aborted first date, but she started anyway. The dinner was so nice. Was she too aggressive? She knew he had been in prison and how that could destroy one's sex life. Maybe she was playing with fire. *But he seemed so calm and in control and not a dipshit! Holy Jesus... what a stupid fucking asshole. He had me for the taking and all he had to do was hang for a few minutes. You don't treat a woman like that. Not me anyway,* she thought with exasperation. A roar of anger inside was keeping back the tears for now.

She would continue to cross-examine herself in the morning, but finally declared a recess and fell into a needed state of sleep.

Dagmar pulled on his shorts after the mess he made and listened to the waves. *I ruined everything,* he thought. He curled up on the blanket and closed his eyes. Like five hundred nights in prison, he wiped his eyes before he could sleep.

He heard some people talking near him which woke him hours later. Like in prison, he learned to be alert even when asleep. He rose grabbed the blanket looked at his phone and saw two a.m. When he got back to the apartment, everyone was asleep, but he took a shower anyway. When he took off his shorts, he saw the remnants of his stupidity. He knew he was excited, but ejaculation? *When did that happen? Peg must think I'm a rapist. I must apologize tomorrow, but I'll clean the blanket first. Maybe she will give me another chance.*

Peg awoke to another free day in paradise. She had nothing planned but to get back to her W's or at least three of them today; Walk, Write, and Wonder. Surprisingly, she felt no obsession, just numbness from anger as she cleaned up the mess she left in the bathroom. A new platform that could make her stronger, she hoped. *Is this how guys go about everything?* She wondered, a first step to toughness, perhaps, as her stomach seemed to agree.

She picked up her dress and turned it inside out to throw in the washing machine. As she shook out the sand, she saw the stain. *How could this be? It seemed like only seconds or maybe it was longer that he was on me – treating me like a fucking dog! Oh my god...is this how Monica felt when she found the stain on her blue dress? These scumbags never stop coming,* she shook her head in disgust as she realized the double meaning. *I suppose it is evidence now*, she sighed. And like a high tide coming in, she felt gravity descend a wave of rage that nearly drowned her.

She managed to seal the dress in a plastic bag. It was time to find the mayor.

Chapter 5

With her backpack filled with essentials, Peg headed towards the beach as she tried to reach the mayor on his phone. She wanted to meet with him about the attack and give him the dress as evidence to run the DNA. Making herself feel safe was her first goal, beyond that maybe this guy was a serial rapist and needed to be caught. She wanted to stamp out the uncertainty about Dragmar and not have it overtake her personality.

As she walked to the crossover on Lincoln Street to the beach, her anger was lifting her anxiety, and already on high alert. *Was this how she felt as a child? Being thrown from adult to adult for attention when her parents were too high to notice her*, she theorized. She had too many questions in her head, like in a queue, from the past at times. *Would it be too hard to make a list?* She thought harshly about herself and wondered why she had not written everything down so far. It was etched in her memory --- every detail, so making notes for the mayor would be easy.

She stuffed her sandals in her backpack and enjoyed the sand on her toes. It never seemed to get old. The warmth helped loosen her calf muscles and then her thighs. Her stomach was in knots and her chest felt compressed by gravity. The back of her neck and her shoulders were aching from the physical force of last night's wrestling match. Luckily, she could bench press 160 pounds, but she was at her limit last night, she thought.

After the first ten minutes of her journey, she became lost in listening to the waves and feeling the ocean lap her feet. The tides were shifting the gravity from her shoulders and letting the heat of the sun do its healing on her as she took expanded breaths to ease her chest. She had a T-shirt and shorts on over her bikini. It felt more secure until she could get closer to the Port and find some privacy.

Her phone was ringing, she answered without looking, expecting to hear the mayor's voice.

"Hey, Peg…this is Phillip. Just checking in on you after last night and wondering if you were walking north this morning. I'm set up in the grasses with my canopy if you want to visit."

Confused but pleased, it took Peg a second to switch anxieties in her head. "Phillip…I'm so sorry about last night."

"My mistake Peg. I'm not sure what I was thinking. I just had you on my mind and I was out for a walk. I hope things worked out well with the lucky guy."

"Not so much, but I'm not sure what I was thinking." They both laughed, hoping to reduce the nervousness of the conversation. "I'm not too far away," Peg said with hope.

"Great I'm just north of the crossover between Buildings one and two…back behind some of the mounds and grasses."

The low tide made it hard to see from the ocean, but Peg had a view of the buildings coming up about a quarter mile ahead on her left. "Thanks Phillip…I should be there in ten minutes or so."

Her stomach felt some relief as she thought about getting attention from Phillip and talking about writing with an adult male that was not controlled by his hyperactive, sex-organ. She felt disgusted at the thought again of Dragmar coming on her like a dog in heat. She felt her phone buzz and saw a text from the mayor.

"Peg...I'm free later today around 4 p.m. Maybe Barry's on the back patio?"

"Great...I'll be there. Thanks, so much Mayor Calvanese." She loved to write or speak his name and looked forward to the treat of being alone with the mayor to help relieve her anxiety and anger.

The phone was tucked into the backpack as she saw the crossover in the distance to Phillip's building. The sand replenishing or dumping as she saw it, had finished three years ago but still looked awkward around some of the high grasses. Overall, it cut down on the tides coming in so far and taking sand away from farther in. Eventually, she believed in ten years or so it would look like it did before. She had spent hours watching the bulldozers work in three shifts, twenty-four hours a day, moving sand reclaimed from the bottom of the Port entrance. It was an amazing project that moved up and down the coast from Cocoa Beach to the Port.

Peg found her way around it, and heading up towards the grasses and dunes, she noticed a turtle, about a foot long, had lost its way in the replenished sand area and was heading in open territory towards the ocean. Peg feared that the sand had been dumped up towards the crossovers covering lots of the tall grasses. Normally these land turtles lived in the grasses with underground tunnels built into the sand. As she got closer to the grasses, she noticed another turtle looking out towards the lost friend. Peg wondered if it was calling the fellow turtle somehow. Suddenly she noticed the wayward turtle had turned around and headed north and west back towards the grasses. Moving at unusual speed, the little terrapin covered almost a hundred yards in under two minutes. *A new world record.* Peg chuckled. Finally, the lookout little terrapin turned and headed its way back to the tunnel that they came from, satisfied its friend was heading home.

Peg felt like Phillip could be her fellow terrapin, calling her back into the grasses to be at home. She was pretty sure that the terrapin was the mascot for the *University of Maryland* and wondered if Phillip had gone there or was a big fan. Seeing that he was very athletic looking, he had the appearance of a football player even at an older age. *So much to find out about him*, she thought, as her energy for their meeting was starting to soar.

She was glad Phillip's area was almost untouched by the beach makeover being behind the first set of dunes. It looked like a natural beach dealing with the sea level naturally from the battering of gravity and tides from the ocean waves. It was much more pleasing to Peg. Finally, the canopy came into view, tucked away nicely behind some small hills in the sands. Ironically, the last few hurricanes had dumped some beautiful white sand that naturally transferred into the area without hurting the growth and gave it a softer feel around the grasses. Phillip was sitting in a chair under the canopy with an empty chair across from him. Looks perfect, she thought, and hoped it was saved for her.

He was reading a hardback book when Peg came up behind him. For some reason, she decided to touch his locks of hair growing down his neck as she walked by. Just a touch with her fingers that Peg could not help. "Hi Phillip," she strolled by and dropped her backpack on the blanket.

Phillip was startled but jumped out of his chair to greet Peg with a big hug, "so nice to see you, did you have a nice walk? I have some cold water," he quickly responded.

Peg smiled broadly, still feeling the strength of his hug to soothe her beat-up feelings. She thought for a moment about getting another one and just crying in his chest, but she regained composure quickly and sat down. "I brought some water…so I'm good. What are you reading?"

"Just some Richard Ford…one of his earlier novels that I found a few years ago but haven't read yet."

Peg was excited that she had heard of the American author during a literature class in college. He had won both the Pulitzer and Faulkner awards for "Independence Day" in 1996. The only writer to do so. The class discussed the Richard Bascombe character that Ford had written four novels about in class, but she had not read any of the books. She did know that Richard Ford's "Independence Day" novel was not the science fiction, action movie hit out when she was a kid. It was about a father in New Jersey dealing with family issues. She finally asked, "One of your favorite authors?"

"Someone I admire and a truly great writer. I'm many, many notches below him." Phillip laughed as he sat up and looked deeply at Peg. She looked tired and of course not as dressed up as last night, but something seemed a little lost in her eyes, he discovered.

"What could I read of yours? Anything new that you're working on at the beach?"

"Well, I have written three novels that were published, one in 2013, 2015, and 2020 and I have finished one more that needs a little work, but right now I have a book of short stories that I'm finishing. These are all for a new publisher. It's complicated…believe me."

"Any success? I would love to read the first three at least."

"The first two did pretty well and are getting turned into movies. The third one may be as well, though it is a bit sexy…. So the new publisher wants to wait to publish this last one and the short stories book after the release of the first movie next year."

Peg felt uncertain about her response. She was percolating feelings inside from the hug and attention, but now to learn that he was rich and famous...*Wow!* She screamed inside her head.

"Holy shit...success would be an understatement...that's pretty cool Phillip! A movie huh?"

"Well, I'm pretty lucky. My sons are famous professional athletes with lots of money and they have turned my books into screenplays because the two main characters are athletes. I told them it's a big gamble, but they're on a roll being famous. One of my sons is going to star in them and the other is going to be executive producer. They secured $100 million from somewhere to make the two movies and have rights to my next two books. Pretty crazy huh?"

Peg opened her backpack and pulled out water, but she needed some whiskey right now. "I'm floored, Phillip...I'm sure you're busy..."

"No, no, no...please Peg, I need the distraction. I'm not doing anything for the next month except the short-story project. Forget all that hype stuff. It doesn't mean anything. I want to be the farthest thing from famous. Besides, you gave me an idea for something last time we met that I can't get out of my head."

Oh boy, she thought, here comes the move on her. Unexpected really...but she might be interested at this point in her life for a fling! Peg closed her eyes for a moment and thought, wow I'm all over the place. She opened her eyes and reset her mind to ask, "What did you have in mind, Phillip?"

He hesitated a moment to see the sparkle in her eyes growing. It was something he had not seen in her before. She was smiling as well, which was new. It gave her an extra dimension of appeal. Her maudlin look at the chicken shack seemed underwhelming but cool in a Lauren

Bacall way, but this was sending a chill down his spine. He decided to go ahead with his idea. "You impressed me so much in our little conversation at Barry's. I started to think of a new character for my fourth book based in the City of Cape Atlantic... I've been around here for three to six months a year for almost seventeen years, and I find the town fascinating."

"A new character?" she was relieved and disappointed at the same time. "What came to mind?"

"A woman character...maybe your age dealing with life issues. I thought we could talk about it...and maybe you could help me write it."

Peg felt overwhelmed by the gravity of the moment and lifted herself from the chair. She stood for a moment but wanted the softness of the sand and fell to her knees right in front of Phillip, her eyes filled with tears. Somehow, she was swept forward and fell into his arms, and could feel an ocean of tears cascading down her face. She curled up in his big body like a baby and just hung on as her feelings came out like the tide rushing in to make a new sea level. Her new wall of anger was underwater.

Part II
Sea Level

Chapter 6

At the age of fifty-two, Jackie Calvanese had reached a level of respect he always wanted – a successful second term as Mayor of Cape Atlantic. Now in his sixth year, he had effectively brought in commerce to lower unemployment to fifty-year lows and raised property values to their highest levels in history. He worked tirelessly to increase revenues from state and federal levels to finish the northern section of Cape Atlantic Avenue and build a new City Hall while updating the Library, Fire, and Police Department buildings.

Running for State Senator to represent Brevard County in Tallahassee was his next conquest, and then a run for Governor. He knew that the four major metro centers in Florida – Tampa, Miami, Jacksonville, and Orlando ranked forty-third, forty-fourth, forty-fifth, and fiftieth out of fifty in hourly-median-wage nationwide and could be a big campaign issue. Bringing high-tech jobs to Florida and increasing minimum wages would be a first step. With so many service jobs in the state because of tourism, people could not work full-time at eight to ten dollars an hour and pay their bills. It had to be at least doubled that, he thought. Making public education excellence a priority for all students and mandating health insurance for the service workers would be his first two priorities.

Campaign money would not be a problem because of his family's wealth. Francis Calvanese was a founding father of Cape Atlantic, helping to incorporate it in the early 1960's. He was part of a group of wealthy landowners concerned that Cocoa Beach would extend and incorporate their property for upper-middle-class homes. His father's group wanted to make their own rules in their community. They wanted to build affordable apartments for working-class folks north of Lincoln Street with nice homes for many, including themselves south of it. They also had a vision of Port Atlantic becoming a major income source for themselves and Central Florida. Currently, he was a quiet billionaire in ill health and dying slowly in a lovely nursing home in Rockledge.

Jackie had big construction plans that would start as soon as he left office. He would create a new southern part of Cape Atlantic Avenue connecting it to the redone northern mile that would showcase the rebuilt City Town Center with four high-rise condominium buildings, beautiful shopping, restaurants, and updated apartment complexes. Citizens and visitors could drive, bike, or walk up and down Cape Atlantic Avenue feeling free and safe. Many of the ten thousand visitors coming every day through the Port would spend their money locally instead of busing to the theme parks exclusively. To get the zoning decision from the City Council to allow these four condominium complexes to be twelve stories high, seven stories above the allowable height in Cape Atlantic, the investors agreed to build the city a hundred-million-dollar, junior-senior high school for free. The location was on city land, just off A1A and State Route 528 as you came into Cape Atlantic, owned once by the Calvanese Foundation and given back to the city.

The current Lincoln Street was an east-west demarcation that was not unnoticed by Jackie during his upbringing. An unnatural line was drawn that was similar to what President Lincoln faced as he fought to unite the country until his death. Jackie was born after the turbulent sixties, but unlike most in Brevard County, he saw himself as a Kennedy Democrat and an advocate of civil rights for all people. He wanted the Cape and the Port to be a model area on the Space Coast for those values.

Jackie had five boys; Paul and the apostles; Peter, Philip, James, and John. The apostles, which they were jokingly referred to, headed his construction, electrical, plumbing, and architectural businesses, while Paul, the oldest, headed the biggest law firm in Brevard County located in Titusville. They all worked as kids and teenagers in Jackie's construction business and now had taken over the day-to-day business with Jackie as Mayor. Through various shell companies, Jackie was free of any direct connection with these businesses. Most of his money was in a trust coming from his father's empire.

South of Central Avenue, running east-west, were streets named after Presidents, starting of course with Washington Street, and ending with FDR Street. Francis Calvanese intervened as the streets were laid out. To make room in the town grid for FDR Street, his hero growing up, he left out a half-dozen presidents that he hated. For Francis, a first-generation Italian, the naming of the Streets was a patriotic gesture by the City Fathers to remind citizens of America's history; or at least his version.

Through the offshore, shell companies, the Calvanese family prospered in Cape Atlantic by diversifying in legal and illegal trade. Besides real estate investment, property management, and construction, they ran every vice on the Space Coast including the Port. They owned legal businesses like strip clubs, liquor stores, and the casino boat out of the Port. On the dark side, they controlled illegal drugs, gambling, and prostitution in the area, but it had never become public knowledge so far.

Barry Hornbaker was the frontman for the gambling and prostitution operations. Publicly he ran Barry's Chicken Shack near the entrance to the Casino Boat in the Port. He had made his money in Las Vegas learning the ropes about investment from the famous developer Del Webb in the sixties. Webb was the construction foreman for Bugsy Siegel when he built the Flamingo in Las Vegas in 1946 and went on to develop mega-communities in Arizona and Florida. Barry and Jackie bonded as New York baseball fans because Del Webb was part-owner of the New York baseball team from 1945 to 1964.

Barry also ran a Taxi business on the Space Coast and used his Chicken Shack to funnel most of his cash made from his gambling and prostitution. Otherwise, he was happy to enjoy the Florida life and women from the strip joints on A1A and sometimes a Caribbean transgender boy when Anmar found him one to his liking.

Jackie was sipping on his margarita on the back porch at the Chicken Shack waiting for Peg to show up for their meeting. A decent crowd had filled the Shack from the first Casino trip of the day that went out at noon and returned at four p.m. The next boat would head out at seven p.m. and stay out until midnight. That crowd would fill the Shack and begin drinking during Happy Hour. The Shack was within walking distance to the pier for the Casino Boat. Even those who were hammered could meander the couple hundred yards for a chance to lose their money and continue drinking all evening.

Frankie was the star of the show from behind the bar, shuffling out drinks and cooking up chicken in the fryer. Barry was generally too cheap to hire an extra person when it was crowded so he would hang out from 4 to 7 pm in case it was too much for Frankie to handle.

She was Barry's favorite, even though she was a handful for him to control. At five-foot, ten inches she towered over Barry who was five-foot, six inches…maybe. She was boisterous to the bar crowd in her criticism of him as he kept complaining about the procedures not being followed. Most of the customers loved to see the soap opera play out every happy hour.

Peg arrived just after four p.m. at the Shack, looking refreshed in her beach attire. Phillip had brought her inside to his condo and massaged her feet, ankles, and calf muscles while she lay on the couch watching ESPN with him. She fell asleep in five minutes and when she woke up, Phillip was sitting at the dining room table working on his computer. She was still in her bikini with the blanket wrapped around her. Phillip was in his swim shorts and looking awesome for his late sixties, she noticed. It dawned on her how nice it would be to fuck him right now but quickly realized how bad of an idea it was. *Fucking your mentor never works out well and besides, they were going to write a character together!* She remembered hastily.

After they talked for a while, she felt like her emotions had been filtered by a guru, someone who had listened to her and helped her to find the truth of what she was feeling. Now she knew what she wanted. And there was no doubt --- it was revenge. Peg wanted Dragmar to feel the same way she felt, being used like an animal. She wanted Jackie to find someone to tie him up and ejaculate their load on his ass and take their time doing it.

At the Shack, Peg wore the same white shorts and a sleeveless shirt she had on all day to show off her biceps. She liked having her bikini on as her underwear. She felt it would be inappropriate to complain about someone ejaculating on her with her breasts hanging out and her pubic hair flowing in the wind. Jackie had never seen her dressed sexy and it would be a mistake to start now, she assumed, but this outfit fit in with a beach look.

"Peg my dear, I've been so worried about you since I received your message." Jackie rose and kissed Peg on the cheek and held her with a long hug.

"Sorry, I'm a little late Mayor…I know how busy you are." Peg said softly as she reluctantly let go of him. She lived for these moments of affection with him hoping someday they could go further. They matched up physically, she thought, because her head could rest just below his ear and her chest could settle into his soft abdomen.

He always moved his hands down her back over her bra strap and just above her tailbone and then rested just above her hips as he looked at her before letting her go. This was Jackie's style with any woman he met who had a tight body like Peg's. Looking into her eyes, Jackie asked, "Peg tell Jackie what I can do for you. Let's sit down. Here… I got you a draft… Frankie said you always drink Stella!"

Peg felt invigorated from her time with Phillip and had written notes of what to say to the mayor. She sat down and took a long gulp. The heat was searing through the shade on the patio. She felt her bikini gaining sweat already because the normal breeze of the shack was not blowing through the patio. Phillip had put her into a short trance to remember things in the past that were troubling her. Without telling him specifically what happened the previous night, he realized she was upset about something. Over the years she seemed blocked by this feeling she had about being abused in some manner. All she could remember was the intense anger she felt when Dragmar pushed her down like a dog and started rubbing on her. It was something that had been familiar in her past. Never had she made the connection before being in the trance. Details were sketchy, but she knew she was pre-pubescent and in her bed. Now she could at least feel vindicated about the feeling in her past. Maybe with some more help from Phillip, she would figure it all out someday, but for now, she wanted to present her case to the Mayor about Dragmar.

"Do you know this new guy that works for Anmar, the Pawn shop owner? His name is Dagmar."

Jackie smiled right away, a little surprised that Peg was so quick to get down to business. Of course, he knew Dragmar and his background. It was his idea to get him involved in the business. He

46

seemed like someone with some brains and ambition. "Sorry Peg, I barely know Anmar and his Pawn shop business. Who is this Dragmar?" Jackie lied so convincingly.

"He's my age and just out of federal prison for some drug business in Baltimore. He has some connection to Anmar and his family. Anyway, he is living in the Neptune Apartments with the drug runners that work for Anmar."

"Wow…Peg, you seem to be up on the pot selling on Lincoln Street. Tell me more."

"Mayor as I have reported to you many times, you know a lot is going on every night on Lincoln Street. Those kids meet there every night and get driven around in a van up to the Port every night and fan out to customers."

"How do you know this, Peg?" Jackie looked innocently at her as he did his best to be concerned about the problems.

"I followed them a few times…but that's not the point. This has been going on for years, Mr. Mayor. Everybody knows about it, even the police I imagine."

"Trust me, Peg, if the police knew about it, they would all be in handcuffs!" Jackie did his best fatherly look at Peg without being angry.

Peg stared back at Jackie without moving a muscle, knowing his statement was total bullshit, but not wanting to press it further she kept silent. Finally, she turned an unusual smile on her face as she turned her head slightly and tried to act sexy for a moment. She gave him some seductive eyes and put her hands on his left hand. "Mayor, you know how much I support you. I'm sure you have too much on your plate to know everything that happens on Lincoln Street. I'm here to ask you a favor."

Jackie felt her warm hands and the stirring in his shorts. "Peg… I'm here to serve you. You know that you can tell me anything and I will attend to it. I want you to feel safe in our city."

Peg opened her purse bag and pulled out her spring dress in the plastic bag. "Here Mayor…take this and run the DNA on this patch of sperm on the dress." She stopped for a moment for dramatic effect. "That scumbag Dragmar tried to rape me like a dog and came all over my fucking dress. I want to see if his DNA is in the Sexual Assault Databases anywhere in the country."

Jackie's potential hard-on went limp. He took the bag and kept his eyes on Peg. "Oh, Peg I am so sorry. I can call the police right now to start a report on that creep?"

"No no…just check the dress. I know he was in prison, but maybe he has never been checked for sex crimes. I want to make sure he's not a serial rapist before I figure out what to do with him."

"Done Peg…whatever you want me to do with him I will do."

"Thank you, Mayor, but nothing right now other than testing the dress. I want it back soon. It's my favorite dress."

"I'll make sure to get it dry-cleaned for you. I'm sure you look pretty in it." Jackie reached out and touched her hand, but suddenly she seemed cold and distant as the sweat poured out on the back of his neck and down his back. She was a complex young woman, he thought. He pulled back and waited to say goodbye. Her rare smile had vanished, and her eyes were tearful. Something terrible had happened last night and he would find out in his way. Peg was special to him, like a daughter, but more like a lost soul that compelled him to help her. Sometimes she was too scary to think about. Trouble with a capital T, he reminded himself.

Finally, Peg looked up at Jackie and responded. "I thought I did, but it was a mistake to wear it last night. He could have had me if he had been patient, but he became an animal and treated me like a dog."

Chapter 7

Jackie Calvanese left the Shack with the dress in plastic and headed immediately to an FBI field office in Orlando. Four lights on George Royal Avenue were shinning green for the mile ride to the exit onto Route 528 better known as the B-Line. It was a warmup lap for the forty-four miles of straight expressway with a suggestion for the speed limit to the Airport. Jackie's BMW, made in America, cruised at ninety without a sweat in the hot sun of Central Florida. The Brevard and Orange County troopers knew his car by now and his frequent trips to Orlando International Airport or downtown Orlando, meaning that stopping him for speeding was a worthless endeavor. Besides, they all liked Jackie, he provided well for all the police unions and supported all their causes.

He pulled into the FBI field office and spent time glad-handing everyone in the building as he moved freely to a Lab office in the back part of the structure. Julianna Martino was the head of the Lab and is currently on the phone in her office complaining about several budget cuts hampering her personnel. She saw Jackie and waved him in as she finished the conversation, "Tell those stupid fucking people that the Lab will not be able to process anything else you send me from out of state, starting July first."

Jackie sat down and watched Julianna Martino in action and was incredibly pleased. She was the daughter of his high school buddy, Paul Martino, who had died in 2003 in Iraq. Jackie made sure that Julianna got through college and got her PhD in Chemistry. She was tough as they came and now lived in Orlando with her husband and two kids. Jackie was godfather to both of her children.

"I'm just warning you…any mass shooting in Georgia or Alabama or fucking Puerto Rico, we're not available after July first, if we don't get our money for the full fucking budget! OK…OK…later."

Jackie enjoyed women using the word "fuck" in several variations. Especially smart professionals. It gave them an edge to their personality and was extremely sexy too. "Whew…nice job Juliana. That phone must be burning up north. I think they got the message."

Juliana burst into a big smile and jumped out of her seat to hug Jackie. "Wow, the mayor in my office. This must be important Mr. Calvanese. How are you doing Jackie?" She held on to her hug as she looked up at him.

"Sorry to barge in like this, but I wanted an excuse to see you." He pulled out the dress in plastic. "I got this 'Monica' dress here that I want you to run the DNA nationally."

"Anything I should know about the cum spot? A friend of yours perhaps?"

"Let's say it will be handled in Cape Atlantic, one way or another."

"So, it's revenge evidence! Ha…my favorite kind Jackie. You know that little town of yours sure has some secret shit going on, doesn't it?"

"Well Juliana…we try to take care of things before they become a problem and if they do become a problem, we find a way to send them back to the mainland…"

"Unless they can't make it out of the Banana or Indian River first."

"You have quite an imagination, Julianna!"

"Well as you heard, we are a little backed up, so I'll have to play with this myself in the next few days. Sound good?"

"Perfect…now tell me about my godchildren."

Chapter 8

Peg was thinking through her options after meeting with the mayor. He had made a quick dash for the door a few minutes after receiving the evidence from her. He said there were some people to meet in Orlando and that he had to scoot. She immediately began to obsess about giving him Dragmar's name in connection with the dress and telling him about the disastrous date on the beach. She thought it might be convenient for the mayor to blow her off and declare there was no connection between the dress sample and other federal crimes. Knowing that Dragmar had been in federal prison and was already in the system with his DNA would be the logical answer. But she trusted the mayor and had confidence that he would get to the bottom of her concerns. He had never failed her yet so why would he start now with such an important situation, she decided.

Being an expert in watching detective shows since she was seven, Peg knew that DNA connections for other crimes did not necessarily happen automatically, especially between State and Federal levels. She had seen too many *CSI* shows to trust that government agencies would talk to each other, especially in New York City, where everybody hated each other. And the District Attorneys were always dropping charges and making deals. Besides, she waited to make sure Dragmar had not fallen through some "juvenile system crack of sealed information," or some bullshit like that before he was eighteen. She had seen enough of *Law & Order: Special Victims Unit* to know all kinds of crap that happened in those hidden-away, abandoned warehouses.

What she needed was Detective Goren from *Law & Order: Criminal Intent* to figure this shit out for her. She always fantasized about working with him when she grew up. He was so brilliant, she thought, and unappreciated by his Captains. Only Detective Eames stood by his side. Though she was jealous of her role, Peg loved her feistiness and thought she was cool-looking. They shared the same body type, she thought.

Peg cried watching the last scene of the series when Goren leaves the therapist's office (for some bullshit anger management sessions, she thought), of course in a brownstone row-house on a quiet Manhattan Avenue with trees, and comes down the stairs to see Eames standing next to her car and says, "How did it go?" Goren shows an unusual smile and says, "Fine." Then she says, "There's a case..." (with more blah, blah, blah, she remembered), and Goren looks at her with unusually kind eyes, suddenly appreciating her beauty as a person and a friend that he discovered from talking in the session, and says, "Let's go!" The partners drive off together to another murder scene and hopefully with peace in their lives, Peg imagined. She had watched this episode dozens of times and got emotional every time.

After thinking about Detective Goren, Peg walked slowly down Royal Avenue towards the Beach. She passed one of the *Holiday Inn* Resort buildings (which she remembered as the *Ron Jon* Resort as a kid) and entered the walkway into Brevard Beach Park. The well-maintained campground was to her left, which was next to the concrete floating fishing pier that bordered the Port seaway as it opened to the Atlantic.

She stayed on the walkway to the south side and went through a cover of jungle-type plants providing a cool space for a half-mile or so before the beach. On the right and mostly covered was the first of the eight condo buildings that continued down to Phillip's building. There was a beautiful, multi-acre-sized lake with wonderful swans swimming and some other long birds she did not know walking around it, that she wanted to learn about someday.

A developer had tried to buy this slice of land of the Park (9.61 acres) from the county and develop it into more condo buildings. She attended many of the meetings and was proud of the mayor's leadership in squashing the moronic idea, she remembered. Finally, in 2018, the Port Authority Commission, which ran Port Atlantic, forked over $862,950 to purchase the slice of heaven and permanently add it to Brevard Beach Park. It was a small victory for the people, her father mentioned one time to her.

Dozens of feral cats roamed through the jungle surrounding the meandering walkway. There were small bowls with cat food and water hidden away under the jungle floor for them. Volunteers came through every day to feed the critters. Peg took time to talk with some of the cats and tried not to touch them, fearful of catching something, even though almost all were treated by the county for disease, she remembered.

Finally, she arrived at a trail of sand that would lead her to the beach. As a child, Brevard Beach Park was her playground and entrance to the ocean for her. Her Dad had one good quality, she thought, getting her connected to the ocean. Many times, after school and on the weekends, he would take her to Brevard Beach Park before middle school started. He would park at the resort garage to avoid the eight-dollar charge to drive into the park. The extra walk never bothered her. By the time she was nine or ten, her father would go to the bar in the resort, and she would take her towel and head through the park, following the meandering sidewalk – like she was Dorothy in the *Wizard of Oz*. Eventually, her father would find her on the beach sleeping after swimming in the waves for hours.

Starting when she was four or five, he taught her to swim in the ocean and then watched her for hours, standing at the ocean's edge. After the first dozen times, he did less and less teaching, and more watching. Then after a year or two, there was no teaching, less watching, and more sleeping. And finally, there was mostly sleeping on the beach, no watching, and "wake me up when you're ready to go home, Peg."

It occurred to Peg, just now, that her dad thought it was normal parenting at the time. He grew up in the Fifties when the outside was the best babysitter in the world. Kids explored all day in their neighborhoods. Worrying about abduction was not on the radar of society. He played war in the woods, fished in the plentiful creeks in Pennsylvania, swam in the local pool, or jumped off cliffs in a quarry filled with clear water and sometimes skinny-dipped in a hidden lake on a friend's farm. She knew Lester played sports every day, but was never on a formal team, By the time he was old enough for that, music took over his life. He loved Johnny Cash, Buddy Holly, Roy Orbison, and anybody else from Texas that crossed over from Country music to Rock n' Roll. He headed south for college, first in Athens, Georgia because it had a music scene and finally transferred to Gainesville, Florida, where he fell in love with being a southern hippie. He never came close to finishing a degree but made a ton of friends playing music. By the time he found Hazel, he had settled in Central Florida working construction and playing music in bars at night. There was so much building going on in the early sixties, that he could work as long as necessary and then quit to travel on a band tour playing music or working in a crew all over the south. Hazel became attached to him and started selling things in the parking lots and then inside the festivals. They became a good team and enjoyed themselves in their twenties. Parenting was the farthest thing from his mind. For Lester, playing music and working for bands turned into a profession of selling things to people following bands with Hazel. Mostly they stayed true to each other, but Hazel kept getting pregnant every other year it seemed. Lester was relieved every time she reported "taking care" of it. Finally, when he thought the possibility of her getting pregnant was over because she went five years without expecting, Hazel had a child at age forty and decided to keep her future daughter. Lester was stunned but made the best of it as a father in his forties. He was surprised at first by how much fun it was and spent most of the decade with his little girl when he was in town, but when he hit almost fifty, something changed; and then for the last eighteen years, he slowly let go of Peg and Hazel and needed to be alone. He was gone for a whole year between fourth and fifth grades or was it fifth and sixth grades? Peg could never remember exactly.

It made her self-sufficient, Peg thought, and she was proud of that as the memory replayed of her first years with her father. She forgot how Brevard Beach Park gave her these memories. As she escaped the jungle of trees and plants, she saw the ocean at the top of the dune trail. It always surprised her to see such a mountain of water stretching across and below the skyline. It seemed ironic to her that her one connection to her father was the beach. She wondered if he had lost it. She had not talked to him since Christmas. It was the first year they had not talked for six months in her lifetime since that year he was gone when she was nine or ten. He would be back in October, she thought, and it might be good to get him on the beach and have a talk about things past, present, and the future before it was too late.

She realized that there was a lot to do to be ready for such a summit. It did of course become an immediate obsession as she walked to the shoreline and headed south as she felt the ocean roll back and forth over her feet. The tide was between the extremes which gave her lots of oceans to play with as she weaved between the beach and the water. She was very alone and evolved into deep thinking about her plans for the next month.

First, she needed a job as a teacher, hopefully in Satellite Beach; secondly, she needed to spend more time with Phillip and learn about her passion for writing and how to get it down on paper. This, she surmised, would help her get organized with her thoughts and get her to figure out what she wanted to learn from her father. Next or concurrently, she needed some affection and sex, so she would not end up fucking Phillip (which she knew would mess that mentor-guru thing up); and at the same time, she wanted to figure out the Dragmar dilemma and get past it – maybe! Finally, and most importantly, if she got her father to open up, she wanted to find out what happened to her as a child.

Chapter 9

Interviewing at twenty schools throughout Brevard and Orange Counties became Peg's full-time job in July. She immediately became excellent at it. Her years of watching television gave her clues on how to handle interviews. Central Florida's *PBS* station taught her many things over the years of how to handle oneself properly during an interview. She was a sustaining member since she could write a check. Additionally, dressing up was her forte and gave her a chance to display her sense of fashion while keeping an appearance of business. She knew that men would be making most of the decisions and that gave her an incentive to highlight her sexuality without making it obvious but noticeable. On most days, she would wear a suit jacket over a skirt or dress, then after shaking hands, she would seat herself and take off her jacket to reveal her bare shoulders and an open-neck blouse or dress. She would leave a button or two undone, not enough to reveal any cleavage, but enough to reveal her beautiful tan and tantalizing collarbone area.

She appeared strong and mature while being older than most just-graduated-teaching prospects; and having sales experience, she could convince many a principal to hire her – especially the male ones. Offers came in from fifteen of the schools. Her obsession with detail helped her be incredibly prepared; and her normal personality, which was mostly sullen, came across as serious and organized. She seemed like a teacher that would never be frazzled by fourth graders.

Satellite Beach Elementary was one of the last two to make an offer, mainly because they did not have an opening for a fourth-grade teacher. She waited out an entire week of offers before getting the call for her dream job. She had not talked to Jackie or Phillip about interviewing there. Both offered to put a good word in with the Mayor of Satellite Beach. Since she was busy for the whole month interviewing, they saw very little of her, so independently they each made phone calls to the mayor to make sure the principal was aware of her talents. After scrambling to reassign some of his teachers, the Principal at Satellite Beach got with the program and offered Peg a fourth-grade position.

Fortunately, when Peg accepted the Satellite Beach offer, she believed it to be all of her making. She was mostly correct, but the Mayor of Satellite Beach and the Sheriff of Brevard County made it clear to the male Principal of Satellite Beach Elementary that she was the best candidate for the fourth-grade school position. Her splendid references seemed to make a difference.

Another by-product of her successful interview process was a chance to get some male attention. A half-dozen, older professional men, in the role of elementary principals, asked her out directly. Another two, who were women, asked to have coffee with her, which she accepted immediately. One seemed intent on giving her the ins and outs of working in the County School system and was glad to be a mentor for her, the other was a lesbian looking for a hook-up. Peg navigated through both of those meetings with little difficulty, pledging to keep in touch with the first and clarifying her sexual preference with the second.

The men navigated a less direct route. She understood that sleeping around with school Principals might become negative news that made it around the county school system even before she started working. They each met with her in their offices, asking for a chance to review her application again. For the most part, the principals assessed her best qualities, and some gave her good advice while two of them talked about teaching but left long pauses between anecdotes to look her over and gaze at her best qualities. This more sophisticated type of sexual harassment made it clear that they were interested if she approached them in the future.

After accepting her position at Satellite Beach Elementary, the week of training for new teachers was held at *the Eastern Florida State University* campus, inland near the City of Cocoa. She made it a little vacation by booking a room at the nearby Americana Motel which was a short drive to campus. US Route One had a familiarity for Peg since she grew up in a trailer park just south of there about twenty years ago. Now her parents lived five miles north where US Route One was full of new communities. As Peg drove to her motel, she could see a decent restaurant or two, a hillside with a cemetery, and lots of warehouses that mostly bordered the west side of US Route One with the beautiful, mile-wide, Indian River-Lagoon on the east side.

After the first day of training, the organizers announced a get-together at *Ryan's Pizza & Pub* which had an open-air, top-level bar with a great view of the Indian River in the old section of the City of Cocoa. A gateway town of eighteen thousand people to the Space Coast beaches, Cocoa had been around in one form or another since the 1890's. It hosted *Major League Baseball* Spring Training for the *Milwaukee Braves* in the fifties and for the *Houston Astros* from the sixties to the mid-eighties, but when a big offer came from the City of Kissimmee they left. The main purpose originally for Cocoa was to be a rail hub for the fruit-picking businesses. Now it was becoming a real college town with the transformation of Brevard Community College into *Eastern Florida State University* with fifteen thousand students at the main campus in Cocoa. Peg liked the energy of the area, but it had too many memories of her hippie childhood to be a comfortable place to live and it was a fifteen- minute hassle of a drive to the beach. Some of the scenery looked the same as when she was young, but most of it had been transformed into suburbia.

She sat at the bar drinking a Stella draft while waiting for the top floor to fill up. Most of the attendees were in the air-conditioning of the first-floor pub, but Peg wanted to be in the open air after a day of attending boring lectures. The sun was low in the western sky as the

60

breeze picked up some speed for the usual round of thunderstorms on a summer evening. She knew by the color of the clouds the storms would wait until ten pm or so and not affect her evening. The heat was the only problem for some but for her, it felt great and soothing. She wore one of her summer dresses but with a bra and panties, which were driving her crazy at the moment. After a couple of beers and a bathroom break, they might end up in her purse, she thought.

A group of new teachers came up the stairs and found a table far away from the bar. One of them came over next to Peg to order a beer. He was too young for her at first glance, she thought and wondered if any of the training staff or principals were joining the party.

"Hi…I'm Joshua from Virginia and new to this area. What did you think of today's training?"

Peg noticed his metro-sexual look and soft eyes and wondered if he was an elementary school teacher. "Not much Joshua…it was kind of boring. Now I remember what High School was like." Peg managed to show a limp smile to Joshua, who looked twenty-four at the most.

"I was impressed with the presentations, especially about the diversity in the students. In southwest Virginia, I went to Christian schools all my life and didn't have the experience with different cultures as I will down here…I'm looking forward to it"

Peg immediately wondered how Joshua would survive in the *Brevard County* Public School system, but on the other hand, maybe it would do him some good. Either way, he was not a good candidate for what she needed tonight or tomorrow night. "Well, that's good to hear Joshua, I'm from this area so I guess it's natural to me. Did you go to *Liberty University?*" Peg knew that was a large conservative Christian school in southwest Virginia. She visited there once after seeing *Charlottesville* with a friend when she toyed with going to the

61

University of Virginia. The city of *Lynchburg* or *Liberty University* was not her cup of tea.

"How did you know…huh I'm sorry I didn't catch your name?" "Peg."

"Oh, Peg…is it that obvious? Maybe you can give me some tips to learn."

"Where are you teaching?"

"Merritt Island Elementary School."

"Well, that sounds perfect for you. I think you'll like it. Lots of rich white folks live on the island, but most of their kids go to private schools." Peg paused as she studied Joshua's puzzled look, "Hey… where are you living?"

"My family's pastor found a nice older couple near the school that I can live with until I get settled. I'm very fortunate. How about you Peg? Where are you teaching and living?"

"Well… I live in Cape Atlantic, just north of *Cocoa Beach*, and will teach at Satellite Beach Elementary…fourth graders – my favorite!"

"Me too Peg…we must keep in touch about our experiences. I know I will need some help." Joshua laughed matching his harmless personality, so Peg grabbed his phone and entered her number.

"Call me Saturday and we'll do the beach and talk about the little rascals we're trying to teach. You do swim I hope?"

"Oh, I love the ocean…thanks so much, Peg. You're quite a lady! I'm going to get back to my gang. I'll see you later Peg!"

"Be careful with that beer Joshua…maybe you should drink some before scooting."

He took a big swig. "Now that's better…I think…right Peg!" Joshua gave her a pleasing look with his soft eyes and chuckled as he proudly steadied his beer – which might have been his first in public, Peg thought.

She finished her draft with a long gulp that sent a cool sensation throughout her body. It was a good feeling to have that ability at the old age of twenty-eight, she thought to herself. Peg once imagined herself to be a champion chugger of beer during her years of chasing young men out of high school. Now that memory was in the rear-view mirror, but it was fun to bring out that talent occasionally. The bartender pointed at her to set her up with another one. Fortunately, it was still happy hour pricing.

A crowd full of talking and laughing was forming behind her. Several of the Principals she interviewed with came to the bar, mostly ignoring her, and ordering for a table closer to Joshua's group. One of them she recognized as being an administrator from the County found a stool in the middle of them. He quickly ordered and downed a double Jack Daniels as the group decibel level increased. Finally, the crowd dispersed and left the gentleman asking for another double Jack as he got padded on the back from several of his colleagues. He seemed close to fifty or maybe just shy of her golden age of recruitment. He had a solid head of hair with a little grey, but not overweight and not much taller than her. It appeared to her that he was a bundle of nerves and not enjoying himself yet. Then he lit a cigarette, to Peg's dismay, disgusted that shit like that can still be legal in public places in Florida. He took only two puffs put it out in his finished second drink and ordered another.

Well, that was progress, Peg thought, assuming he was trying to quit, as she could see he was about to join the crowd he came in with. She hopped off her stool and quickly moved in before he had a chance to escape.

"Hello there...you're from Titusville Elementary...right? Counselor person or H.R. person? Francis Richards?"

Francis looked like a deer caught in Peg's headlights, trying to avoid a head-on collision with a young woman and her chest within inches of his left shoulder. He tried not to panic as he managed to turn without rubbing into her bra, which he would have been entitled to because of the proximity of her chest to his shoulder, but his constant awareness of the harassment issues helped him gain control of himself. "Oh...well you have a good memory. Yes, I'm Francis Richards, head of Human Resources for the *Brevard County* Schools. My office is out of Titusville Elementary... And you are?"

"Just a new employee...I thought your presentation was the best of the bunch today."

"Thank you...well once a year they drag me out to this training you know."

Peg moved closer making sure her chest made contact this time as she whispered in his ear, "I'm in room two-o-six at the American Inn on Route One. You're invited to meet me there at eight pm." She moved away went back to her stool and took a nice chug on her second draft.

Frances knew better than to approach her because everyone would see it, but if he left soon and joined the group, nobody would know what just happened. He would have about ninety minutes to drink some more and get some dinner before he would decide to be foolish or take an Uber home.

Peg ate pretzels and peanuts from a bowl offered by the bartender and watched as her potential catch for some affection joined his group of fellow rule enforcers for the school system. She knew during his presentation; that Mr. Richards would make the perfect foil for her needs. And being a top-ranking administrator could not hurt her employment situation. He seemed like he was once handsome and nice but had become cautious and a ball of nerves enforcing an impossible set of rules that led to a constant fear of lawsuits against the school system. She was sure, he had never been propositioned before and therefore would not be able to abstain from accepting such an idea. His sullen penis would be sending signals to his brain like sonar signals from a submarine. Luckily, he showed up at the bar Peg was sitting at and left himself alone for an attack. Her plan was working well.

During the next hour, Peg drank another draft as the salty pretzels and peanuts increased her thirst. Occasionally a fellow new teacher would come by and say "hi" while they ordered something and even Joshua stopped by to say hello again and thank her for her invitation. The beers seemed to affect him as he asked about what SPF he should wear to the Florida beaches in late July, among other things.

Finally, Peg paid her tab and caught the eye of Francis Richards, as she sauntered like a showgirl in her high heels towards the stairs and slowly worked her way down them to get outside and to her car. She knew three drinks was too much for her one-hundred and fifteen pounds to pass a legal alcohol limit in the time elapsed, but it was a short distance, and she was a great impaired driver, she assured herself. The key, she believed, was to drive slowly, cruise just under the speed limit, and always stay in the right-hand lane, she reminded herself.

She felt relief when she opened her motel room door and cranked up the A/C in the room. It was surprisingly clean and comfortable; and opened directly to the outside, so she put a chair under the doorknob and double-locked the door. She decided it was fifty-fifty that Francis Richards would come by, but she wagered he would be on time if he did. Quickly she removed her dress and hung it over a chair, removed her underwear, and took a thirty-second cold shower.

Feeling clean and rejuvenated, she put on the TV and found a baseball game. She put on her dress, pulled back the bed covers, propped up the four pillows, and crashed on the bed. Ready for some pleasure, she thought about touching herself but decided to wait until after eight p.m. Part of her felt ready to explode if she got some affection, but another part of her wondered what the point would be because it would only leave her wanting more. It reminded her of a conversation she had with Phillip when he said, "You cannot occupy two opposite emotions at the same time. For instance, the moments before orgasm, a male reaches an unexplainable set of pleasurable emotions, something that they want to stay with forever, but they go ahead with their climax because at that moment they have very little decision-making power to halt – no fear of what is on the other side because they feel unstoppable. Then in ten seconds, it's over and they feel a vacuum, a great feeling of despair that it's over, and then they think, *that can't be possible*. The feeling they just experienced is nowhere in their consciousness until they achieve it next time."

From that talk, she concluded, that experiencing emotion is all you have – positive or negative. To decide to forgo a positive experience because it becomes absent soon after, goes against the idea of living day to day as a human. We might as well be that turtle, she witnessed, who rarely ventures towards the ocean and only stays in the comfort of the grasses. Then he does and it may change his whole future. Peg smiled to herself at her perception.

She decided to stop arguing with herself and try to think of something positive. She liked to think of Phillip because it made her happy. She tried to not fantasize about him, but he seemed to always make her content inside her head, so lately he was at the center of most of her sexual forays replacing the mayor as providing her sexual self-pleasuring.

She closed her eyes for a fifteen-minute nap and tried to see the ocean playing with her feet. After fading into her thoughts, she suddenly she sat up and looked at the clock next to the bed, it was 8:10 pm and assumed quickly that Francis had declined her invitation. She opened a cold bottle of water from the refrigerator and guzzled half of it. The coolness down her throat helped calm her. She walked to the back wall of the room to the right of the bathroom and looked outside through the high part of the window over the air-conditioner facing west. The sun was still working its way down to a clouded sunset she was loving the cold blast of air on her chest and below. Leaning on the A/C unit, she lifted her dress and started to find her favorite spot for pleasure. The last remnant of the sun's orange glow was mesmerizing as the cold air continued to blast her core. The pleasure was quite different but steady, as she pictured a cowboy riding in from the west, hopping off his saddle, ready to be her toy. She was soon mounting him and finding a beautiful rhythm when she heard a loud knock on the door. Quickly, she backed away from the cold air blasting and looked at herself in the mirror. She decided to accept the look of a cold-hard-bitch without touching up her make-up and was ready to meet her cowboy.

Francis came in carrying a bag and flowers. He apologized for being tardy almost twenty minutes, "I'm so sorry to be late…I'm never late, but the new *Cumberland Farms* on Route One, just down the Avenue, had a load of kids in there. It's quite a super convenience store!"

"Oh yeah, we got one in Cape Atlantic on A1A and North Atlantic, you could spend twenty minutes in there before deciding on something. Kids see it as a night out. They have a freezer room that you can walk right into to buy beer. On most Florida days that is awesome." Peg looked at Francis with a cold smile, "Sorry for my bad manners at the bar, my name is Peg Patterson."

"Nice to meet you, Peg, thanks for the invitation." He said quietly as he pulled out some wine and handed her the flowers. Peg moved slowly to find the ice bucket, filled it with water for the flowers, and put it on the table provided in the room. Francis nervously found two cups poured out some wine for each of them and laid out the goodies he brought: including cheese dip, *Doritos*, *Cheetos,* and amazingly four pieces of fried chicken with macaroni and potato salads.

Peg's pulse sped up as she spoke with an unplanned alliteration, "How did you know all my favorite foods Francis, you're fabulous." She glowed with a suddenly warm smile, realizing that nothing got her going like chips and dip followed by deep-fried chicken with mac and tater salads. She lunged at him with a big kiss on his lips for several awkward moments. Francis managed to balance his wine in his right hand as she pulled away and sat in her chair.

For a moment, she pondered the idea of getting past the nightmare of Dragmar. This would be different, she confidently thought. Going on interviews helped her feel assured to move on. She still wanted justice and was certain the mayor would come up with something.

Francis looked like a young boy at a birthday party as he sipped his wine. Peg heated the cheese dip and took a big Dorito chip to scoop a glob out and balance into her mouth. The taste was extraordinary, she did not realize how hungry she was and grabbed the Cheetos bag and opened it. She finally looked up at Francis and asked, "How old are you, Francis?"

"I'm forty-six, two kids in their early teen years, and divorced."

"I'm twenty-eight, single, and finally graduated from *Eastern Florida State*. I think I started when it was Brevard Community College," she laughed.

"Nothing wrong with that. I finally got my master's degree about ten years ago. How long have you wanted to be a teacher?"

"When I got tired working retail out of high school and went to part-time, I started some nanny work and liked being around kids, especially a nine-year-old. They're smart, but not cynical quite yet."

"Wow...I like that description and now you get twenty-five or more of them in a classroom. Should be interesting."

Peg decided she was done with the chips and would wait on the fried chicken until after some fireworks happened with Francis. She got up and straddled his legs as he sat on his chair. They met eye to eye as Peg took her hands cradled his face and kissed him full force.

Francis lowered his wine and took in her tongue while he gasped for air. She pulled back for a moment as she wondered if his sullen penis had gotten the message yet.

Francis reached around her with his arms and pulled her in for another kiss. He felt her bare shoulders and neck. Peg was already wet from her A/C experience, as she rubbed herself on his crotch center that seemed to be showing some life. Francis moved his hands down her dress lifted it and discovered no panties or bra. Suddenly his members started growing at an exponential rate. His last girlfriend of six months last year was cautious and always on the bottom type of gal, he recalled. He was enjoying Peg's leadership and wanted to please her.

After another long kiss, Peg got up and grabbed his hand, turned off the light, and guided him to the bed. They embraced for another kiss, just long enough for him to remove his pants and shirt. She noticed that he was impressively hard and straight as she pushed him on the bed. Flawlessly, she stepped out of her dress and easily mounted him. She hung over him and barely noticed his hands all over her breasts and his fingers hardening her nipples. Her hair hung over her face as she slowed her breathing as she felt him move deeply inside her. She moved up and down and sideways to get every morsel of pleasure she could from inside her vagina.

Francis was amazed at such a lovely creature above him. He knew the climax was near, but he hoped it would take an eternity. She seemed like a gift from the heavens after years of crap and drama from his divorce over eight years ago. He forgot what youthfulness was like and sexual freedom with a woman. His experiences in his twenties were sporadic and not plentiful. He married his wife because he feared at thirty-three that he would be alone forever. Now he was, for the most part, having given up on the idea of a meaningful relationship again.

"Oh my god," he screamed out as an orgasm was upon him and seconds away. He had no choice; she was in control, and he could not stop it. Peg bent over and kissed him as he pumped a volcano of past frustration inside of her. Her lips were luscious and soft as she slowly left his lips. Peg rolled off of him and stayed close. She reached over his chest for his right hand and slowly led him towards her clitoris. She guided him to the right spot, and he gently complied. Her head settled back as she felt mountains of misery fall off her. Francis found a perfect rhythm and softly kissed her face as she uttered sounds of deep resonance like a bad-ass woofer sending out a thumping bassline. Finally, her voice changed to a higher octave as she battled to reach a feeling above all the misery. She had finally reached her pleasure dome and a great sense of freedom.

It was well after nine p.m. when Peg turned away and Francis pulled back the sheet and covered her. He quietly put on his clothes and then laid down next to her as he put his arm around her and the sheet. Tears were rolling down her eyes as her breathing steadied. He pulled out a handkerchief from his pants pocket and wiped her tears. She gladly took it from him and quietly blew her nose. Finally, being prepared as a gentleman paid off for Francis.

After both Peg and Francis rested motionless in bed for another hour, she stirred and found the bathroom and a robe. Francis rolled out of bed and found his seat at the table, turned on the light, and poured some wine. In a few minutes, Peg appeared and immediately grabbed the chicken and nuked it for 30 seconds. She waited quietly as she looked at herself in the mirror to see what a satisfied but hungry woman looked like. Without much conversation between them, the food feast happened quickly, first, the fried chicken and then the mac and tater salads were all gone followed by a car ride to get ice cream. Peg then dropped off Francis near the Pub to get his car.

"Will I see you again Peg?" Francis asked before he left the car.

"If I have a Human Resource problem, Francis you will be the first I will call." Peg smiled with an extreme look of satisfaction. "With me, I think my life is just starting and I haven't written the first chapter yet, but you could be a good character." She said with a more serious look.

"I'll text you, so you'll have my number. Let's be in touch when you write that chapter. I would be a great supporting character." He leaned over and kissed her on the cheek and held her chin for one last look.

Chapter 10

Juliana Martino contacted Jackie Calvanese from a burner cell phone she purchased for just this type of occasion and left a message for him to meet her in Titusville. She could make it to Titusville in twenty minutes from her Orlando FBI office during her lunch hour and get back in time.

Jackie made it to Vito's Restaurant in Titusville in fifteen minutes, wondering the whole way what the secrecy was all about. The message said it was important. The restaurant was their spot to meet for years in between her work and the Space Coast. Jackie entered through the kitchen back door to get to the owner's office. He was an old friend who provided his location for meetings that Jackie needed to take without notice. It was furnished with a nice daybed for certain discreet situations that did not currently involve Jackie.

For a short time, Jackie and Juliana had an intimate relationship that was ended because Jackie knew it was a mistake. She was currently happy in her marriage and wanted it to stay that way. Still, Juliana felt a deep love for Jackie whenever they met outside her office. He was so charismatic and loveable that at times when she had a few drinks, she still wanted him deep inside of her. She knew it seemed incestuous, but he pulled her out of many wells of depression that saved her life. There was no amount of love that she could repay Jackie and she was happy to provide him with anything he needed at any time.

It had been over a month since Jackie handed over the evidence on Dragmar to Juliana. It was something he had not given much thought to since having only seen Peg once since their Shack meeting in late June. He was concerned something had happened on the date that was not legal, but since she seemed busy with her job search and being successful as well, he was not worrying about it. He was looking forward to celebrating with her and seeing her again. Peg provided a diversion at times for him – a young obsessive woman who thought he was a rock star. He enjoyed helping her and seeing her become successful. Watching after her was important. Occasionally when they met, he would think about sex with her, but he knew deep in his heart that would be a big mistake. He had other distractions for that.

Juliana looked white as a ghost as they sat down in his friend's office. She was all business as she handed over the evidence and the DNA report. "This is a bomb ready to go off Jackie and you may be the target." She said sternly. "What is going on at the Cape and the Port, that would cause this kind of mess?"

"Jules, what kind of mess are you talking about? Who is this kid?"

"I'm not sure we will ever know for certain. The name for the DNA is Alejandro Majada, who has a Peruvian mother who immigrated to Baltimore in the sixties. Dagmar has been his cover for over a decade…maybe longer."

Jackie looked at the report and saw DEA Files highlighted several times, "What the fuck does this mean Juliana?"

"It means that he is their property, and they are most likely coming after you. Are you involved in selling drugs Jackie?" She knew better than to ask that question, but she was pissed to be drawn into this, even if it was her mentor and friend – the mayor.

"I'm trying to run a city and keep the Port clean from that kind of shit. My father would shit if he knew the knuckleheaded crap going on in his properties, but our police, the Port police, and the County Sheriff are all over that crap. Hopefully, re-development will get that thing cleaned up, but we do our best to keep this kind of shit out of the press and certainly away from the hard-working citizens."

Juliana knew the difference between the truth and a politician talking, but in this case, she believed Jackie. She knew how much he cared for Cape Atlantic and the Port development.

"Okay...well be careful... here are the main points. At some point, the FBI got this kid as a juvenile sex offender and trained him to infiltrate "The Turk" in Baltimore, who is probably his father, and helped take him down. The eighteen months in prison was a cover to get him back out as an undercover guy for the DEA in a drug organization. The sex cases are sealed and never will see the light of day to the public. Most likely the information on them and evidence is long gone, except I have a friend who knows the guy who ran the whole Baltimore City joint-task-force operation and is now a big-wig in the FBI. My friend is going to see if we can get an M.O. on sex crimes. This Alejandro was thirteen or fourteen, when he was first adjudicated to juvenile hall in Baltimore, then got busted out by "The Turk" and hidden away for a couple of years, and then was rearrested for the same shit and put directly in the FBI's hands. It was during this time he was broken down and allowed to re-enter "The Turk" network after they brain-washed him into believing that "The Turk" was behind him being sexually assaulted when he was ten to twelve years old. "The Turk" had 20-30 kids that he fathered, living like dogs, and taken advantage of by his soldiers." Juliana adjusted her chair feeling sick to her stomach reporting such a thing. "As far as "Dragmar's" victims are concerned, that prisoner is still in federal prison and named Alejandro. The FBI was totally against using him as "Dragmar" by the DEA, but in Florida, they have lost their power to the drug enforcers. If anybody knew what I knew about this latest "assault" they would probably have him wiped out."

Jackie tried to hide his concern, but his head was spinning with questions. "So other than the fact that there might be a sexual predator on the loose in my town and the DEA watching and listening to me, what should I be worried about?"

"I'm not sure Jackie…to be honest. I have never seen anything like this. Who knows, this might be a vacation for him before another assignment or "THE ASSIGNMENT." He does seem to be an offspring from the "The Turk" probably sired from one of his Peruvian women in his harem in Baltimore. It may be the only reason he is still alive, and they had no idea of his FBI connection. Also "The Turk" had no clue about Alejandro's second arrest, it was handled so quickly and made to look like a drug sweep with a weekend jail stay. The FBI must have put the fear of God into him to get him to flip, a salary, and a ton of bonus money available to him as well when he's finished. Either way, he's out there and we don't know the specifics of his crimes as a youth yet. I'm working on that, and it may take some time."

"OK, thanks Juliana for the heads up. We'll get surveillance on him and let me know anything else."

"Well…one more thing Jackie…I would suggest keeping it on the down-low with any surveillance, the DEA may have him in their sights for now."

Jackie tried to stay cool and gave Juliana a big hug and kiss, "Thanks sweetheart, let's get together soon with the kids. Sorry to drag you in on this."

"Anything for you Jackie…you know that." Juliana squeezed him hard and kissed him on the lips with affection. They embraced for some lingering moments. She wiped her eyes as she headed off.

Chapter 11

Paco Lawrence, a DEA agent in Central Florida, was spending the morning with his informant, Dragmar, in Cape Atlantic. He worked the Space Coast and the rest of Brevard County along with Orange County for the past thirty-five years tracking down informants and keeping them from going down the gutter. He was close to retirement and had seen almost everything. Previous to 9-11, the nineties were the worst, because federal funds were low, and the informants were coked-out, speed-freaks – the definition of unreliable. He started during the HIV epidemic in the late eighties when crack was starting to take hold. With the rich kids in Melbourne living off the meth derivative for years, the behavior of the under-twenty-five drug user at the time was erratic and off the scale. Self-mutilation was the big scene caused by too many stimulants and crashing in between. It was ten times worse than the cocaine scene in the early eighties and that was bad, he reminded himself. Luckily, money to fight terrorism, after 9-11, helped stem the tide of the craziness, because most of it went to the DEA in Florida. Now it was back to alcohol, cocaine, pot for pleasure; and fentanyl for people trying to deaden their pain quickly. The millennials were not as reckless as the Generation X kids in some ways, he thought.

As he pulled up to the twenty-year-old condo complex facing the Banana River, he tried to recall an informant of his getting such a nice place and a sweet ride to boot. *This Dragmar kid must be something special*, he mouthed without a sound. So far, it had been vacation time for him since his prison release in June, now he was supposed to get working and come up with some information on the drug supply network in Cape Atlantic. Personally, Paco did not understand the big hoopla about putting an informant on this Anmar Douglas, the A1A Pawn Shop guy. He was small time, and under the radar, in his opinion. Paco was not sure it was worth the DEA's time, but that was not his call and frankly, he was glad to have a low-energy assignment for the summer. Dagmar was well-mannered and disciplined; not a problem like most of his informants over the years had been. Shows up on time and is not a drug addict. *Now that was hard to beat*, he laughed.

They met in the parking lot and headed inside the lobby and up the elevator to the three-bedroom furnished condo. Dagmar opened the door and headed directly to the balcony to see the fourth-floor view of the mile-wide Banana River with Merritt Island in the distance. Paco was impressed and a little jealous. Dagmar was originally slated to move inland, closer to Titusville, but he demanded to stay in Cape Atlantic. He had fallen in love with the beach and the quiet but active nightlife on the upper Space Coast. *Who could blame him?* Paco shook his head in agreement.

They sat on the balcony quietly as Paco read through some notes from Dragmar. Every other line included the reference "Calvanese family,"

"Dragmar… is this the same as the mayor's family?"

"Yes, it is Mr. Lawrence. They own a substantial amount of property in Cape Atlantic and Jackie is the mayor."

Paco knew about the history of the old man Calvanese and being a founding father of Cape Atlantic, but was not versed about his extensive land holdings, "How do you know about all this?"

"Hours online and at the library. The family owns half of the Cape and is involved in businesses from Cocoa Beach to the Port and land holdings throughout Central Florida. Slum-lording, gambling, prostitution, drugs, alcohol; you name it – they do it. Lots of legitimate stuff…restaurants, strip malls, shuttle transportation, taxi service, casino boat, luxury boating, fishing trips, property management, land development, and of course politics! You know it's like playing on the

77

beach near the ocean, as a kid you dig out a big hole in the sand and get your arms, legs, and chest full of granules while you wait for the ocean to fill it up with water. Then the tide comes in and wipes it away like it was never there, but you still got sand all over you. That's how deep they are in this town. They are so entrenched that the details have been washed away like it never happened. And today is a new day and tomorrow is a new year."

Paco was not sure he followed the metaphor, but he got the idea from Dragmar and was impressed with his knowledge. He took notes as he asked questions on the specifics he brought up. They parted after an hour and Paco was pleased with the new information, though it was not his job to follow up on anything. The higher-ups had Dragmar on a certain mission that he was not in on, right now. His job was to be sure that Dragmar was working and safe to bring them new information. He could do some digging on his own about Jackie Calvanese and see what he could find out, he pondered, as he headed back to the mundane of the mainland.

Dagmar spent the morning moving his stuff in while saying goodbye to the Neptune Apartments. The boys thought he was moving back to the mainland, not some hot-looking condo on the river. He might run into them some time but most of the time they were sleeping during the day and working at night.

He relaxed on his new king-sized bed in the large master bedroom with sliding doors opening to a balcony. There was a nice field and park between his building and the Banana River. He decided to get a soccer ball, so he could practice some moves out there and maybe a bike to journey around the Avenues and down to the Manatee Sanctuary just south of him or head over to the Beach about three-quarters of a mile east of him.

The memory of Peg still haunted him. He had met a couple of women at bars and the beach lately, but nobody stood out, and no physical contact. His performance with her had shocked him. It was something that he hoped was behind him from many hours of therapy, but he knew prison had screwed up things for him. The affair he had with the transgender inmate left him questioning his manhood at times. It was just one time, but it was him being forceful after some cuddling and kissing. It was like his teenage years when he lost control and rubbed himself on girls with them facing down. Most of the time with their backside bare and his member reaching orgasm. It would always happen so fast, like it did with Peg. The embarrassment would always overwhelm the seconds of pleasure. Even when the girl seemed understanding, he would never see them again, fearful of their judgment. Later when he forced a girl down in an alley after walking her home after a date, he was arrested for sexual assault and taken away by the Baltimore Task Force headed by the FBI agent Brooklyn O'Malley.

The complex deal set up by O'Malley, directly with Alejandro Majado at the time, was done because he truly felt his contrition and he was willing to have the GPS chip installed to accept the delayed prison sentence. He was all in on getting revenge on "The Turk" and saving his mother. He had no clue if she was still alive.

Before entering prison at twenty-five, he had several years of regular sex with women and two long-term relationships. After the FBI got a hold of him when he was still a juvenile, they sent him to behavioral therapy for three years while he worked his way up "The Turk" network in Baltimore. He was injected with hormones to lower his testosterone, put on beta-blockers, and of course, the GPS chip put in the back of his neck to keep track of his whereabouts. By the time he was twenty-one, he was allowed to see women on his own and was successful in avoiding his fetish for anyone.

Now he was uncertain of what to do. He was ashamed and angry at the same time about how he treated Peg, but he still wanted a chance to talk with her. So far, she had been unavailable and hardly ever on Lincoln Street or the beach when he was around. He had left a couple of notes for her but avoided physically seeing her.

He needed a plan to see her and change her mind. She was perfect for him and seemed to be mature, unlike most of the women his age. She was in charge of her sexuality and knew what she wanted. That detail stung like a long needle in his spine for not realizing that at the time. *What a stupid shit I am*, he berated himself repeatedly like an old vinyl record skipping and replaying a verse endlessly.

He was proud of her for finishing her degree and starting a professional career, something he wanted as a teenager before he got arrested and was sent undercover. He had two years left in his commitment and then the money would be available for school. Studying to be an engineer was his life ambition, but he knew time was running out.

Even though Peg's face was not a classic beauty, Dragmar was obsessed with her. He was convinced her sullen personality kept her from looking beautiful to others. He saw a flower ready to bloom into a rose. And her body was perfect for him, toned and tanned with dark hair around her face that turned him on. He was not necessarily a breast man but loved the concise size of her breasts and how they would fit softly in his hand. Picturing her confidently displaying them clinging to her bikini top, he wondered if she could teach him about finding his sea level.

Chapter 12

Peg was glad to be home after her mini vacation in the Americana Motel in Cocoa attending the week-long training at the *EFSU* campus. Her night with Francis seemed to clear her head and fulfill an internal need deeply seeded years ago and growing like an unkept lawn for months. The last six years had been full of disappointment in romance, but finally some success in her professional growth. It was a tough road that she navigated to graduate after losing her way several times. She had a small sense of pride to have accomplished her goal of teaching fourth graders. In nine days, she would be in the classroom trying to change young lives at Satellite Beach Elementary.

This weekend was time to enjoy the beach and get back to her sea level. She wanted to re-connect with Phillip; and then find out from Jackie about the evidence on Dragmar and figure out what to do about him. Since her sexual experience with Francis, her strong exterior of anger towards Dragmar had developed some cracks. Had she overreacted to the situation? He had left several cards that were sweet, asking for forgiveness. Should she reconsider her strong sense of revenge? Unlike Francis, Dragmar turned her on. That was a fact she could not ignore for the moment. *Maybe he needed some understanding*, she considered.

She settled herself in her chair after laying down a blanket and putting up an umbrella. It was now officially a beach day. The mornings in the summer were the only times to be out on the beach on the Space Coast. The sun could be a brutal weapon of destruction, and the air was too hot and humid after noon time. The afternoons were full of thunderstorms with wind and uncertainty in the air for hours. If you could scoot in a hurry, it could be fun to watch the fronts move through, but Peg would bring a chair and a book after 6 pm if there was some clearing and it was low tide.

With her eyes closed, she felt the warmth on her face and her body. It would be nice to get toasty and hit the ocean for a cool down even though the water was over eighty degrees. Deeply in a trance, she thought about her father coming in October and spending time with him. She had called him after getting her job and finally talked to him. He was unusually supportive and sounded upbeat for the first time that she could remember. Lester said that he loved her and looked forward to seeing her. It was a shock that gave her chills.

The sound of the surf was climbing towards her, and the smell of the air made her open her eyes to see the parading of people that moved consistently north and south on the shoreline. Closer to her was a super-white-skinned, young man cautiously navigating the sand while carrying a heavy bag of stuff and a chair. Peg recognized the non-Floridian and shouted out, "Joshua...over here!" Surprisingly, she was happy to see him after totally forgetting about her invitation. She looked at her phone, which was on silent, and saw a text from him an hour ago telling her he was coming by.

Joshua looked relieved and joyous at the sight of Peg. He attempted to speed up his gait to reach her but fell to his knees awkwardly. She decided to get up and help him get settled next to her. For some reason, she felt a kinship with him, basically a total stranger, and looked forward to his company.

They talked non-stop for the next hour about settling in for their new jobs. Joshua acted like a kid in a candy store for being free of his conservative Christian, Lynchburg Virginia with all of his new experiences in Central Florida. He had spent several days at Disney World and Universal Studios for pure fun, the Kennedy Space Flight Center for exploration, and rode his car on Daytona Beach as an adventure to the wild side where he barely got out of the car, fearful he might catch a tattoo or body hair he never knew existed. For him, it was a tour of the gates of hell, but he loved the excitement. Joshua was discovering some of the many non-Christian things to do in this state.

Peg loved his enthusiasm and tried to learn from it. She knew teaching youngsters was all about energy and being positive. She had energy, but not always positivity. Joshua like most conservative Christians had a lens of belief that filtered out certain horribleness of the past and helped construct an optimistic present – their world guided by the idea of Faith.

Peg always had trouble with Faith, because she learned to have none in her parents and most of her friends. Her building blocks were constructed with concrete facts that led her to new levels of truths she could trust because they were based on solid foundations.

She realized that spending time with Phillip gave her Hope about her talents and the future. Joshua's personality or view of the world could give her a foundation of Faith to mix in with her concrete facts. A formula that could help her with her creativity and vision of each day.

Joshua was hidden from the sun and covered with 100 SPF but was still showing signs of redness. Peg rose from her chair and grabbed his hand, "Joshua let's get you in the water to cool off before the sun turns you into a shade of watermelon." He happily agreed and ran with Peg into the ocean. They played for twenty minutes with Peg swimming circles around Joshua. He ventured passed the breakers, where he could still stand with the water at his chest. He could swim but was not much of a diver or explorer. For Peg, having a playmate in the ocean touched a memory or two of making friends in the ocean when her father would bring her to Brevard Park as a kid. Jumping on Joshua from behind or swimming through his legs was entertainment for her. Joshua, being much more of a kid at heart, loved the attention and the new feeling of salt water on his body. He was feeling relaxed in the water with Peg around.

They headed back to their beach spot, catching their breaths after escaping the waves. Joshua fell straight back onto the blanket as Peg dried off her body. His ultra-whiteness was getting pink on his shoulders and feet. She knew he needed to be out of the sun as soon as she settled in her chair.

She opened her first beer of the day at 11 am and was barely satiated by her first gulp. The coldness down her throat felt wonderful. Quickly she took three more and almost finished the bottle, when she saw a familiar face, "I thought I might find you near Lincoln Street. You're ready for the weekend I can see!"

"Phillip…what a surprise!" She shot out of her chair and hugged him tightly. Tears came to her eyes as she was caught off-guard by her overwhelming emotions. He was wearing an Australian sun hat and sunglasses that hid his eyes, but his size still towered over her. Joshua sat up to learn about the commotion, "Phillip this is my teacher friend…Joshua.

We met at a teacher training last week. He's also teaching fourth grade but at Merritt Island Elementary." Peg tried to shrug off the awkwardness that she felt and her over-explaining of the situation.

They exchanged pleasantries as Phillip noticed Joshua's pinkness, "Peg we need to get him inside soon or he'll be toast for the weekend!"

"You're right Phillip. Let's go to my place and do some lunch or something?"

Quickly they assembled their stuff and headed to Lincoln Street. Peg was happy to get into a summer dress and put some icepacks on Joshua's shoulders and feet. "I can make Iced Tea for everyone and some Tuna Fish sandwiches...I got some chips, pickles, cheese, applesauce too."

"This is quite a treat Peg... can I help at all?" asked Phillip

"Just clear the table for me and make sure Joshua ices the tops of his feet as well."

Joshua, with an ice pack on each shoulder, was feeling well taken care of but was a bit confused with Peg's relationship with Phillip. He was feeling some strange activity below his waist as he watched Peg prance around in her sun dress... braless. "Phillip how do you know Peg?" he finally volunteered.

"I'm a writer and met Peg getting some chicken one night and realized we both had a passion for creating stories, so we decided to collaborate on a project...possibly a novel."

Peg chimed in, "Joshua... he's been kind enough to mentor me on my ideas about writing. He lives up the beach about a mile and has been extremely generous with his time. And Joshua don't tell anybody but he's kind of famous!"

"Oh... my... Peg. I'm very good at secrets," Joshua blushed," I'm so happy you met him."

"Well, I'm sure he can mentor both of us if we behave ourselves and not ask too many questions!"

"That would be wonderful Phillip."

"Anything I can help you with Joshua let me know. Peg has been a joy to meet. and I am so proud of her for getting her degree and a teaching job. This should be a fun, but hard year for both of you. Maybe we should have Tuna Fish lunches once a month or so!" Everyone agreed as the food was served.

"So how ready are both of you for nine-year-olds to take over your life?" Phillip asked. Both Peg and Joshua looked at each other in between bites and laughed.

"I mean do you know their music...their culture...what's in, what's out?"

"Well, I listen to all kinds of music, but I have to admit I'm not up on the latest Justin Bieber type or the current British Boy band," Peg said with some seriousness. "Now Joshua over here will be blindsided because he grew up on Christian music!"

"Oh, Peg... that is silly! Okay somewhat right I guess... but I like pop music and do Snapchat, Instagram, and Facebook!"

"Well, guys...seriously... study up the next few days. It won't hurt and clean up your social media pictures and content...if you have any." Phillip remarked.

"So true...I will make sure I do that Phillip. That makes so much sense Peg... doesn't it?"

"Yep...I only do Facebook so I'm in good shape. But...you should know Phillip... the curriculum is so set that you don't have much time for chit-chat with these kids." Peg declared as she got up and took her plate into the kitchen feeling like a professional teacher already, "Any more Iced Tea for you Phillip... Joshua?" She enjoyed playing hostess and having company in her little place. For once in her life, she

86

felt confident having two of her new friends in her abode without feeling embarrassed. Luckily, she had spent some time cleaning up over the last month. The place had a little shine to it, she assured herself.

Just then, there were heavy sounds of feet on the stairs coming up to the apartment and then a thump against the decking like something had landed. Then some more feet down the stairs or maybe up again with some muted voices exchanged, then a stumble and more noise outside the door. Finally, a light knock landed on the door.

"Peg, I think you got a package…Amazon maybe." Phillip announced a proud Amazon Prime user himself. It seemed miraculous that you get almost anything you wanted the next day for so little cost, he thought, feeling a kinship with Peg's package already.

"Oh… maybe my new shoes are here already, how exciting! We should all go dancing tonight," she exclaimed. "Phillip, can you check the door for me." Peg turned to the refrigerator to get the Iced Tea as she heard Phillip unlock the door twenty feet away.

"Is Peg available?" Said the voice of the good-looking fellow, who looked familiar," Phillip smiled without placing the face. "Here's a package for her." Phillip reached out for the package as the man stepped inside taking his cap off his tightly cropped dark hair. His eyes had a purpose and a smile burst out on his face.

Peg came out of the kitchen with a pitcher of Iced Tea to pour when she saw his handsome face again.

Chapter 13

Dagmar looked more attractive than Peg remembered. His arms and chest looked stronger while his neck and shoulders looked carved like a bust of a god-like face. She steadied her legs as she poured Joshua some tea.

"No tea for me Peg," Phillip said trying to stifle the awkward silence of the staring. He finally figured out the puzzle about the date that went awry and caused Peg to be a basket case for a day at his condo. He had been glad to be there for her, but he knew something had gone wrong. As he stepped behind the young man, he closed the door slowly, waiting for some movement, but mainly to keep the hot humid air from stealing the comfortableness of the apartment. Though he was in his late sixties, he was still a force of humanity at 6'3" 210lbs with a loud bark if necessary. If protection for Peg was needed, he had no doubt he could pin the young man on the ground in seconds and control him as she called the police. In all of his years of athletic competition and manhood, Phillip had never punched anyone or started a fight, but as a high school wrestler and a football star, he knew how to get people down to the ground if necessary.

Joshua would not be much help, but he could tie some knots around his feet and hands if necessary. Within seconds, Phillip had it all planned out in his head while Joshua seemed not to have a care in the world while he finished his Tuna sandwich and thanked Peg for some more Iced Tea. This Florida sweet tea was something else, he thought to himself. He did start to wonder if the young man was the delivery man and needed to get paid or sign something. Peg seemed to be in suspended animation and the young good-looking dark man seemed to be patiently waiting.

Peg thought of a thousand responses in a second or two as she put down the Iced Tea flask on the counter. Finally, she realized it was too complicated to confront him immediately. "Can I get you some Iced Tea?" she said forcefully.

"That would be lovely Peg!"

"This is Dragmar, he lives in the apartments next door...these are my friends Phillip and Joshua. We were out on the beach this morning and decided to have some lunch. Would you like a sandwich? I have some Tuna Fish left."

"Why yes...thank you if it's not too much trouble." He stepped forward towards the table and kitchen area. "I am so sorry to drop in on you like this, but I saw the package come to your door and I had not seen you for over a month and wanted to make sure you got it. You can never be sure in this neighborhood." Dagmar said convincingly.

"That's so sweet of you Dragmar...Luckily, I've never had a problem with folks around here," she lied. "Most of the people on Lincoln Street behave themselves..." Peg gazed at him with her normal smile-less face to emphasize the point.

"I have moved to a condo on the Banana River. I just got a new job at the Port and a car. I decided to stay in Cape Atlantic, it feels like home. You know a little bit of paradise."

"I agree with that Dragmar. I'm a ten-minute walk from the Port. Are you in those condos near the park over there?" Phillip entered the conversation.

"Oh yeah...I got a soccer field, a putting green, the *Manatee Park,* just south of me, and a great view up on the fifth floor. I saw my first rocket launch last week from my balcony. It shook the place...like God was speaking to us."

"That was gravity…" Peg sharply retorted.

Everyone stayed silent as she pulled out a seat for Dragmar to sit at the table. "You see Dragmar, gravity is so powerful that it drags all that water in the ocean back and forth almost a hundred yards on the beach four times a day. And when we try to leave the surface of the earth and go faster than the speed of sound at 767.269 miles per hour it fights back with terrific strength causing the air to shake and the sound to boom because we are breaking free of that power in that moment." Peg was in a teaching moment with a young man who needed to learn about the environment around him including the female race. "We all possess gravity because our bodies have mass and when one body tries to take over another body, it fights back unless it's a good match like Hydrogen and Oxygen or Sodium and Chlorine. They have atomic structures that easily come together and stabilize each other to make useful compounds like water and salt."

Phillip was able to follow the metaphor by Peg but was not sure Dragmar was smart enough to catch the imagery. Joshua was intrigued by the science lesson, not being his forte, and kept his eyes on his fellow teacher.

Peg stepped back into the kitchen, made a sandwich flawlessly, put it on a plate, and passed it to Joshua to give to Dragmar. She washed her hands in the sink forcefully like a surgeon.

She watched Dragmar take a bite of the perfect sandwich as she walked back to the table, across from him, and then put her hands on the back of her empty seat at the table and leaned over, almost horizontally, waiting for Dragmar to finish chewing his first bite. "Enough mayo on the tuna Dragmar?" She asked as her half-unbuttoned dress exposed cleavage.

"Just perfect Peg… can we talk for a minute after lunch?" He asked softly trying to keep his eyes on her face

"We can talk now if you want, my friends won't mind, I'm sure."

Joshua looked unsure as he sucked down his Iced Tea and Phillip nodded affirmatively to Peg. He knew it was going to be a showdown and he was ready to referee if necessary.

Dagmar stared at Peg for a few seconds then Phillip and Joshua and finally answered, "Well…okay I guess…" Dagmar cleaned his mouth and sat back from the table for a moment. "If this is my only chance, Peg?" His eyes fell from her face to her cleavage as her beauty overwhelmed him for a moment he got up from his chair and walked behind his chair to face her at eye level without distraction.

Peg stood up straight and folded her arms over her arched chest. Her eyes were intense and her mouth was sullen as normal.

"I wanted to apologize for the other night on the beach… I lost."

Bang, Bang, Bang came a hard knocking that almost buckled the door. Peg got behind Phillip as he quickly rose and went to the door. She followed and yelled, "Who is it?"

"Peg it's the mayor… Peg it's Jackie…"

She moved ahead of Phillip and opened the door herself and let Jackie inside. She could see two Cape Atlantic Policemen on the deck outside the door.

He turned around as he entered and barked out, "Just listen up boys if I need you." As Jackie pointed to the police radio he carried.

Peg welcomed the hug and offered quietly, "We're having some lunch Mayor...can I get you some Tea or Coffee?"

"No Peg...so sorry to interrupt. I came over as soon I got some information for you."

Peg kept close to him and whispered, "Not now Jackie."

She stepped away from Jackie and turned to introduce him to the players in the current drama. "Mayor this is Joshua, a teaching colleague; Dragmar, a friend on Lincoln Street; and of course, you must know the famous author, Phillip Finelli, a half-time Cape Atlantic resident!"

"Phillip it is a pleasure to finally meet you." Jackie looked amazed at how tall he was as they shook hands ferociously. "We have to do dinner sometime or have some drinks. How are those famous sons of yours? I'm a big fan of Guy... not so much Alex for beating my New York team...Hahaha!" he bellowed.

"Thank you, Mayor, a real honor to meet you. I love this town as you must know by now."

Jackie moved to the table like a seasoned politician looking for votes. "Hello, Dragmar, and Joshua very nice to meet you. Where are you teaching this year Joshua?

"Merritt Island sir... Mr. Mayor...fourth grade, like Peg." Joshua stumbled over his words with his nervousness, confused about Peg's popularity and what Dragmar was apologizing about.

"Here's my card Joshua, if you have any problems as you settle in don't hesitate to call my office and I'll help you. Best of luck this year son."

Peg made a quick decision and looked at Phillip for his support. "Let's all sit in the living room for a few minutes…Please!" She said loudly looking directly at Jackie and Dragmar. They all followed directions and found seats on the couch with Joshua ending up in the middle between Jackie and Dragmar. Phillip sat in the comfy TV chair and Peg grabbed a dining table chair and sat across from the couch.

Immediately she took control. "Since I have all my friends here, I'm wondering if you can help solve a problem for me."

"Anything Peg you know that but is this the best…" She put up her hand to Jackie.

"Sorry mayor but can you help me?" He nodded yes as the rest agreed without a sound.

"Here's my problem. I like Dragmar but unfortunately, he is an asshole!"

Jackie leaned forward as Dragmar's head dropped to his chest. Joshua showed some leadership and put his hand on Jackie's shoulder.

"The question is do I give him another chance? Or should I demand that he get help first?"

"Excuse me Peg but you asked me for some help and I…" Jackie hesitated as Peg gave him the stop sign like a school patrol at an intersection.

"Sorry Mayor… but that was over a month ago and I have moved on. Now he's here and all of you are here. And he just apologized before you banged on my door! Now at least he had the balls to do it in front of two of my friends in my apartment, so I need to answer him."

Peg felt overwhelmed as she finished but fought back her tears and pain. She felt like gravity had just kicked her in the stomach as she fought for air in her lungs, but she refused to give in. She reached for Phillip's hand on her left and Joshua's hand in front of her as he knelt.

It was quiet in the room as Peg felt strength returning to her chest as Phillip's big arm went around her shoulder and Joshua hugged her thigh. Jackie reached out his handkerchief marked with his initials to Peg's face and dried her tears. She finally retrieved her hands and took the cloth to dry her eyes and finally found her voice.

"Dragmar, I accept your apology, but you hurt me deeply and I think you're wounded in some way like me. And maybe like me, you need some help. So, I cannot be with you right now. Maybe we can write to each other over the school year through e-mail or text or even a real letter or a card occasionally. And learn to become friends maybe or maybe not. Then by next summer, we can try again if it feels worth it." She quietly blew her nose and stood up with her chest arched forward, feeling proud of herself. The room was noiseless except for the air conditioner humming like a beat in a slow dance. "That's the best I got for you. What do you think?"

Dagmar rose from the couch and bowed at the waist. "Thank you Peg for listening...I will count every school day off the calendar and write each week for another chance sometime. May God be with you Peg." He stared for one more moment at her loveliness and lodged it in his memory. The tears were just behind his eyes being held back by his manliness. He nodded to her and walked to the door, then outside past the Cape Atlantic police and quickly to his car. The tears finally came as he tried to find his keys. His stomach cramped in pain. Not even prison felt like this, now that he was a free man without love.

The mayor waited for a few moments and grabbed his radio. "Boys, has the male cleared the floor?"

94

"Yes… Mr. Mayor."

"Let's tail him without being noticed…10-4?

"10-4"

Chapter 14

"We need to know where he is living Peg. I have reason to believe that he is involved in something on the Space Coast."

"Mr. Mayor, he said that he is living in a condo near a soccer field, just north of Manatee Park." Joshua chirped in, trying to be helpful. "He seems like a nice person."

"Well, he's not son..." Jackie was losing his patience with the naïve schoolteacher. He then looked to Phillip for some help. "Phillip...I'm so sorry you had to be a part of this. Maybe it would be better if you could show Joshua around the neighborhood for a few minutes while I talk with Peg." He hesitated a second, "There's a rumor going around that your next novel is situated on the Space Coast, maybe I could give you some good fodder on our history sometime."

Phillip understood the assignment and turned to Peg to assure her that he could stick around. "Peg, you have my number...I'll check in with you a little later...OK?"

Peg mustered up a nod as Joshua hugged her and headed towards the door with Phillip. She found a pillow on the couch to hold and pulled her knees to her chest as she wept.

Jackie sat in the comfy chair and gave her a few moments before he asked her to listen for a few minutes. "Peg, I am so sorry it took so long, but it was complicated, and you were in training and so forth." He waited for her to look up, but she was still crying into the pillow.

Another ten minutes passed, and finally, the radio beeped him to crack the silence. "Mayor, we have secured the location and the car. No activity on the fifth floor at this time."

"Thanks, boys, you can leave the surveillance...10-4."

Jackie took a walk around the apartment and into the kitchen. He opened some cabinets and found some Jack Daniels. "You mind if I help myself to a drink?"

Peg lifted her head with a surprised look and watery eyes and quickly said, "Sure Mr. Mayor and make me one while you're at it... a double on the rocks."

Jackie smiled, relieved that the flood of tears had been interrupted, and brought identical drinks to the couch, where he settled himself closer to Peg. "You know you can call me Jackie," he took a big gulp and put down his drink on the table. "Peg we are suddenly actors in the same play. Dagmar is not who you think he is. It's an alias, he's Peruvian."

Peg finished her drink and stood up to blow her nose and clean up her face. She hated crying – period, the swollen eyes, the red nose, the snot, the stomach spasms. It was all bullshit that she decided to forego as a young teenager because it never got her anywhere. Being left alone a lot or with others at times, made her feel like an orphan living in foster homes. She was left to navigate guys by herself before, during, and after high school. Luckily, there were some teachers and school counselors who were pretty cool and helped at important times. Her goal was to keep from living in the streets and going to college. Her parents would wake up and show interest in her enough that keep her from the depths of despair. So, she learned to expect despair and work from there.

Rarely would her feelings rise to the level of disappointment or hurt. Sullen became her expertise. The problem was that she was still an interesting person. Teachers found her smart and mature; and guys, not looking for the cheerleader or a popular girl, found her somewhere between stimulating and sensual. Her body seemed mature even at the beginning of high school.

Growing up around "Free Love", she wanted to be anything like her mother, who seemed to have a lot of partners, whereas her dad never showed any of his possible lovers. She assumed he had many but kept it private. So, in high school, she kept herself busy and waited late in her senior year for sex, just in time for prom, and continued to like it during that summer with one boy. Then he left for college out of state, and she moved on to one boy every month or so for four years. Were we going out or was this a break-up? Was never an issue. She made sure of that. Her look was popular and fashionable, so she could be selective. By twenty-two, she ran out of boys to be interested in and decided to change her attitude towards life.

Dagmar was the first one that caught her soul. He happened to be her age but maybe that was not just a coincidence now that she thought of it. She just realized it when he stood in front of strangers apologized to her and walked out without whining. She thought it was just sexual between them, but he had somehow gotten through her armor. She felt beautiful around him and calm even if it was just a few hours. And now the mayor was going to tell her something to blow her mind. With a double whiskey down her throat, she was ready.

Peg sat back down on the couch and turned to him and asked him, "What's the play we're in...Jackie?"

"His real name is Alejandro Majada, his mother was one of several women connected to a man named "The Turk" who ran a major drug empire in West Baltimore until early 2020. "The Turk" was most likely his father. The organization is still on the East Coast and has kept him safe even now as he is out of prison." Though that might be true, Jackie did not want to mention him being undercover with the DEA and after his ass. He hoped she would focus on his sins and scare her away from him. "He was a sex offender as a teenager but went through therapy and then got involved in the drug world. Mainly as a driver from what I could tell. Whatever happened to you could be similar to his past and maybe the prison thing screwed him up again. Either way Peg...you did the right thing. I hope you know that my dear girl, just stay away from him."

Peg knew liars and Jackie was a good one. Politician, she thought, always peppered their bullshit with some truth, but always are trying to make you believe what they want you to believe. She loved him for it, but now this was different, and she had a decision to make. Suddenly she remembered her dad telling her about punting in football. It seemed odd at the time because she did not know much about sports. He liked to bet on sports, according to her mother. He explained to her once when she was a kid and a game was on in a bar and her dad was uncharacteristically seated and paying attention to the game, that the reason they call it football was because of punting, "Peg, the worst thing you can do in a game is going for it when the odds are not in your favor. Playing defense and extending the game, even when you are losing by less than a touchdown is better than making it worse."

Peg smiled at the memory but used it to cover her lie to Jackie, "You're so right. It's time to move on. He might be dangerous...no doubt. That's why I wanted you to check it out. Thank you, Jackie. I hope I didn't cause you too much trouble."

The bullshit was too convincing to consider not believing her. Jackie was relieved and felt like he wanted another whiskey and to get after Peg, but he knew that was a huge mistake and quickly got to his feet. "No trouble my dear...keep in touch Peg. Let me know how the job is going."

Chapter 15

After Jackie left her apartment and headed down the stairs, Peg looked through her blinds and saw Phillip and Joshua walking up Lincoln Street from the Beach. Phillip hugged Joshua and continued walking towards A1A. Joshua headed up the stairs to her apartment. For some reason, she felt relieved. He seemed like a young puppy dog ready to make his master happy. She felt like having a human around would put no pressure on her and provide some much-needed companionship. Besides, she thought, he needed an explanation and an apology for being put in the middle of this mess. She made a note in her head to call Phillip later and thank him for his support. He would understand, she surmised.

She let Joshua in the door and sat down with him on the couch. They talked for hours on the couch about the current Peg situation and everything about Joshua. He supported her decision with great enthusiasm about Dragmar but wondered if guys ever really change. He revealed that he had never been with a woman but had no doubt about his sexuality. He liked women, but his religious beliefs and his not-necessarily attractive features kept him from ever having any kind of sex with a woman. He had kissed a girl in college on several dates and liked it, but it went no further.

Peg was not sure about his reality. He seemed a little gay, but it was hard to tell these days and to each his own, she thought. It gave her a perverse thought to try to entice him and get him turned on. He might just need a hand job to gain some confidence in pursuing women or find out it did not turn him on. She liked that kind of challenge, but right now she was extremely tired and wanted to take a nap.

"Joshua, would you stay around until the evening, so we could walk on the beach or take a dip in the ocean?"

"Sure Peg...that would be fun. You look pretty tired. Do you need a nap?"

"You're a genius Joshua...would you hold my hand while I went to sleep in my bed? I just need to feel safe before I fall asleep."

Joshua took her hand and walked into the bedroom with her. She found a spot in the middle of the bed and put her head on the pillow. Joshua kept connected with her hand as he sat on the side of the bed.

Peg closed her eyes and after a minute said, "Joshua...you're welcome to lay down if you want to rest." Joshua squeezed her hand and enjoyed the moment. Peg was asleep in minutes. He flipped off his shoes and nestled in next to her. He always wondered what it would be like to sleep with a girl or anybody. It had been since camp in elementary school that he slept in close quarters with anyone. His parents had paid extra for a single dorm room at school, being an only child. They wanted him comfortable in college.

Before he realized it, he was dreaming of swimming in the ocean with Peg and being touched by her and liking it. He could see her body without her bikini and felt excited by it. He felt for his swim trunks and they were gone. His member felt like it did when he came in his dreams.

An hour passed, and Peg fell awake and saw Joshua's eyes fluttering in a dream. She rolled over and inched gently closer to him, then softly rubbed his shoulder down to his hips placed her hand on his shorts, and unzipped them. She could feel his hard member just below his underwear as she got closer to him. She kissed him on his ear as she found him and stroked him softly. She whispered in his ear, "You can touch my breasts, Joshua," but he did not move. She took his hand and placed it inside her dress and on her breast. His hand seemed to naturally latch on as his fingers moved on her softness, exploring every part of the primal feeling. Finally, his eyes opened as she kissed him on the lips.

He let her tongue play in his mouth for a short while before he experimented with his own.

Peg felt him responding and started to slide up and down a little harder on his member. She knew he was getting close, as his head fell back showing euphoria and his hand pulled tight on her breast. He made a cluster of sounds as he climaxed for almost thirty seconds. Peg laughed to herself about how she had struck an untapped well that exploded all over her hand and the sheets. She rolled away from Joshua as he curled up to deal with the aftershocks of his eruption. She cleaned her hands in the bathroom and returned with a roll of tissues. Acting like an attending nurse, she cleaned him up and assured him that he would be alright. Finally, as the dripping stopped, she made sure the member was put away and his pants zipped up. She sat comfortably next to him on the bed.

"Are you okay Joshua? I know you weren't expecting that, but it seemed to help me if want to know the truth."

Joshua looked relieved, "Yes Peg it was quite unexpected… why would it help you?"

"I needed the distraction and you seemed to need the help getting past something. It was just a guess, but I think you do like girls and sex is healthy – not a sin."

"I do like girls Peg. I just never thought I could be with you."

"I don't see us as partners Joshua, but sometimes friends have to help out in strange ways."

"Well, that was strange...but wonderful. I was dreaming about you when you started touching me. How did you know?"

"Well... let's just say it was a leap of Faith!"

Chapter 16

The school was in session and the first month was not going well for Peg or Joshua. They met every Friday during happy hour at *Coconuts on the Beach,* literally on Cocoa Beach, to drown out their concerns for the week. Joshua was having a tougher time than Peg.

"The staff is mostly older women who have not experienced a young male like me!" He laughed as he chugged down his first beer.

"You mean the metro-sexual look?" Peg added joyfully.

"I think they're jealous of my fashion sense!" Joshua was getting to like the sin of alcohol every Friday and feeling sarcastic. "The boys are pretty nasty but at least the girls like me! Maybe that's a good start!" He bellowed out with a giggle. "Who knows it could be a lot worse…at least the janitor likes me!" He was on a roll and Peg loved it. She liked having a colleague to sink or swim with every week. "How about you Peg, are the parents still on you?"

"Some… but I can handle that, it's just a lot of listening and nodding. The kids are just different than I thought they would be…especially the girls." Peg complained.

"I think the Merritt Island girls are a little more sophisticated than your normal fourth graders, but it may just be they're testing you. How are you dressing? Conservatively? Or showing some cleavage occasionally?" Joshua laughed again as he started his second beer.

"So, you think if I show some cleavage, the girls will like me better? How does that make any sense, Joshua…I think the alcohol is getting to you?" Peg said with a laugh.

"Conservative huh? I thought so. Girl... you have to open it up some. You're a fashion icon...give them something to look at. The girls love that stuff, and it gives you some panache with the parents."

Peg looked confused. It was something she had not thought of, but Joshua was correct or at least on the right track...maybe. She was still unsure, "I may need to give it a go, my friend. I'll let you know how it goes next Friday. Can we order some nachos or something? I'm starved!"

"See...like you have been teaching me...sometimes you have to think outside the box. They say if you got it, flaunt it! Right? I should know...those babies are soft and sweet...and bigger in person...whew!" He slammed the table with his hand as he drank a big gulp of his beer.

"Joshua...are you becoming a male chauvinist pig? What have I done?" She leaned over and kissed him on the cheek. "I may be driving home tonight. Anything else you got for me?"

"Are you texting with Dragmar yet? Oh yeah...how about that HR guy you slept with at the summer training...any communication there? You may just need some more of that!" Joshua needled Peg. "I mean...of course, I would do it, but that might ruin our friendship and that's too dear to me to ever screw up." Suddenly transforming into his most charming character he touched her hands for a moment. "You have been a great friend Peg!"

She was unsure how to continue. So, she grabbed a server and ordered some appetizers and two more beers. "Thank you, Joshua, you are one of a kind! And I haven't answered Dragmar's weekly texts yet but maybe I will this weekend... That seems like a good idea. And Francis has left two messages for me, but I have not answered him. Maybe I need to catch up with him. Not a bad ally to have. Maybe a date and talking would be therapeutic."

"Yes, my dear…and maybe in more ways than one!" Joshua smiled in his dearest face to his friend.

"I have created a monster!" Peg laughed. "I hardly know him. And I was in a different place when I met him before. If we go down that road it will be because we have a relationship. I don't need him to be a fuck buddy." She sat back and looked towards the ocean as the light of the day was starting to wane. This spot, right on the beach, was beautiful on a night like this. Maybe she could walk on the beach tonight when she got home and think about what they had talked about. Four weeks into her profession was something to just survive but not enough time to change the world. She was still confident in her abilities and there were a few kids she had connected with.

Finally, the nachos arrived and then some broiled shrimp showed up. She finished her beer and gladly took a new one. All this talking had made her famished. She started shoveling some nachos down as Joshua was talking with the server. A petite kid about his age looking a bit disheveled with her hair and one tooth that needed fixing, but a nice smile. Was Joshua flirting with her? Peg wondered. The server stayed longer than was needed and came back quickly with some extra napkins and sour cream for the nachos and never even looked at Peg.

After ten minutes, Peg finally felt nourished enough to check in with Joshua who had gone to the bathroom and bumped into the server on the way back. She could not wait for his response.

"So, what's her name?"

"Who?"

"The server Romeo! I guess she assumes we're not together." Peg tried to look annoyed.

"Becky…I think! She pretty cute?" Joshua reported.

"If we get her a dentist and a hairdresser and a trip to the mall for some clothes, I think you got yourself a partner. Did you get her number?

"I think I'll need another beer to be that brave!"

"You're doing pretty well right now Joshua…you should go for it before you stagger out of here."

"She probably gets hit on all the time!"

"I doubt it and you weren't hitting on her. You were talking to her like a gentleman. Which are few and far between around here. And shit you have a job and a degree!"

"Okay…I'll go for it. I guess we both have challenges ahead. Thanks for the encouragement, Peg."

"Anytime my friend."

Chapter 17

She looked over the texts from Dragmar over the past month. One every week, usually on Friday night, but sometimes over the weekend.

Week #1. "It was great to see you last week…good luck with the kids!"

Week #2. "I hope you had a good week…I'm staying pretty busy."

Week #3. "We got lucky on the hurricane going west…the beach was beautiful this week."

Week #4. "I hope the rain stops this weekend…I could use a beach day Sunday."

Never any pressure to respond, just short and sweet to get her engaged. After the second text, she had started to look forward to seeing them each Friday night after a long week of toiling and was disappointed now that he had not sent one after talking about it with Joshua, but it was only eight pm, she could still hope for one tonight.

She started thinking of responding to him and what she would say. Maybe it would be better if his text came tomorrow, tonight she was a little drunk when she got back to her apartment after leaving Joshua. She decided to grab a water bottle and hit the beach for a walk and get her ankles wet by the waves. It was a beautiful night, very much like the night they went out. She thought of that feeling she had before his attack. For a few minutes, it was magical, she wanted him desperately and felt connected to him deeply. She wondered if she was over-emphasizing the feelings during a short period. But it was all she had, she lamented.

After a City Council meeting two Wednesdays ago, she talked to the mayor and assured him she of no contact with Dragmar. He seemed pleased. After a lot of thought, she was certain he was an abuse victim like herself. Maybe he had been in therapy and just had a relapse. Jackie knew more about him than he reported, but she was not going to bring it up again. She wondered why he was so anxious about this kid working undercover for the DEA. He should be ecstatic, she thought. Jackie cared so much for the city, that getting a handle on Anmar Douglas and his Pawn Shop which controlled drug activity should be great news. Talking with him after the City Council meeting gave her the chills. She stopped asking him questions after he said for the third time, "You're better off not knowing this guy…he's trouble waiting to happen, Peg."

"Thanks, Mayor," she responded obediently and went home that night more confused than ever.

She had made it to the beach with her water bottle and found the tide pretty high and jumpy. After a short walk, she found a place to sit and looked at the work of the ocean. She became mesmerized by the cycles of power created by the gravitational forces of the Earth and Moon, two worlds in a single-sun solar system, which was a tiny part of a ginormous galaxy in an unending universe. In life, there were forces outside her little Cape Atlantic that she could not control, but like the tides, there were four cycles that she could control. Work, Write, Walk, and Wonder came to her mind again. She liked that rotation of W's because it was endless starting anywhere. Working all day can lead to writing followed by a walk and wonderment or writing and walking can lead to wonder and work and so forth. Her emotions had come full circle. The summer had provided a boundless amount of turbulence that she navigated, now she wanted smoother sailing. She hoped to see Phillip soon and spend time with him. He could help her focus on her cycles of energy and work on what she could control. The rest of the disruptive energy around her were forces of the universe that she could not regulate.

With her father making his return to Titusville sometime in October, she wanted to organize her thoughts. He might give her clues about her upbringing or non-upbringing. She wanted to remember what happened to her. Right now, it was a horror show she could not watch, but she wanted it to become a mystery she could solve.

The rolls of the waves started to calm a bit. The apex of the high tide had been reached. She could tell the pull of the energy was going east away from her. The water was reaching out with smaller waves from different angles. She decided to get her feet in the water and walk along the edge for a while.

Lincoln Street was quiet after 9 pm. Peg had no anxiety about walking the three blocks to her apartment. The Neptune Apartments were showing no signs of life. The power of the tides had calmed her and maybe the effects of the alcohol helped too. She headed inside and went to her couch to plop down with some pillows. Excitement crept into her body as she opened her phone and pulled up her texts. There it was… an unopened message from Dragmar… or would it feel like Alejandro?

Chapter 18

She hesitated to open it and thought about her response. What if he had lost his patience and lashed out at her? She romanced the idea in her heart to call him, Alejandro, but that would be a mistake her head responded. Somehow the knowledge that he was Peruvian made her feel more comfortable. She realized that was racist and tried to re-frame her feeling to something more acceptable, but she could not. For her, it felt true. She liked Peruvians, they were a peaceful culture from a magical place in the world, she surmised. A place Peg had wanted to visit in her early twenties. In her studies, she always read or watched on cable anything that involved Peruvian culture. It was just a thing that she liked; Peg relented.

Her body let out a sweat from deep inside. An anxiety that she was not aware of had increased her body temperature. It could not be helped, she figured. He had responded and that was all she cared about it. She continued hesitating, wondering if she could she wait another week to hear something new from him. It felt like being sucked into a dark hole. His patience and discipline had been impressive. He had pursued her for months to talk and then came to her like a real man to apologize. She dared him in front of others, and he responded with calm but not fear. He went all in, and she was on the edge ready to dive in after him. Would she swim in his love or drown from his control? She sat back and took a deep breath. Her strategy would be important. How she responded would set the stage for their relationship. Latin American boys needed to be shown strength, she believed. She had to show her discipline with her response no matter how she felt inside.

She put down her phone sat back on the couch and closed her eyes. Who was she kidding? She had no plan. Suddenly the anxiety came over her like a wave she had not seen coming. Her throat felt like it was closed, and her air was getting cut off. Her chest felt like gravity on Jupiter. The pressure inside her head pushed her off the couch to get a glass of water. She leaned over the sink panting after a big gulp of water. Finally, she headed back to the couch and got horizontal.

She wanted to call someone, but it felt foolish. This was something only a girlfriend or a mother would listen to and unfortunately, neither was an option at this time. She had no friends right now who were girls, and her mother was terrible at listening for more than thirty seconds without going on about something in her worthless life. Why was she in this situation, she asked herself. Having friends after high school became boring quickly for her and she was horrible at following up with people. She had learned to be alone as a kid and never cared too much about friends. Since she was nine, it had served her well, she realized. What the hell happened to me?

Chapter 19

"I have decided this is too hard for me. I want to hear from you. I will never quit, but tonight I am feeling some weakness and I could use a friend."

She did not know what to feel. First, it was fear and sadness, then a shot of adrenaline with hope, followed by confusion. This would call for drastic action as she got up off the couch and grabbed money. Quickly she was down the steps heading out to A1A going north. Peg needed some ice cream. The half-mile walk to the *Tastee Twist* would give her time to clear her head and think about a response. The ice cream destination was a cone with swirls on top and a back to it. An adorable place you might think to find in the Midwest, it had little metal tables with umbrellas on one side near the parking lot and a drive-through on the other side. Like her fried chicken fetish, Peg tried to limit her visits, so she made herself walk to this place. She looked forward to the shot of sugar, one slurp at a time of a vanilla and chocolate swirl cone that would cool the fire burning in her soul.

As she crossed North Atlantic Avenue at the light, her phone buzzed in her pocket. Praying it was someone she could chat with; she was excited to see Joshua's number light up as she answered. "Hello, Joshua…are you okay?"

"Oh Peg…I'm so glad I got you. I had to tell someone!"

"Joshua…what happened?"

"I kissed her…can you believe it and my hands were all over her."

"What…who Joshua? The server?"

113

"Yes...Becky...Becky Baker-Winters, but she goes by Becky Baker. Her parents did the hyphen thing. I'm so happy she dropped the Winters...kind of like the Space Coast seasons," Joshua laughed, "Isn't that the cutest name?"

"Where are you?"

"I'm home now...but she called me when I was just leaving and asked me to join her for a cigarette during her fifteen-minute break. And before I knew it... We were making out in an alley between restaurants. I'm glad we had some practice...whew!" Joshua paused again with a loud breath. "You know she is thin as a rail, but she has some cute breasts when we hugged and think I touched them... on the outside of course, Hahaha!" he bellowed with laughter over the phone.

Peg was smiling like a happy half-moon and glad to be annoyed by his bellow, wondering what in the world was happening in Cocoa Beach. "Congratulations Joshua...I'm out for a walk to get some Ice Cream."

"I wish I could join you but I'm already in my pajamas playing with myself. I can't help it...I'm so excited."

Peg winced at the thought of that scene but continued forward trying not to howl at her new friend finding love. "Well, best of luck with that Joshua."

He continued with his monologue, "But here's the best thing Peg. She runs a little coffee shop a couple of blocks south of you on A1A during the mornings and serves at Coconuts in the evening. You should stop by this weekend and see her. She thought you were really pretty."

Peg was floored by the flattery and excited by the news. "Sounds good I'll call you this weekend to catch up."

Joshua undeterred by her attempts to end the conversation, continued. "She's very industrious and a super hard worker. The Café has books to read and borrow, and games to play. There's a wall for community goings-on, up and down the Space Coast and Merritt

Island. It's for the community. A place for people to hang out in the morning. Her Dad got the lease dirt cheap for 18 months to see if she could make a go of it. The whole thing inside was her idea. She bakes all the stuff like pastries and cookies to sell and is starting some morning sandwiches soon…I can't wait to see it."

Peg was pleased to be distracted by her friend's excitement. She reminded herself that she did have a girlfriend, it just happened to be a boy! She said goodbye and walked up to her cone place. They, of course, had sundaes and other combos of ice cream, and even sold hot dogs; but she came for the medium swirl cake cone under three dollars with tax. She waited patiently for her prize while her mind wondered. After she secured her cone, she sat at a table and watched families play with the toys set up in the sitting area. She could not imagine having kids anytime soon. Dealing with herself was a full-time job.

The idea for her response to Dragmar's text was starting to become clear. It would come tonight but show that she did not jump in with a quick response and did not want to continue to ignore him either. It would show she had another world other than him on a Friday night after a hard week of work, maybe even a date. It would be cautious but sensitive to his concerns.

She was already several blocks down the road as she licked most of the ice cream down to the cone cake structure. The sugar high was incredible like riding a wave on the shore. There was great technique in getting the cone ready for its final bites as she got closer to her apartment. The last two bites had an amount of ice cream meshed into the cake cone bottom. Overbiting a section might cause a severe brain freeze but an underbite would betray expectations of the final sugar high. As she headed up the stairs, she looked at the cone ready for chomping but turned towards the road and looked at the southern sky of stars for one last look before she proceeded with the culmination of eating a great cone. As she swallowed the last part, the freeze in her sinus area hit the upper temperatures of freeze-dom but just below the threshold of a brain freeze. It was a successful cone experience from start to finish. She felt ready to respond as she flopped down in her spot on the couch and looked at her phone. She finally wrote: "You are not alone…friend. The world can be a hard place but living in paradise is not a bad start!" She sat back and looked at her masterpiece text, then thought to herself, *take that my dear Alejandro…and already…I cannot wait for your response!*

Chapter 20

It was another magnificent day in wonderland, as Peg rolled out of bed wanting to be productive. She needed coffee, but she was not ready to go to the Café quite yet. If she was going to meet Joshua's new girlfriend, she wanted to look presentable and clear out the cobwebs in her brain. Her phone was void of any texts from Dragmar as she made herself a cup of coffee. She was relieved but curious about his next response. She put together a cute blouse and shorts and some make-up. Brushed out her hair and hit the road.

As Peg walked south on A1A past Johnson, Grant, Hayes, and Garfield Streets, she would remember each President for those few minutes after passing their signpost and recall their Presidencies to test her historical knowledge. Johnson was a horrible President, she would plainly remember, but was impeached for something stupid because he was from Tennessee and tried to gum up Lincoln's legacy. Peg hated him. Grant was a Civil War hero whom she loved and did many great things to undo Johnson's blunders but was drunk and had an administration full of corruption which reminded her of LBJ somehow. Hayes was the first President who lost the popular vote and won the Presidency when he agreed to the Compromise of 1877, even though he was a staunch abolitionist; the Compromise ushered in the era of Jim Crow in the South and ended Reconstruction. Peg hated him with a passion. Garfield was one of her favorite Presidents and unknown by most for his greatness in a short time as President, she thought. Before being shot, he accomplished amazing reforms in the government and championed civil rights for African Americans. She would get emotional sometimes when she washed her hands thinking of the filthy doctor's hands that operated on him to remove the bullet. Garfield died of a simple infection because of their extreme thoughtlessness, she remembered sadly.

The Harmony Café was the only occupant in a small set of storefronts on the north corner of the block. The Café was tucked into the edge behind the beginning of the next set of buildings in the middle of the block. It could only be seen from the northern side of the highway traffic. It had grey trim on white vinyl siding. The sign above had been hand-painted which added some originality to it. The main area of tables was small in the front along with a counter that ran for thirty feet or so. The back of the room had more tables and a wooden bench coming out of the corner for ten feet either way. A circular table had magazines scattered all over it. On the opposite side of the counter, the wall was lined with rows of shelving scattered with books, half of them paperbacks, that ran for twenty-five feet. The variety was impressive as Peg quickly scanned the collection. Beyond the shelves was a display of bulletin boards with various activities and one with loads of business cards from local customers.

Peg took her time reading the events and activities as a line of people waited for their orders to be filled. Luckily, she was in no hurry to get a coffee. The twenty or so people sitting in the Café were talking or reading books. A couple in the back had the benches to themselves as they laughed at the latest People magazine together. Peg noticed two people behind the counter taking orders or making coffee. The display of homemade baked goods was mouth-watering. The older men and women, probably in their late forties, smiled warmly at the customers they served and seemed to be enjoying themselves. Finally, Becky appeared out of the kitchen carrying a tray of turnovers that smelled delicious. Probably apple variety, Peg thought. Her parents Buddy Baker and Beth Winters, both helped her empty the tray on the counter. A half dozen of them went immediately to customers. The rest would not last long, Peg assumed.

She waited for Becky to take off her top apron as she gave instructions to her parents to go in the back for a break or preparation of some more baked goods, as she took over the counter. Peg finally joined

118

the line. Becky seemed to know every customer and enjoyed filling their order as a personal favor. Peg was sure Saturday and Sunday were her big days and guessed that her parents were happy to help her. Becky had a sun-filled face with blond streaks of hair that were cut in awkward lengths. She was thin and taller than she seemed as a server but much prettier in the daylight. Even without mascara, her eyes were striking, and her lips looked sensual. Imagining Joshua kissing her seemed strange because he looked so different than her. Sometimes opposites attract, she thought. Becky's smile was cautious because of the tooth that needed repair. As Peg got in front of her, she noticed several of her upper teeth had been capped already with the one needing more work. On closer inspection, the bottom teeth would be next to be capped. She wondered if Meth use in her growing years had rotted her teeth. She would not be the first kid on the Space Coast to experience it, but one of the few to recover from it.

"Hi, I'm Peg... Joshua's colleague and friend. I saw you last night at [AF1] [PF2] [PF3] Coconuts during Happy Hour. Joshua told me about your Café, it's lovely! I live three blocks north of here on Lincoln Street."

Becky seemed a little embarrassed but happy to meet Peg, "Thanks for coming by...it's nice to meet you," she expressed authentically as she extended her hand, "sorry about the flower on my hands." She laughed.

It seemed serendipitous to have a break in customers for them to greet each other and talk for a few minutes, but neither of them noticed as they were deeply engaged in learning. "This place seems very special Becky, I'm happy I found it," Peg admitted after exchanging pleasantries for a few minutes.

At 24, Becky seemed a bit older than her age and as experienced as Peg with boys for several years. Their eyes seemed comfortable

119

staring at each other. It was a calming experience for Peg to gaze at her. She wondered if this was what a great friendship felt like with a woman because she had never really experienced it. Finally, a customer appeared inside the door and Becky quickly asked Peg what she needed and ordered a Latte' along with one of those delicious turnovers, which she enthusiastically pointed at. As Becky filled her order, Peg moved down the counter towards the register. She wanted to say more to her about something but could not remember specifically. It was like an itch she needed to scratch but could not find it on the surface of her body. And she wanted to listen to find out so much more about her. Becky quickly returned with her order at the register, rang up a total, and gave her full attention. She wrote her phone number on the receipt and spoke softly, "I would love to spend some time with you as a friend. Do you like the beach?"

Peg was floored and excited at the same time and uttered, "Let's do it today or tomorrow if you want, I could use a beach day. I'll call you!"

Becky winked at her and smiled fully without hesitation. Peg felt a warm heart and an itch scratched as she thought, "A girlfriend...possibly...at last!"

Chapter 21

"Have you ever done a woman?"

Becky asked Peg quietly after an hour on the beach and three beers. Normally Peg would be appalled by such a question but was excited to answer Becky. Their conversation so far had been so interesting and deep. In some ways they were quite different; like their fashion sense and music, but otherwise, they shared the same philosophy about men – the older the better. Except right now Becky fancied Joshua because he was unique and kinder than anybody she had ever met. "No...never thought of it to be honest. But I have to say... I do love your lips!" Peg laughed as she cracked open another Coors Lite.

"I bet you kiss better than Joshua!" Becky fired back with a cute smile.

"O god I hope so that boy could use some experience...you could mold him any way you want him, Becky."

"That sounds like a good thing...I hope?"

"Yes, it does...he's a good kid but has all that conservative Christian crap to escape from."

"I'm used to that down here...religion has a stranglehold on most of us growing up."

"Luckily, that missed me. I had hippie parents who left me alone after I was nine or ten."

"No brothers or sisters?"

"Nope...how about you?"

121

"An older brother and sister who are very successful and live up north. I was the mistake child ten years later."

"That sounds familiar." Peg clicked beers with Becky.

"Maybe that's why we seem to connect so well Peg, we're both cute and skinny, our girls look good, and we're great kissers!" Becky laughed. "How about shaving down there? I'm kind of minimalistic, you know as long as I can wear a bathing suit without the pubic hair showing."

"Agree with that. I like the bush look as much as possible."

"Amen to that!" Becky clicked beers again. "Hey, I'm ready for the water."

"Let's hit it Becky the Baker!" Peg laughed at her silly joke.

The afternoon went beautifully as they came back to Peg's apartment and napped for an hour before cooking dinner together and watching a movie. They laughed and cried together during the entire day sharing stories and watching the movie, something on *TCM* from the fifties with *Gloria Grahame*. Becky crashed on the couch and Peg promised to wake her early for work. They talked for another hour as Becky closed her eyes and got settled under a blanket. Peg was so comfortable in the comfy chair that it was hard to get to her bed. Each of them would mention something after minutes of silence and then the other would answer. Finally, sleep came over them but Peg shook herself out of it and got up and pulled the blanket up to Becky's neck and kissed those beautiful lips. She smiled as she went to her room, got under the covers, and set the alarm on her phone for 5 a.m. Before falling into a deep sleep, she thought of Becky at the Café and how she had jumped into her life, like a sister she never had. What was October going to bring? Work, Write, Walk, and Wonder she hoped. It was a perfect day.

Chapter 22

Peg pondered the weekend hours she spent with Becky, getting to know her new friend. Being at the beach together, hanging at her apartment, seeing her at the Café, and meeting locals was all full of pleasure without drama. She had a wonderful experience with almost three days of interaction. As she sat in the City Council room waiting for the mayor after the Wednesday bi-weekly meeting, the good feelings kept going through her head. Her sullen-looking face was starting to create new muscles from all the smiling she had done.

Seeing the mayor was not the highlight of every other week anymore, but she did not want him to know that. It was important to act like there was nothing different between them. As they talked and hugged, she was relieved to see how busy his face looked. No questions about Dragmar as he was focused on a few concerns about the new City budget for Fiscal '23 that had just been passed. She was good for the next couple of weeks, she predicted. In another month or so, Jackie would sit down with her and want an update on her life and any contact with Dragmar. She had to be ready because something was happening in his life concerning Dragmar and it might be scary. More reason to connect with Dragmar, her Alejandro, and her potential dream relationship, she reminded herself. Somehow, she had to learn the information about both men without getting caught in the middle of it.

There was only one route for her to go and she knew what it was. She needed Phillip to get her focused and she needed her father to get back in town and talk to her. Just that was close to an impossible task. It had been eighteen years since they had been pals, now they were strangers trying to get in the same zip code.

Her job was in the second month and becoming tolerable. The fourth graders were starting to act like the nine-year-olds she knew and loved. The girls were melting their frozen personalities and warming up to her presence and the boys were settling down and enjoying her attention. They liked it when she played with their hair. It would happen innocently before, during, or after class and have calming results.

During the second week of class, two boys were fighting in her class. Instead of sending them down to the principal, she talked to them during recess and rubbed their heads as she stood behind each of them, alternately. It mesmerized them, and both hugged her after they solved the issue and went running out to recess. Since then, she picked out two boys to work on each class day for the opportunity to play with their hair or rub their buzzed heads. About a quarter of the boys believed buzzed haircuts were the best way to handle all the outside activities. By fifth or sixth grade, they would discover girls and then let their hair grow out.

The hugging afterward seemed important since most of them were just tall enough to reach her bust line. Each boy found a way during the day to get one. The smell of Miss Patterson and the thought of being close to her breasts would keep them engaged all day. She would take any advantage to get these boys to focus on her in class. It seemed to be working.

During the back-to-school night, she hit a home run. She dressed like a knock-out, fashion icon and prepared her presentation like a CEO. Her PowerPoint slides were well-organized and fun at the same time. The men were drooling over her copper-toned body and the women loved her shoes, outfit, and hair. Any problems they discussed were dealt with by Peg like a politician spinning slogans. The individual conferences were concise and full of optimism for every student. These parents had not seen such professionalism by a new teacher at Satellite Elementary School in recent memory. It did not hurt that her new friend Becky catered her room with homemade baked goods and beverages from The Café. The publicity would start a buzz in Satellite Beach about the new Cape Atlantic coffee shop on A1A.

Peg wanted to be alone by 8 p.m. on Friday. She sipped at her beer with Joshua at their end-of-the-week Happy Hour at Coconuts on the Beach in CB, but her heart was not into it. She played the role of a good listener, as Joshua reported about seeing Becky several times during the week and how his back-to-school night went with his class at Merritt Island Elementary.

"Peg you should have seen it. I had those parents eating out of my hand after my presentation. It was all fire and brimstone about how important their kid's education is. Some of the men didn't take to me that well but most were congenial, and the moms were lovely."

"And the kids?"

"We had a great week…I seemed to have so much get-up-and-go." Joshua whispered the following, "I didn't know sex would give me so much energy!"

Peg smiled but did not react like she would have two weeks ago talking to Joshua. She knew Becky had changed her life, so it was not unexpected to see Joshua in la la land. "Joshua some things are better left unsaid!" She playfully pushed him away.

"I hope you're not jealous. I hear she spent the night at your apartment after your Beach Day on Saturday. Wait a minute, maybe I should be the jealous one!" He laughed boyishly.

Peg wondered for a minute what she had gotten herself into but pulled out of it when she saw Becky coming. She looked a little different Peg thought as she said Hello.

"Hey, two of my favorite Space Coasters! Joshua are we on for later tonight?"

"Of course, my dear."

"And Peg… a beach day this weekend?"

Peg hesitated a moment and looked again at Becky. Her hair was different…styled and cut a little less ragged. But there was something else and then she smiled as she asked again, "Peg this weekend?" The tooth was capped, maybe not permanently, but addressed…finally! She was even more attractive than before. "Let me text you after tonight. I must set up a couple of things this weekend when I get home. My father is coming into town soon and I should talk to my mother about it…ugh!"

Becky leaned forward and squeezed her chin, then brought her luscious lips within an inch of Peg's. "Well… don't leave me out of the schedule. I need some beach time with my girl." She winked at her as she pulled away. "Got to get back to work!" She pounded her heart and pointed to her girl and boyfriend as she walked away.

Joshua started more conversation that became a monologue, Peg's sullen face broke into a smile occasionally, but her mind was elsewhere.

Chapter 23

Paco Lawrence was driving his ten-year-old Toyota Prius over the Indian River bridge forsaking the government-issued black Chevy SUV because he had his DEA boss with him and did not want to be noticed by any look-outs early Saturday morning as he headed to meet with Dragmar or the real Alejandro Majada in his condo on the Banana River in Cape Atlantic. It was a surprise visit because there was heat on the mayor, that Dragmar had uncovered, and just in case there had been leakage, they wanted to be unseen by the mayor's men.

They parked in the lot next to the soccer field. It was still dark at 6:30 a.m. as they headed towards the back of the condo building. Checking for any vehicles anywhere, Paco led his boss, Cheverly Santiago, who went by Chevy (pronounced like the car), into the building and up four flights of stairs. Chevy was a firecracker of energy and hopped up the stairs in double time, laughing as Paco walked slowly up each step like it was an epoch of time. "Paco you look like you're climbing Everest, let's go, go, go!"

Paco had known and mentored Chevy during her career. At thirty-eight and fifteen years in the DEA, she was a new breed of action agent who administered programs but also took to the field and got her fingernails dirty. He was proud of her quick advancement to the top. At his age, he could not keep up with her. All he could do was flash that smile of his, full of teeth. When he got to the top with her, he went over the assignment. "It's the fifth door on the left... number 505. I'll slip the key in and let you in first. His bedroom is in the back. Try to be quiet."

She nodded and followed his instructions. She moved like a cat inside the condo, noticing the mess in the kitchen and shoes and clothes thrown on the couch. His bedroom was just off the living room twelve feet or so before the balcony sliding glass doors. The door was cracked open, and Alejandro was sleeping like a baby curled up with several pillows. They both stepped in as Paco sat on the bed and quietly called out his name. Surprisingly, he opened his eyes as though he was expecting them.

"Paco…why is there a woman in my bedroom?"

"This is my boss DEA Special Agent Cheverly Santiago. Listen, we had to be careful to get in here just in case somebody was watching."

"Can I pee first…excuse me Special Agent Santiago." Alejandro grabbed a shirt and shorts and made it to the bathroom. He relieved himself, washed his hands and face, then combed his hair after putting on his shirt and shorts. "Let's go to the kitchen and get some coffee…anybody need a cup or some tea?"

Chevy and Paco followed him to the kitchen and found two spots at the counter. Paco answered, "We're good Alejandro, but please help yourself."

"Sorry about the mess. I usually keep a pretty clean place. Saturday is my clean-up day. The crew was out late last night, so I got in about two a.m. Who are you avoiding?"

"Don't underestimate the mayor, Alejandro, he must know by now you're on to him."

"How would that be possible?"

"He is spending more time with the Pawn Shop guy according to our wire in his shop. He knows something about you. Somebody from the FBI ran something and then met with him. They are old friends, so it may have been nothing, but we can't be sure. Especially if they found something special."

Alejandro took his coffee black and sipped it softly. He thought about everything that had transpired since he got out of prison and appeared in Cape Atlantic. Then he thought of Peg, She knows the mayor, but why would she tell him about the incident, at least in detail? All he knows is that I apologized to her about something. If he did know about it, he might have run a check on me with someone in the FBI or even DEA, but how could he get my real name and information, that's impossible, he felt certain. "I appreciate your caution Paco, but I assure you no one knows my connection to you guys."

"Fine...Mr. Majada tell us what you have found out so far about the mayor or his organization." Chevy was a dark skin Peruvian like Alejandro with her black hair tied in a ponytail. She had very strong cheekbones and deep dark eyes. Her body was petite and strong-looking at the same time. Her mannerisms were unemotional and minimal. She was not a lesbian but had not been with a man in a decade. She had a teenage boy from a failed marriage who took up all of her social life.

Alejandro picked up a file and dropped it in front of Chevy and Paco. "It's better if you read through it as I talk it through. There are two copies there of everything. Everything the mayor has his hands on goes back over sixty-five years. The old man Calvanese started everything. He is on his last legs at a retirement home in Rockledge about twenty minutes from here. He's on the penthouse floor of the place. It's quite a palace. Jackie has gone there every other day mostly but every day for the last two weeks. His sister and brother are not involved anymore. They are down in West Palm Beach in beautiful residences, each with a beach house as well. The real estate holdings are the central tenet of their power. Not only in Cape Atlantic but across Central Florida. The brother and sister have already been bought out. The estate is worth at least $500 million maybe several billion or more – all goes to Jackie through a trust. Tons of money in off-shore accounts buried many, many years ago." He took some time to let things sink in and then he continued. "The drug empire is not a big thing. He does it to control the drugs in the city. It's weird but he loves Cape Atlantic and the Port. Every once in a while, he has to reign in Anmar at the Pawn Shop about the supply. Anmar had been adding fentanyl patches to his supply and Jackie went nuts on him. The last thing Jackie wants is dead cruise ship visitors in the Port or the Cape." Alejandro emphasized. "You know, he's a pretty good guy according to everybody in the city that works for him. He wants to take over Florida with the Governorship and try to flush out the corruption, as crazy as those sounds. The last three terms of Governor have just about ruined Florida, he believes. He plans to run in 2024 for State Senate and 2026 for Governor. He wants his rebuilding plan, done by his companies and run by his sons, for the city to start right after he leaves office in 2024 and becomes State Senator. It should be mostly done by the time he is in the Governor's office by 2026. It will be another money maker to pay for his campaign, but more importantly, the Cape and the Port will become the jewel of the Space Coast to show off state-wide. He plans to spend $20 million for a state senate race in 2024, which is crazy, but he will spend it for statewide name recognition and then budget $200 million in 2026 for the Governor's office."

"So, you think other than his Space Coast operation, his drug operation is minimal," Chevy stated sarcastically.

"I did not say that…Miss Santiago."

"Please Alejandro…Chevy. You're both from Peru…I believe?"

"Oh well…Chevy that's good to know." Alejandro was drawn to her eyes for the first time. She seemed pretty tough but was trying to show some softness. He thought she needed a good fucking, if she was not a lesbian, as he primitively assessed her sexuality.

"What we don't know is what's coming through the Port. That's the operation that has increased tenfold in the last decade. In 2012, three Cruise ships a week were going through the Port, mainly *Disney*. Now

30 a week with the new ports for *Carnival* and *Royal*. The word is that everything for Orlando is now coming through the Port. Jackie gets a cut but has nothing to do with day-to-day operations from what I hear."

"We need more intel on that Alejandro. Miami has dropped operations in Orlando, and we suspect Tampa and the Port have taken over as supply routes. Fentanyl and its derivatives have been flooding Central Florida for years. All ages are dropping like flies. More than traffic deaths now." Chevy paused for a moment to look at the young stud in front of her. He was ten years younger than her but seemed extremely mature. How does a kid like that get caught up in this drug world as a kid? She wanted to know more about his past, as the file did not tell it all. Surprisingly, she was very attracted to him. The deadness in her body felt some life for the first time in a while. Maybe it was the fact that they shared the same tribe, she thought. "What about the gambling stuff?"

"Again, small time…just the casino boat and some games in his strip joints, which are all pretty clean by the way. In his way, Jackie is controlling the vices in the town, making money, but keeping them in check and free from violence for the most part."

"I hope you're right. He may be the person for us to get behind to run this fucking state." Paco piped up his opinion. "The working folks in Central Florida have been getting fucked for so long, it seems like normal. Do you know that forty percent of black men are felons and could not vote in the last election even after the referendum was passed giving them the right to vote? Tallahassee held it up for two years. At least this sounds promising bizarrely."

"Yep…I agree Paco…Chevy. Let me know how you want me to proceed."

Chapter 24

The 'Join US 1st Diner' just south of Titusville was close enough for Hazel Bannister to walk to from her trailer park home because it was located just across the US Route 1 highway, but at age sixty-eight she would have to navigate 4 lanes of highway to get to her server job. Instead, she still drove her 1969 Oldsmobile Cutlass Supreme with a 350 V8 engine and a 4-speed manual transmission to work every day. Because of the highway divider blocking an easy crossover from her residence, she joyously drove almost a mile to the first place to legally U-turn, shifting aggressively through all four gears to hit seventy mph quickly before the U-turn. She always hoped the "coast would be clear" to peal a U-turn, downshifting into second gear, before resuming acceleration to seventy mph; and finally turning into the parking lot to find a spot behind the Diner so no one would get close to her classic car which was worth around sixty-grand, according to Lester. The car was in Hazel's possession for life, now fifty-three years old, after buying it new, just before she was sixteen with her Daddy's help and her babysitting savings. It still had less than sixty thousand miles and would likely outlast her. It was the one thing Lester addressed, like religion, when he returned home each year. It had its own garage and concrete driveway that he had built next to her trailer park home.

At one time Hazel was as hot looking as her car, but the wear and tear of hippie life and her love affairs with drugs gave her a look of almost eighty. She did her best to look good, but her hair was too thin for coloring to make sense and her skin was too wrinkled for make-up to hide it all. The silverness of her thinning hair gave her a realness that allowed her a credible, elderly status that she lacked at other stages in her life. She added small bows to her hair to add color and distraction to her silver-thinness reality. Amazingly, her teeth had survived and prospered with her constant whitening of them to show her sweet smile. Her hazel-green eyes were also still vibrant, giving an observer a window into her past as a younger woman. Living on stimulants for years helped her figure stay slim; and during this century, finally wore bras that held together her once-hanging breasts in her tight blouses and skinny jeans. It was still hard for Lester to keep his hands off her whenever he was in town. Surprisingly, since Peg was nine or ten, she stayed celibate when Lester was away even though she had plenty of suitors after her – even now.

Peg had recruited her new friend Becky to visit Hazel with her at the Diner and find out what she could about Lester her father returning home. She knew Hazel worked Tuesdays and Thursdays, lunch and dinner shifts, and one brunch shift on the weekends. Getting there after school around 3:30 p.m. would be her break time. More than likely, she would find Hazel smoking a cigarette out back near her car with a friend or two.

Hazel would easily clear over two thousand dollars a month as a server, to match her income from Social Security. She had less than five hundred dollars in bills a month, which gave her over fifteen hundred dollars in spending money a month. Since Social Security started to come in to direct deposit over four years ago, she had not touched that account, giving her over a hundred thousand dollars in the bank. She had some other savings in a mutual fund Lester set up years ago, the classic car, and paid-off trailer home and garage worth at least a hundred thousand dollars. On the other hand, she spent her leftover income easily every month, enjoying a bevy of activities with her girlfriends. Little did Peg know that she would inherit a nice chunk of change when Hazel's heart finally might give out in the next decade or less. All of her money would bypass Lester and go directly to Peg. He made certain of that in Hazel's Will that she signed a decade ago with a glancing look. In Peg's mind, Hazel as a mother had been worthless in making her feel protected, in her death she might finally get some of that security.
Peg pulled up behind the classic Oldsmobile Cutlass, remembering that she had learned to drive with a manual transmission in that car only a dozen years ago. Handling that clutch *made a man out of her*, her mother

would say. It was one of the better moments she remembered with her mom. Unexpectedly, Hazel was never nervous about Peg learning to drive her masterpiece.

As she had guessed, Hazel was pulling every ounce of nicotine from her cigarette when she saw Peg. It had been months since they had seen each other, but Hazel acted calmly like it had been yesterday. She was the exact height of Peg as they met with a hesitant hug. "Peg, you look great. Let me look at you." Hazel said in a surprising tone as she held on to her biceps and at arm's length, she gave Peg an up-and-down, look-over and squeezed her shoulders while breaking into a prominent smile. Always surprised by her fashion sense, she hugged Peg again with passion and stayed together for almost ten seconds. Peg felt her mother's breasts deep inside her chest and finally let her hands feel her mother's body which felt void of fat and full of bones.

"Mom…this is my friend Becky. She runs the Harmony Café on Garfield and A1A and does serving at *Coconuts on the Beach* in Cocoa Beach."

Hazel knew the Space Coast like the back of her hand, she took a long, final drag of her burning cigarette and let it drop as she exhaled and stomped it out. It was a move she had perfected over the years, like a movie star in the nineteen-forties or 1950s. "If that's a hopping place, you can make some real money, Miss Becky," Hazel winked at her, "What are you doing with the Café? That location is hidden driving from the south if I remember correctly."

Becky was pleased to fill her in on the details as Hazel tried her best to look interested. She was surprised to see Peg with a friend and assumed it was a good thing. She never would judge Peg if she was experimenting with her sexuality, but she was pretty positive she liked guys, exclusively. Sometimes Hazel thought Peg might be happier being with a woman. In her own experience, she knew men could be tough to live with or without, "My girlfriends and I will have to descend on your place some morning after 10 am. Can't wait to see it. Best of luck with it, young lady...Becky the Baker," she laughed as she touched Becky on the shoulder and then guided the two of them inside. "Let me get you girls inside to a booth with something to drink, so we can chat a bit."

They settled into a booth far away from any activity, sipping green tea that Hazel had made for them with their pot from the kitchen. Peg quickly brought up her reason for being there, "Mom...when does Dad come in town?"

"I thought we might catch up a bit, hear about your new job, your new friend, romances..." Hazel turned her eyes downward and sipped on her tea, clearly disappointed.

"I'm sorry Mom, I just don't know how long you have to talk, and I wanted to be ready for Dad when he visits."

"I see," she paused to collect herself and gained a smile again, "he could be in town as soon as this weekend, but he has some business to take care of that will take a week or so." She stared directly at her daughter to make sure that "some business to take off" would not be discussed. Peg knew about Lester's business and thought it was pretty harmless. She had no idea the volume of pounds being moved to the Space Coast.

"Wow...so I might be able to see him by the weekend of the twenty-first and second of October."

"Well, Peg...I'm sure he'll want to see you as soon as he can, but I can't speak for him about his schedule. I learned that a long, long time ago." She said with a hardened smile.

"I understand Mom…with work and stuff, the weekend would be the best time. Can you tell him to call me, so we can set something up?"

"Absolutely Peg…now tell me about your job and your friend here."

Surprisingly, Peg had her mother's attention for the longest time in her adult memory. She went an entire half-hour without asking for a cigarette break out back, and then they all continued to talk while she leaned against the Cutlass [AF1]. Something about having Becky there seemed to make her mom feel more comfortable and able to focus on listening.

Could she be approaching this whole mom relationship wrong all these years? Peg wondered. Did she need to feel some competition or did Peg seem more interesting now that she had a friend and a professional job? At least Lester called to congratulate her on graduating, she remembered as an annoyance, so she never bothered to give her mom the details of the ceremony. Not that Peg wanted her to go to it, but she thought, what was the point without family to see her walk across the stage? Isn't that what families do? To be twenty-eight and graduate with a bunch of twenty-two-year-olds was not a ceremony she would attend without a reason to feel proud, she decided.

Instead of heading back in, Peg gracefully let Hazel get back to work and thanked her for talking on such short notice. Hazel again hugged her daughter with intensity, told her not to be such a stranger, and promised again to get her dad to call her. For a moment it seemed that Hazel had a tear or two in her eyes, but maybe it was just the cigarette smoke, Peg decided it was the former.

On the way home, Becky went on about Hazel. How nice she was and an assorted number of observations. Peg nodded a lot and wondered if her fog of anxiety had kept her from seeing the reality about her parents at times; or how easily she could make friends, or enjoying sex, or just about everything that she was suddenly good doing. What had changed? Finally, graduating? Meeting Phillip? But maybe it was real…meeting Dragmar and the disaster of getting assaulted then giving evidence to the mayor, and now forgiving him. *What was all that?* She took in a long breath and wondered if she was in charge of herself sometimes.

Wanting to talk to her father to find out what happened to her was becoming an obsession, taking over her idle time. Why now, she thought. Was breaking through the cloud of anxiety just a matter of courage or newly found confidence because she persisted in finishing her degree; and was now making something out of herself, by really becoming a teacher? An interesting theory she pondered.

Whatever the reason, Peg knew things were different now and her anxiety would not stop her from finding out the truth about what changed her innocence and taken away her courage. Over eighteen years of feeling lost and close to no one. It took a stranger to change her life and now she needed his help to get her dad back into her life for good – and for the bad.

Part III
Rip Tide

Chapter 25

Mid-October was always a high point of trepidation on the Space Coast. If the hurricane season had bypassed the area so far and the two-week forecast showed little activity in the warm seas west of Africa, where those terrible tempests seem to gain a passport for obliteration, a collective sigh was calmly exhaled by those natives aware of the reward – the pleasant beauty of the Florida Fall. As the temperature on the Space Coast settled into perfect days of mid-eighties and nights of low sixties with no rain except for a rare shower at night for an hour or less, Jackie Calvanese was feeling the heat from the multifaceted inquiry observing his existence. His father had worked out a perfect system for years to keep the DEA at bay in Central Florida. It was a brilliant maze of offshore payoffs, real estate deals, and construction at a discount; but this new operation was giving him more heartburn than usual. He had never been in on any serious action destroying human life in the past. As far as he knew, Francis was a mellow operator who made everybody happy to avoid violence. He always outlasted any heat on him because his business interests were so diverse. But now Jackie had to figure out the seriousness of this rogue interest in his empire and the combination of mob interests in the mid-Atlantic and the FBI/DEA operation backing this alias of Alejandro Majada–Dragmar. He wondered if Dragmar was being set up by the Baltimore family including Anmar, in retaliation for his take-down of "The Turk" or did the DEA wanted to simply use him to continue to infiltrate his operation as Dragmar. Jackie's discovery of Dragmar's creation by the FBI through his friend Juliana was his trump card. No one in the DEA would know that…he was certain. But his mind these days would uncharacteristically wander into new baseless theories. Could the Florida political machine be that smart in taking him down before he got started politically statewide? He knew they were formidable but were they that brilliant? When it came to holding on to power and corruption, anything was possible politically in the Sunshine State, but brilliant – he did not think so.

His schedule was full of fundraisers for delegate and state senate races in Central Florida for the mid-terms. He was determined to make his 2024 run for the State Senate, a runaway against a Republican incumbent. His support from the local mayors, city managers, educators, and the business community throughout the County would be unquestioned when he planned to announce less than a year from now. His platform would be all about Education because he wanted Brevard County and all of Central Florida to become the mecca for public education in the state. It would be the perfect platform and a stepping-stone for his gubernatorial run in 2026. The key for Jackie, he concluded, was to avoid the rip-tide, a dangerous undercurrent that he could not see coming. Did he need a plan to eliminate Dragmar or convince his DEA handlers he was doing good for the people?

The last City Council meeting in October would leave only two more for the rest of the year. With the budget set for the 2023 fiscal year and the holidays in November & December, meetings had limited agendas and were sparsely attended. Peg brought her friend Becky to her first meeting and of course to meet the mayor. They exchanged pleasantries and Becky's business information.

"We're heading up to the *La Cantina* if you two want to join us for a beer or two since we ended early. It's my favorite dive bar in Cape Atlantic." Jackie smiled.

The two women looked at each other and Becky stated, "We're in! Mr. Mayor."

Jackie leaned in and got his strong hug from Peg gave Becky a special lean-in and whispered in her ear, "It's Jackie, my dear."

"I think we'll walk up there Jackie…it's so nice out and we can drink as much as we want."

"Sounds good…I'm all for being good citizens!"

La Cantina was a mile north on to North Atlantic going towards the Port. It was a one-story building, a few feet below the road with gravel parking all around and a sign that blared out Warm Beer, Cold Food, and High Prices for those with a sense of humor. It survived hurricane damage in 2016 to the roof and floor. The bar was in the middle, creating two separate seating areas with a backroom for a pool table. You could sit out front on tables if you wanted to watch the slow and sporadic two lanes of cars and bikes go by, but most people sat around the U-shaped bar. The food was Mexican and surprisingly good along with great fried chicken. Domestic beers cost two to three dollars all day with a limited variety of fancy beers for four dollars. It had a dozen televisions around with sports on but most of them were old-time televisions with smaller screens. The owner, since '91, was a hippie surfer type who had one big screen HDTV if you were that serious about a game on the left side of the bar. The jukebox was playing with an occasional couple dancing on the right side of the bar area. It attracted the trailer park folks up and down North Atlantic Avenue and older folks who enjoyed a sixties-type bar. Canadian snowbirds staying in the condos always fell in love with the place, getting a *Bud* or *Coors* for two bucks a piece felt like home.

Jackie had a couple of tables with City employees and friends on the left side near the pool table room. Baseball playoffs were on with Jackie's New York team pounding Cleveland as usual into submission. He was feeling like a champion, standing at the table, showing his smooth political moves between voters on different ends of the table and the spectrum of partisanship.

"Peg and Becky welcome…these are the folks working hard for the city." Jackie nodded over to the bartender for another bucket of beers for the table. Jackie walked around the table put his arm around Becky and said, "I'll bet you're a pool shooter…Am I right?"

Becky was looking prettier tonight than usual, wearing a full display of make-up and her hair looking a bit longer. She matched Peg's fashion style for the night with a nice tight blouse and short skirt. Peg was not surprised that Jackie would give her his full attention. He liked them young, she thought. She grabbed a *Coors Light* from the bucket on the table and walked over to the other side to check out the digital jukebox. She pulled ten dollars out of her purse and started pounding out numbers for songs to replace the Country Western nonsense playing that she grew sick of after ten minutes.

"Hey, make sure you play some *Beatles* or maybe some *ELO…*"

Peg heard loudly before she turned around, hoping it was Phillip. She ran over to his bar stool and hugged him as she barely reached his chest. "I never thought of meeting you at this dump. What brings you here?"

"The Seaport entrance is just a hundred yards north of here, making it about fifteen hundred steps from my Condo. It's between here and the *Holiday Inn Resort* Bar to get a drink and this is always more interesting. I think any novel we write about the Cape would have to include this place somehow."

"What a great idea…hey the mayor asked my friend Becky and I to come with his employees up here. I usually bypass this place, but it's an acquired taste and it's better than Barry's!"

"It depends on what you're looking for," Phillip suggested, "Barry's is about watching Frankie work her magic and Barry complaining, here it's about being unnoticed unless you try hard to talk to someone."

Peg loved to listen to Phillip talk. Her face felt different now because the muscles stretched into constant smiles around him. She could not help herself from getting his attention, "hey help me with my selections." They stayed in close quarters to each other for the next ten minutes haggling over songs. Peg was feeling high from the alcohol and from being around such maleness. She kept holding his arm and rubbing his back. Finally, Becky found her and broke up the lovefest.

"Here you are Peg...wow I thought you left me. Let me guess...this is Phillip?"

"Yes, it is...can you believe it? Phillip this is Becky, my new friend that runs the Harmony Café down at Garfield and A1A."

"Oh, my wife loves that place! We haven't been by for quite some time...but next week we'll come down and see you."

"That would be great. I have heard a lot about you. Peg needs to talk to you."

"I admit I've been missing you Phillip, but with school and everything I've been so busy. We need to talk about my dad soon. He's coming in town next week."

"This weekend would be perfect, I'm free as a bird...okay Becky you pick some tunes."

"There we go '*Free Bird*' by our boys from Jacksonville!" Becky cheered.

"Way before you two were born, I had their first two albums on eight-track tapes the first time I drove through Florida in May of 1974. Back then I couldn't get enough of them. They made five great albums before the plane crash in '77. Lots of memories for me."

Both Peg and Becky had one arm draped over Phillip's back and waist. The alcohol was helping them feel the love between the three of them. "Girls you better give the mayor some love over there or you could be in trouble. Come back and check on me later."

"Becky goes back and keep him busy. He wants you all to himself. I'll be over soon." Peg smiled.

"You are so jealous, Peg...I like that! Take care of Phillip. I'll bring you another beer."

"Good idea. Thanks, Becky!" Peg waved as she snuggled back with Phillip to ponder more selections. He simply felt like a teddy bear that she could not squeeze hard enough and felt happy that he was unfazed by her affection. She could use a big brother or Uncle type right now. Jackie was a little challenging because she had wanted to fuck him at one point but not now. Phillip was different, more loveable, because he was one of the nice ones, so she could look past it. And he was not interested – at all, she predicted.

"Okay, I think we nailed that...I guess it starts in the next half hour or so. Maybe you should check in with the mayor and come back when our songs start playing. Dancing might be possible!" Phillip gave her a wink that chilled her spine. It was not the usual *This is going to be great sex tonight tingle* it was something that went down a different neuron path. Something she had not felt in a long time. The path of trust, where pleasure was not invasive, but mostly available if you wanted to share it. For some reason, she was sure of it.

The mayor had an unlit cigar in his mouth as he leaned over the pool table ready to pocket the nine-ball for another match win. Jackie had been playing since he was seven and could beat almost anyone with his eyes closed. On his backstroke, he looked up at Peg coming through the door and smiled at her as he stoked the cue ball smoothly to ram the nine-ball in the corner for another win. He grabbed Becky with one arm around her waist and snagged Peg with his other to go outside for a celebration cigar. Becky had the drinks and Peg had hers as they watched Jackie light his cigar while spinning it like he was licking an ice cream cone, which Peg was craving about now. "Well, girls this is what it's all about…community! People say family first, but that's a given, at least where I come from, community is what makes a home. Where can you do shit like this on a Wednesday night?"

Becky handed Jackie his drink and went in for a hug. She was right, Peg was jealous. It was interesting to see how quickly she could be replaced. For some reason, her jealousness never felt painful, just a little numbing. She was still on a high from the tingle with Phillip.
Maybe she was finished with her crush on the mayor and needed to move to some higher ground. Either way, she was glad Becky was getting needed attention. Jackie could make or break her business in exchange for a little affection.

Jackie talked for ten minutes as he smoked his cigar, mostly with Becky, then said his goodbyes and headed home. Peg got her hug and turned to go inside before he finished up with Becky. She found her way over to the dance side plucked Phillip off his stool at the bar and slowly danced with him. She nestled her head in his chest and tried to bury her fear of the world in his fortification. It was a wonderful five minutes to be lost in his protection. Finally, she let go of him and grabbed another beer to start a big gulp. Becky showed up with her face redder than usual and grabbed Phillip for the next dance. She looked satisfied and ready to celebrate.

Peg realized that Becky had decided to be with the mayor. It would be a slow burn of time to get all the way there, but her Café could become successful and open four locations in Brevard County and then more in Orange County. Meanwhile, her teeth could become gorgeous, and her wardrobe could become anything she wanted. These could be the fruits of becoming his mistress. It could be a fun and prosperous thirty months, but when the Governor campaign started, Jackie would become a family man again when he moved upstate – at least politically.

Chapter 26

For an entire weekend, Peg had turned off her phone and assumed residence in Phillip's front bedroom. He wanted her to write about her childhood through her teenage years, as much as she could remember. Phillip served as a chef and a kind ear when necessary. Walks were encouraged as well as time on the beach with a pad of paper for any memories recovered.

She spent hours walking through the Brevard County Park walk-through and the beach in front of it. Many things looked different, but the smells seemed the same as did the look of the beach. The crowds were thin with an isolated child or two swimming in the beginning of low tide where the water was barely a foot or so. She focused on one young girl about eight or nine diving into the breakers without much attention from her mother a good eighty yards away in front of the dunes, reading a book. She had a young one digging up sand just in front of her that was taking most of her attention from her reading. The young swimmer was quite agile in taking on the slightly, more-than-normal surf. She would be lost for a few seconds and then appear, hopping up and down before the next wave approached. Neither the parent nor the young daughter seemed to care if either were interested.

Peg kept watching, trying to walk as slowly as possible. She wondered if this was how she started to learn her independence. Of course, her father never had a young one to worry about in addition to her. The joy being expressed by the young girl was endless in time. It might be thirty minutes before she realized that she was tired. Time back then for Peg was endless. A half-hour could have felt like an eternity. At some point, she would have come back to her blanket and dozed off in the sun for a bit before attacking the surf again. Luckily, her dad would always leave a cooler of food and drinks, even if he headed off to the bar at the Resort.

As she headed down the shore, there were several examples of kids in the water: wading, jumping, swimming, diving, and surfing at different depths and distances from the beach. Some had adults within reach, but others were alone exploring what they wanted without a watchful eye. It made her feel more comfortable about her upbringing. *Maybe her father was ahead of his time*, she joked to herself.

When she arrived back at Phillip's place, her phone was on her bed with a note from Phillip, "There are some messages you should check, I'll be back for dinner time. Enjoy your nap." Joshua and Becky had both called to check in on her weekend and wished her well. The third message was from Hazel. She reported that her dad was home, and did she want to meet for dinner? Peg was incensed. How could her mom be so callous? Never had she been invited for dinner when Dad was home. Was it her way of trying to include her? Peg had said she needed to talk to her dad, not the both of them!

She wrapped herself in a blanket and began to cry. *My Mother is such a fuck-up!* There was no point in answering the message. She could not text her mother (Hazel could not figure out how) and she did not want to yell at her mother on the phone. After ten minutes of letting her tears flow, she decided to call her dad after dinner and find out when she could see him – alone! But for now, she decided to let go of her anger at her clueless mother and take a nap.

It was still light out when Peg heard the front door open and saw Phillip walk into the kitchen with several bags of groceries. The time change was still two weekends away, so the light lingered past seven p.m. Taking a two-hour nap was so unusual for Peg but it felt great as she slowly got herself sitting up on the side of the bed. She wanted to take a quick shower, but it seemed like too much trouble, and she liked the smell of the ocean on her body. Her bathing suit was dry and comfortable, so she threw on a red Maryland t-shirt that Phillip had given her for the weekend. It was oversized but fit her like a mini-skirt in case she decided to lose the bathing suit underneath at some point to be more comfortable. She was totally at home with Phillip.

"Can I get you some wine, a drink, or bottled water?" Phillip asked as Peg shuffled by the island in the kitchen, he put away some groceries and got ready to cook some fish and vegetables. *It looked yummy*, Peg thought.

"A water would be great, and I'll do wine if you share a bottle with me."

Phillip grabbed a water out of the fridge and in one motion flipped it to her behind his back about twenty feet away as she headed towards the couch. Peg proudly snagged it and plopped on the couch. She gulped about half of it and smiled across the condo at Phillip at his talent. "Hopefully you'll hand me the glass of wine when you're ready…or I can come and get it!" She laughed.

"It's on the table if you want to open it and pour me a glass. Dinner will be about twenty minutes."

"Great!" Peg finished off the water and found the wine at the dining table and opened it up.

"So, what did you learn today on your little adventure through Brevard Park?"

"Can you put me in a trance? I think I remember something."

"Before dinner?"

"Yes, right now…please?"
Phillip turned off the stove top led her to the couch and sat to her right on the loveseat couch. "Close your eyes and focus on your breathing."

Phillip waited for twenty seconds and spoke slowly, but in clear tones to relax her face, down her neck, across her shoulders, down her forearms, throughout her fingers, to expand her chest and ribs and let go, settle her pelvis, quiet her thighs, release her hamstrings, let go of her calves, extend her feet, open her toes and then all the tension out. He waited for her breathing to be a whisper and then suggested, "Tell me what you remember today."

Quietly, just above a whisper, Peg spoke, "I saw a girl playing in the surf, it felt alone, but then I saw her confidence and it felt calm, then she played and swam and battled the surf. It was lovely. And her mother was up against the dunes, not aware of her daughter's world, just tanning."

"What did it make you remember about the past?"

"At home…when my father left…I had no protector…no one confident in me when he was gone for months."

"What made you feel unprotected?"

"My mother…had these men…and these parties"

"Where do you feel unprotected?"

"In my back…it feels weird down there…someone's breathing on me."

"How do you feel now?"

"I'm okay…I feel protected."

Phillip took extra time to reinforce that feeling with a metaphor using symbols that were reassuring for Peg like feeling the Sun, hearing the waves, and touching the sand with her toes. He also talked about writing down her feelings to save her thoughts. Slowly he started to wake her from the trance. "Feel your breathing slowly increase…let the blood go everywhere in your body. Wake up your toes, your feet, your legs. Feel your energy move your fingers and move up your arms and shoulders. Slowly move your facial muscles and when you feel ready…open your eyes." Peg slowly awakened and looked satisfied. Her stomach was talking to her loudly, I felt hungry. She looked at Phillip and spoke clearly, "Let's eat!"

Phillip was happy for Peg. He smiled and agreed, "Okay…work on the appetizer dish and wine. Let me finish the pasta I added to the meal."

Peg felt free from anxiety for the moment. It was so unusual that it felt like dreaming. She sipped her wine while Phillip cooked and stared straight ahead. Her brain was recharging and seemed to be uploading memories from the last eighteen years and it felt okay. The silence continued as Phillip finished cooking. The smells coming from the kitchen helped satiate her hunger along with the appetizers.

Phillip announced that dinner was ready as Peg poured more wine. He served her the meal, held her hand, and closed his eyes as he meditated for a moment in silence. They sat together quietly and ate everything on their plates. After Peg finished tasting the last morsel of salmon, she reached out her hand and touched his as she smiled. "Thank you," was all she could say. Phillip nodded and beamed with joy.

After they ate, they took the rest of the wine and sat on the balcony to view the ocean and the sunset on different sides of the Space Coast from the fourth floor of the condo building. She was curious to hear from Phillip and finally asked him what he thought. "Phillip…I understand you're not my therapist and you're just trying to guide me along in my journey, so just tell me what you thought during the trance.

I free you of all responsibility for your opinion!" She touched his shoulder playfully.

"We both know that something uncomfortable or maybe abusive happened to you when you were young. But more importantly, your father abandoned you because of it and your mother, well... she just faded away because of it. They were happy parents and partied a lot, and they were approaching fifty and older. Maybe something went wrong in their relationship. Your father knows a lot more than your mother does, that is my guess. It could be guilt or just selfishness, but they made you become an adult before you were ready. You and your parents have a lot of explaining to do."

"Thanks, Phillip...now it feels okay," she paused and tried to sound organized, "that helps me get my brain in the right frame of mind. I'll need some courage when I talk to my dad and then I'll have a heart-to-heart with my mom."

Phillip smiled, wondering if Peg knew what she had referenced, "maybe if you follow the yellow-brick road Dorothy...you might get home again."

Peg almost spit out the wine she was sipping and howled at her statement, "Maybe I do need a brain, a heart, and some courage...thank you Mr. Wizard!" She stood up and bowed to Phillip, "And getting a good meal makes me so happy."

Chapter 27

Cheverly Santiago had flown into Reagan National several times during her training years with the DEA. She loved to visit DC, but it was too cold in the winter and too humid in July and August. This flight was going forty miles north of the tiny airport on the Potomac into the busiest of the DC airports, BWI Thurgood Marshall Airport. It would be her first-time landing just west of the Chesapeake Bay at BWI as she looked out her seat window and gazed at the massive estuary to six states and DC while spanning two hundred miles from its thirty-mile opening into the Atlantic Ocean just north of Norfolk to the Susquehanna River in Pennsylvania. As the plane made a hard left turn, the massive twin spans of the Bay Bridge covering almost five miles connecting the Eastern Shore, looked like a *Lego* toy in a bathtub. She then noticed the U.S. Naval Academy, where she trained one summer and enjoyed a sailboat ride or two under the twin spans that made her feel like an ant.

Brooklyn O'Malley, the acting FBI director, had called her into his famous Beltsville warehouse hideaway that headquartered his takedown of Baltimore's Drug Lord "The Turk" in 2020. Cheverly had complained to her supervisor that she wanted to be in on the mayor's takedown or ascension from the Space Coast. Director O'Malley had gotten wind of it and decided to put her in charge of it at this meeting as he was heading to another venture away from government in two years.

The twenty-mile ride south on the picturesque B-W Parkway with the leaves changing, shocked her. It was something of immense beauty she had never witnessed first-hand. The Parkway owned by the Federal government had two lanes in each direction with a sizeable, wooded medium between and woods on each side of the road. Most of the overpasses and walls were done in large stone making the spectrum of colors seem like a fairy tale scene.

The second shock she had, after arriving at the warehouse bunker in Beltsville, was seeing Anmar Douglas sitting at the table as she shook hands with Brooklyn O'Malley. Her escorts and security left the three of them alone. The room was secured like an underground tunnel. All weapons and phones were outside.

"I guess you two know each other," Brooklyn smirked. "Sometimes in this business, up is down, east is west, and so on.... Anmar has put his life on the line to put away the most heinous individual in American history, "The Turk", who took over West Baltimore as the shipbuilding business closed and the middle class moved south to DC for jobs or to the Baltimore suburbs to build businesses and homes while he built an empire that destroyed the lives of thousands in the under-class who were without education and jobs. Now he is a part of a strategy to change the most important and corrupt state in the nation. We know, politically, Florida can't be run like the wild, wild west anymore."

"I'm sorry Director O'Malley, but why are you telling me all this now?"

"Because we need somebody, who is a native Floridian, and incorruptible to take over this operation."

"How do you know that…Sir?"

"Ms. Santiago, I know everything about you. When Mr. Lawrence brought you in on the Dragmar meeting, you knew something wasn't right, but you still kept your mouth shut and talked only to your supervisor. Over the past few years, we've had people come after you many times with enticing situations and you always did the right thing. This will take a decade of your life and then when you finish, the DEA would be lucky to have you as Director."

154

"So, let me see if I can get this right. You used Anmar's connection to "The Turk" to turn Alejandro Majada into Dragmar and get him back into the family somehow as a soldier to bring him down. Then put in jail as a cover after "The Turk" takedown and then brought him into Jackie's world to figure out all the leads that Anmar had discovered in his years running Jackie's drug business. And somehow Jackie doesn't know all this and is going to use all of his wealth to buy the Florida Governorship and wipe out corruption in the state." Cheverly stood up and walked over to get some water. Her head was spinning in so many directions that she needed a compass to see where she stood.

"Ms. Santiago…if I may say something, Director?" Anmar asked Brooklyn who nodded, "Things kind of fell into place because of a lot of hard work by the Director and some rare cooperation with the DEA in Baltimore. I got caught up in it and was encouraged to go south in the 90s and got involved in what I was good at…you know the Pawn Shop. Francis Calvanese helped me get successful and then it became easy to run some drugs on the Space Coast. Port Atlantic was being expanded and the concern in the DEA and the FBI was about the drugs coming in and who would control it. We have control of that, and the Director never lost connection with me and frankly, he saved my life. When he first asked me for help and then again after 9/11, I was glad to help my country. By running things as a business, you know supply and demand stuff…we kept out the mob from up north and the scum in Miami."

"No disrespect Mr. Douglas…," as she turned to Brooklyn, "but Director O'Malley is this the new patriotism?"

"Cheverly…let's not be naïve about what the country is facing. Since the bitter election of 2000, Florida has become the battleground for Federalism, and its composer, Alexander Hamilton, one of my heroes, predicted this mess when the checks and balances of the States versus the Federal government got out of whack. It's bad enough that a great state like Texas is run like a whorehouse in a saloon, but that state is too big to tame right now and needs another decade to right itself from within. Florida is our only chance to get our federal government back on track. It's just not working when one side that believes in laissez-faire government controls the Supreme Court, the Congress, almost the Senate; there is no balance, and greed is totally in charge. The reason for government is to make sure capitalism is fair and not a monopoly dominated by the few with all the money. That's the difference between a democracy and a monarchy. Hamilton, Madison, Jefferson, Adams, and Monroe all agreed on that." Brooklyn stood up got some coffee and let his sermon settle in on Cheverly. "By the way you can call me Brooks when we meet like this…Okay?"

"Sure, thing Director O'Malley. Oh, Sorry Brooks…" she winked at him and smiled. "Listen I'm Chevy, like the car!" Laughter finally cut the tension in the room. "Well, what is the game plan? Do we bring Jackie in on this plan?" Chevy inquired.

"No…that might be treason or something in that ballpark…Chevy. We have to stay in our jobs and guide the situation when we can. Anmar does what he does best, and Jackie has his ambition. He has money, so he's not driven by that. No, no, no… he realizes how terrible Florida's schools are and that the lack of a state income tax puts tons of pressure on the Counties to take care of public education themselves. Something has to change there. He loves the environment and understands the peril that Florida is in with the shorelines and the Everglades being destroyed. Those two issues should put him in Tallahassee." He sipped on his coffee and thought for a moment. "The only problem right now is Dragmar. I think he has to get out of there. Jackie must know about him somehow. He has an FBI chemist friend who did something for him and may have gotten to Dragmar's cover. It seems impossible, but we cannot let him take any more heat. We can't let Jackie do something stupid and put Dragmar in danger. His father would never do something that stupid."

"Well, good luck getting him out of there Director, he's got a thing for a local girl," Anmar admitted.

"And you're just telling me this now? Where is he living? In Orange County or something inland…right?"

"No sir…he got a place on the Banana River just below A1A in the Cape," Anmar reported.

"Yes sir, it's a pretty nice place…Brooks!" Chevy added.

"Paco took you there…did he lose his mind?" Brooks implored.

"It was dark Sir, nobody saw us." Chevy knew it was stupid as soon as she said it.

"Dark?" He pulled on his full head of hair trying to calm himself down as he put his coffee down. "If Jackie Calvanese had eyes on that building, you guys are busted. Let's hope your little parking down the Avenue before sunrise and coming in through the back venture fooled anybody watching." Brooklyn spouted out sarcastically and followed it up with a very large exhale. "Chevy… get on the next fricking flight and get Dragmar out of there. Get him to the safe house in Winterhaven and let the heat die down on this thing." Director O'Malley never cussed in front of a woman but was mumbling something to himself that was not describing a pretty picture. In a word, he was furious. "I'll meet you at the safe house in Winterhaven next week and we'll map out this thing."

"Yes sir!" Chevy hopped to her feet and hit the road running. She had her orders and wanted to correct the mistake that Paco had made. Well, she made, it because she trusted him and should have known better. She had no idea of the magnitude of the operation but loved the idea of being in the middle of it.

"Chevy…wait…come with me. Let me take you to Andrews and get you on a jet ASAP! We can talk on the way." He wasn't smiling but she could see trust in his eyes. She had heard about his voice box reconstruction surgery and how he sounded like a concrete grinder with his voice. It gave him character, she thought. He was an American hero in her eyes that no one knew about. He was running the FBI because the Senate would not confirm the President's choice. He would do it for two more years and then move on to private foundation work, but then still have his eye on his Florida project. Cheverly Santiago would be in charge and have the FBI and the DEA behind her. He would make sure of it.

Brooks took Powder Mill Road through the expansive sixty-five hundred acres of the Beltsville Agricultural Center as a way to bypass some Beltway traffic. This was where President George W. Bush rode his bike for hours after his doctor told him to stop jogging. It was a security nightmare, especially after 9/11 but it was usually traffic-free. He started filling in Chevy on Dragmar as he took the turns at plus sixty mph in his BMW. "The Turk had at least thirty women over his tenure that sired children from him. Most of the women were stolen or sold from Columbia or Peru. Maybe fifty, or sixty kids or more were born during his reign of terror. Most were killed in the line of fire or by him, but Dragmar and a few others survived but were physically and sexually abused by his old-time soldiers when they reached puberty. It was part of his initiation."

Chevy already felt sick to her stomach but knew it was just the start, "That sounds beyond brutal."

"This guy invented the word… when Alejandro was thirteen, he was seen holding down girls in alleys and rubbing on their bare asses on enough occasions that the word got out from the snitches to the Police, who eventually caught him and booked him on two occasions. "The Turk" got him out both times and the prosecution got lost in the system through bribes, I'm sure. He was probably beaten to within an inch of his life, but "The Turk" saved him because he was a good worker. Years later, he got caught again doing the same shit and that's when the FBI stepped in and sent him to a facility for three years until he was eighteen. We kept it out of the media because we were thinking that we were closing in on the operation."

"Were you?'

"Not even close. He had built layers upon layers to shelter himself from the operation and money was drying up on fighting drugs in Baltimore. It felt hopeless, but we kept plugging along with the resources we had."

"So how did you create "Dragmar"?'"

"I met with him several times and realized that he was brilliant and extremely personable. His sexual deviation was extremely specific to reach orgasm. He felt that touching himself was wrong and he never had intercourse of any kind. As long as his abusers did not anally penetrate him, he would cooperate as a kid and most times would also reach orgasm by rubbing on the sheets. It was the first way he reached orgasm at around ten years old. We developed a relationship and he started talking about going back in as someone else. I thought he was crazy, but over the years in treatment, he became a man and looked completely different. He started reading the Koran and told me, he could be a Sunni Muslim from Iraq. We started building a whole back story and spent a semester at a rural high school and dated a girl. They had supervised sex at the treatment center. She was very eager and signed a bunch of forms. It was pretty risky, but it worked. She went off to college and has done well. We found Dragmar a rat hole to live in Baltimore with some real users who were snitches and started to do some drug running. He looked amazingly Arab and had Arabic down and all the prayers too."

"The kid must be a genius!" Chevy was amazed. She remembered his poise when she met him and his report. It was shocking because most undercover guys are bad at writing reports. She was impressed.

"He picks up languages like eating candy. I think he's got at least six down at the moment. Anyway, in a couple of months, we got him in as a soldier, because he was so convincing, and then he advanced in a year or so to the gang of six that terrorized uncooperative customers and others. He drove the van and planned out the assaults."

"Did you know all that or learn it as it played out?"

"I'd rather not comment on that."

"Yes sir…I mean Brooks…that must have been hard on you."

He finally pulled over under some trees on a gravel area and looked at Chevy. "I have been privileged to work in the FBI and lead heroic men and women to battle evil. Something being "hard on me" has never been a thought. Imagining this kid at eighteen taking on the most powerful criminal in the nation is four billion times "hard on him." I got credit for putting him and others in harm's way. Now I need to save him, so he can live a life as a person without constant strife."

"I understand Sir."

Brooks put his BMW in gear and tore up some gravel. He continued once he hit seventy mph, "We believed that his mother has been dead for years and he had no other family. That has never been verified by DNA on bones that we have found so far. During the whole operation, we kept in constant touch with him."

"Was he involved with the FBI woman that got murdered in 2013, I believe?" Chevy inquired cautiously but felt that she had to know.

"Yes…but that was a botched operation. "The Turk" had ordered intimidation, not a murder. Dragmar was driving and not outside the van at any point. Two of the other "gang of six" members lost control of the situation and gave Anna Cobb an opening to attack them. In addition, they miscalculated the strength of Guy Finelli." Brooks turned to Chevy with a sullen look of pain.

"I know us women are taken for granted as being weak and she was almost nine months pregnant, but I guess they weren't football fans and hadn't watched him play."

"Dragmar will never forgive himself for it. He took the entire blame even in front of "The Turk", but "The Turk" had two others that "miscalculated" the situation, killed." Brooks had tears in his eyes recalling the situation but continued, "The gun that went off was her own in the altercation. "The Turk" took the FBI agent's gun from the altercation and kept it like a prized possession when the media reported the incident with the slain FBI agent and the famous football player. It empowered his masculinity and kept the gun hidden on the Eastern Shore at a gunsmith's shack in the middle of nowhere, where he would visit it twice a year to fondle it and shoot it. It was good fortune that we found it, but Dragmar gave us some leads that helped us narrow down the location. Otherwise, he reported stuff weekly for his seven years in the organization of hell, that gave us the whole set-up, by the time we connected "The Turk" to the gun, we took the whole operation down." Chevy was speechless. It seemed impossible to spend that much time on someone without giving up. Brooks was relentless and was uncertain she could have the same determination.

"The Florida Project is quite different. Why do you want to make it happen?"

"Somebody has to…the whole country is on the line this decade. We are close to anarchy with all the hate in the citizenry and non-cooperation in government. A couple of us had our eye on Florida for a while. Central Florida is still up for grabs politically. And the Space Coast is a sleepy area, but ready to boom with the Space industry taking off. The mayor seemed like a perfect character, a guy with his hands dirty but with a heart. And with his money, he is pretty much incorruptible, unless his personality takes a U-turn!"

"That's some crazy logic, Brooks. But for some reason, I follow it and agree with you. In Florida politics, you got to be able to play in the trenches, like in football or mid-field in soccer. And at the same time, look clean and above the fray."

"But having the heart to care about people is the real thing. Joseph Kennedy was selling alcohol during prohibition a century ago and God knows what else as a rich banker and used his wife's family, the Fitzgerald's, to politically win in Massachusetts as a jumping point for his sons to lead the country. His plan took thirty years to implement." Brooks pulled up to an airplane hangar and spoke to a soldier out his window, who then came around and opened Chevy's door. Brooks shook her hand and then pulled her in for a kiss on the cheek, as he felt an uncharacteristically emotional moment. She hugged him closely and held on awhile as his voice box seemed shut down. Finally, he managed to whisper in her ear, "Remember Chevy, we don't have thirty years to save the country."

Chapter 28

Hazel insisted on driving Lester to Port Atlantic to meet their daughter at the *Rising Tide,* a Restaurant and Bar rebuilt from the fabulous Italian Bakery storefront and kitchen that went under because of a divorce between the owners after the big Recession. The new classy-looking facility was not the type of place Hazel and her girlfriends would normally visit on the Space Coast, but she figured this was a good opportunity to observe the new well-paid millennials who worked in the Space and Tourism Industry. Port Atlantic had also opened a dozen or so shops facing the row of restaurants on the Port. After meeting Peg, she figured she could waste a couple of hours shopping and drinking and checking out the massive ocean liners parked at the Port. The timing was perfect for Happy Hour.

Peg was sitting at the luxurious oval-shaped bar in front of a bank of twenty-foot-high glass panes. The view of the architecturally impressive Port Atlantic Tower building, surrounded by a large moat shooting fountains of water, was part of the Master Plan to make the Port a place to visit. She was dressed in one of her nicer summer dresses, a kelly-green color with a lower-than-usual neckline with a bikini top and bottom underneath and a beach towel in the car in case she and her dad ended up sitting on the beach for a while.

She hoped Lester would be interested in walking down to the Space Coast Brewery tucked in between A1A and North Atlantic Avenues in an old rocket assembly plant. In it was a game area to play and watch sports and a giant circular bar to taste any of the twenty beers and ciders that they made for various companies located in Florida. You could tour the giant vats and learn the process of brewing as well. Her Dad was big on that phenomenon before it had swept the nation in the last couple of decades with all the microbreweries throughout the country. As much as he was a stoner, he was also a connoisseur of beers as well, but never had more than three total beers at any sitting, which could mean nine, four-ounce samples of beer.

Peg was certain that her dad, in all his travels, had never been there because he had not been to visit her in Cape Atlantic since she moved there ten years ago after high school. She was right about him not visiting her and seeing the brewery, but he had been to Cape Atlantic during the last decade to bring the product to Anmar Douglas twice a year. He had been bringing major amounts of marijuana during the twenty-first century.

Her Dad was a walker like Peg and kept in attractive shape. Walking the two-mile loop from the Port Atlantic area to the brewery and back would not be a problem for him. She hoped on the way back they could head East on Central Avenue to walk on the beach for a mile or so to Brevard County Park. It would add a couple of miles to the trip but to her, it would be worth it to bring up some memories, good or bad.

She could see the class Cutlass '69 car make its way through the parking lot, and with the windows open in the restaurant, she could hear the rumblings of the old four-barrel carburetor and dual exhaust pipes. The old-fashioned noise turned a lot of heads. It was not every day that folks saw a sixties vehicle looking for a parking space. Several of the men sitting outside rose to their feet pointing at the stylish-looking vehicle. Hazel took her time standing at her car door, surveying the redone building and the attention of the men. The smiles and howls from men never got old for her. She grew up when catcalls from some men were expected by Hazel. Lester came around the car from behind and took Hazel's hand to lead her to the restaurant. Even as a hippie, he was always a gentleman to her.

Peg could not remember the last time she had seen the two of them as dressed up as they were at the same time. Her Dad had shorted a golf-type shirt with a collar and walking shoes. She was shocked. Her

Mom had a skirt on with a sky-blue blouse showing more cleavage than she could remember. *Is my mom wearing a push-up bra?* Peg was stunned and smiling at the same time. She hugged them both graciously and said, "Let's order a drink at the bar before Dad and I go for a walk."

"Whatever you say, Peg...I'm not in any hurry." Lester suggested.

"I'll take an Iced Tea for now; I still have to drive home you know," Hazel said sheepishly.

"Dad picks a beer; they have a ton on tap. I'm taking you down to the Cape Atlantic Brewery for some tasting after we leave here."

"I know you like that *Stella* draft and I'll take a *Blue Moon*," Lester said with a smile. He looked his daughter over and liked what he saw. She seemed happy and healthy. "You look great Peg. Staying in shape and working hard I guess?"

"Yep, Dad...those fourth graders keep me on my toes."

"She's always been a pretty girl, Lester. You just never noticed." Hazel said jokingly, "She has been smiling more the last two times I've seen her."

"Anyone special in your life?" Lester asked.

"Just some new friends and finally getting a teaching position."

"Still on Lincoln Street?"

"Yep...three blocks from the beach. You should visit sometime." Peg said with her sullen face.

"You right Peg, I should. I'll be in town for a while and would like to see you at the beach sometime."

"Any Saturday or Sunday would be great."

"Hey, do I get in on this party?" Hazel laughed.

"Mom…remember the beach has sand on it." All three laughed.

They caught up on Dad's travels and Peg's new job and friends. Hazel complained about her crazy friends as well. After they finished their beers, Peg signaled to her father that it was time to go. He pulled out a twenty and signaled to the bartender. "Take care of this son…Hazel behaves yourself and keep your phone on."

"Take your time and have fun you two. Call me if you need me to pick you up."

"Maybe at the entrance to the Brevard County Park would be good that would save us a mile of walking or so."

They all hugged again, and then Peg and Lester headed out the door as Hazel finished her Iced Tea and surveyed the restaurant.

It took a few minutes to get to A1A for the fifteen-minute walk to the Brewery. Lester took out a good old-fashioned joint and lit it. He did not offer it to Peg because it never occurred to him that she might smoke pot. She was not a smoker and was now a teacher. Smoking in public mostly anywhere on the Space Coast was tolerated. After five drags, he pinched it with his fingers and put it in his pocket as he was now fully relaxed.

Peg wanted her father to feel comfortable and being stoned was part of that. It was weird having him smoke while they walked but no one was around, and it was a short minute. "Dad at some point, I need to ask you some questions about my childhood. I thought after the brewery, we'll go for a stroll on the beach and talk for a while."

Lester tensed up for a moment but kept quiet. He knew at some point this moment would come in his life and he was relieved that Peg brought it up. He just did not know how to talk about it, but before he died, she deserved to know the truth. He might not be around forever. This prostate thing had him a little worried even though the doctor said it might be two, five, ten, fifteen, or twenty years from now. He had taken care of things financially for his wife and maybe he could stay around all the time in a year or two. But Peg was not talking about those things. She wanted to know the truth of what happened to her eighteen years ago. The real truth she did not know… Her Dad was a killer!

Chapter 29

Chevy had the condo building staked out. Dagmar was not answering his phone and was not in his condo. She was sure he was sun tanning on the beach or in search of this girl he was fixated on, according to her intel, but either way, she was worried about his safety. She put a wire on his door, so she could get lunch and check out the beach area off Lincoln Street. It was a beautiful day, and she did not mind a stroll on the sand after a nice salad from *Wendy's*.

She found a spot across from the Neptune Apartments, where she had spent plenty of time watching in her past. Groups were heading down to the beach without a care in the world. The south side was quiet with their lawns cut nicely and their shades drawn.

Amazingly she saw him, his car rolled down Lincoln from the beachside passing her and the apartments without noticing her. He stopped at the small four-unit apartment building in the next block. *Was that where she lived?* Chevy thought as she looked in her rear-view mirror. He stayed in his car. *This was too good to be true.* Nobody had eyes or info on this woman, but she needed to get him out of town as soon as possible. She chewed her salad slowly and checked her messages on her phone. Brooks was coming into town Monday and expected Dragmar to be secured by then.

A couple was headed up the stairs to one of the units. She tried to take a picture, but she had no straight angle. Dagmar was interested as he opened his car door as they went in. She could not let him go up there, so she got out on the passenger side of her car and stayed low until she got in front of Dragmar's car and hustled him across Lincoln to confront him. She was ready to take him down, if necessary, but luckily no one was around. "What the fuck are you doing Alejandro?" she shouted at him right in his face so no one else would hear it.

He stepped back to the car as she came at him. "What do you want Chevy?"

"I want you to answer your fucking phone and get back in your car. What are you doing here? Is that the girl that you fancy? You're going to blow this whole thing up because of her?"

"OK OK…calm down." Dagmar retreated to his car.

Chevy leaned in and read him the riot act. "Go to your condo and get some things. I'll meet you out back in fifteen minutes. Got it?"

"Yes ma'am…but I want to know who she's with."

"Jesus, Alejandro it looks like an old guy, but sorry that's for later. Let's go. The heat is on!"

Peg and Lester left her apartment with a blanket for the beach. "You've done well Peg. I'm proud of you and a little jealous!"

"Dad you can come over anytime now that you're in town. Just give me a call."

"Thanks, Peg. I don't deserve that kindness with the way I've acted all these years."

They strolled over the crossover to the beach and found a nice spot as the ocean was at high tide. "Yeah, about all those years," Peg asked as they got comfortable and opened some beers.
"Why did you leave me? We were pretty tight when I was in fourth grade and then boom you were gone from my life, even when you were around."

"It's a long story and you're not going to like it."

169

"Well let's at least start?"

"OK." Lester took a big swig from his beer and a deep breath. The smell of the ocean air and the feel of the sun were perfect for the painful subject. "I'm going to tell you the big parts first and then if you want to still talk to me, I can fill in the details."

Peg nodded her head in agreement. She could see the struggle on Lester's face trying to put words together for something unspeakable.

"This guy…well your mother and I…well we weren't doing so well, and I was…away." Lester took another swig and lifted his shirt to his eyes which were shedding tears. "And then I came back and found him…on you." Lester covered his face with his shirt again, then looked up and straight at Peg, "I lost my mind and before I knew it, he was dead on the floor, and I was on top of him."

The worst that she feared was coming true. Her ears were burning from the words "on you" and "he was dead." She dreaded listening to the details because it might make her pass out. Outwardly, Peg tried to stay calm but did not know what to say. Her throat was closing from anxiety because the memories that would be stirred up were frightening and would haunt her forever. At least now, the complex levels of anxiety she had constructed to obstruct her memories had been working, or had they? Would her newly constructed team of friends help her deal with this? *Not really*, she thought. How could she tell her friends that her dad killed her attacker? She drank a whole beer and finally forced out a question to Lester. "Where was Mom?"

"She was gone all night and left him to watch you. I put you in our bedroom and luckily you fell back asleep. I spent all night cleaning up and getting rid of the body. I put him in the van and the next morning I left for six months."

"Did you see Mom?" Peg asked as her eyes were on fire from a lack of tears.

"I told her nothing initially because she was scared shitless to find me home. I told her to get some sleep and I would call her at 7 am. That gave me four hours to get out of state. I called her and told her what I found and what I did. I told her it wasn't her fault even though it was. She was sobbing on the phone, and I told her it would be alright and to get strong for you."

"What did I say when I woke up?"

"You were confused to see Mom and wondered where I was. Mom told you it was a dream and that I was never home, and I would be gone for a while." Lester was looking straight down while speaking in a very low and cautious voice.

Peg did not want to know any more at this time. She needed to digest this disaster that ruined her life, but she did want to know one thing. Without prompting, her father answered what she was thinking.

"Mom took you to the hospital and a doctor friend of mine checked you out and found no penetration. He broke the law and did not report the incident."

Peg was relieved but curious. *Do I want to know why this doctor did not report this assault of an almost ten-year-old girl?*

"Listen, Peg, you should know this now. I worked for Francis Calvanese bringing pot to his suppliers. This was the first guy I ever killed, but I needed protection for my family after this, so my role expanded."

Peg's head was ready to explode, "what the fuck does that mean Dad?"

"He was not the last guy I had to get rid of for Francis Calvanese."

"So that's how you got away with it by becoming a hitman for the Calvanese family?"

"Not really…it was just a couple of guys they wanted out of the area for good reason. Francis used that as a last resort to keep the peace on the Space Coast. The drug trade is ruthless, and he was protecting the Port from being overrun by the usual drug cartels that invaded Miami. I didn't do the killing, but I was there, and I got rid of the bodies." Lester was gaining back his settled emotional state. "Peg…your mom got involved with a grifter and a drug runner, who went from town to town, job to job, and met your mother at a concert while I was gone. She fell for him when I was away. She trusted him to watch you several nights while she was serving and once while she was out with her girls. It was stupid… but she had no clue he was a Frottage freak. They never had intercourse; the guy got off rubbing on his asses. It's complicated…maybe your mom can fill you in if you want." Peg turned her head down and let out some air, seemingly to blow off that suggestion.

"I found out later he had done time in a Florida prison. That's probably where he learned his perversion." Lester was in storytelling mode and not aware that Peg had checked out. "I had a gig with a band on tour for a month and some supplies to get in from New Orleans and bring to the Space Coast. I got back a little early and thought I would surprise Hazel… it was a bad mistake by two distracted parents."

Peg looked up and tried to comprehend such a messed-up situation. "You know Dad, it could have happened hundreds of times when I was young. You guys left me with all kinds of floating-around friends." She paused for a moment and tried to collect her emotions; she knew this was not the time to blow Lester out of the water. This was just the beginning of learning about her life. "But I appreciate you telling me. I'm sure it's been a nightmare for you and Mom as well." She hugged him, which surprised her dad, who latched on to his daughter like a life jacket. As she pulled back, she tried to joke about the immoral nightmare that changed her life, "So, nobody missed this guy after you left?"

"Francis took care of that trail and I left pieces of him in the bottom of lakes and rivers in Georgia and South Carolina."

They continued to talk, mostly about Peg's new job and the interesting friends she had met. She did not mention anything about Dragmar but did go on about Phillip, her mentor. Lester was impressed and told him about how famous Phillip's two sons were in the world of Baseball and Football. For all of his travels, Lester was still a big sports fan. Ironically, he had become a Washington football fan in the sixties because of their great passing game with Sonny Jurgensen, Charley Taylor, Bobby Mitchell, and Jerry Smith. Before Atlanta and Miami joined the *NFL* in the late sixties, Washington was the team of the south and was shown on the *CBS* network television in Florida every Sunday. He was quite a football player in high school before smoking pot and listening to music became his passion by his senior year.

In 2005, Baseball finally returned to Washington and their Spring Training site was fifteen minutes away from their trailer home. Until 2017, he made sure he spent March at home to see baseball. It was a real treat, and he became a big fan of Phillip's boys but tried to act cool about it to Peg – as he did about most things.

Lester and Peg walked up the coastline to Brevard County Park beach at the rocks that held open the Port. Peg spent so much time there as a kid learning about freedom, it gave her chills being with her father again strolling with her feet being lapped by the in and out motion of the tides. They found the walkway to cross the rocks, with the Port opening on their left and the ocean on their right, and walked to the end of the concrete pier, hundreds of yards into the ocean to a place where the waves were just starting to form. A place where they watched many Space Shuttle launches and landings which seemed like magic to Peg in her youth. The sonic booms always were scary. She remembered, with fear waiting for a landing, that the boom would come before the shuttle was visible, making her fear the worst; but then a dot in the sky would appear (she always tried to be the first to yell it out) and then started to grow to the size of the shuttle, as it swung around to land like an alien spaceship.

These memories were swirling in her head as they talked about the present like it was a normal relationship. Peg felt an evenness to Lester's voice and emotion that was calming to her. After the second mile of the walk, she was finally feeling peace inside her soul like being in the eye of a hurricane. When she was alone, she would try to process the story and what it meant to her. For now, she wanted to enjoy being with Lester and soak up the years she had missed with him. Like feeling the sun entering her body and feeling the heat that at first feels good on her shoulders and back, but eventually leaves a burn that can hurt afterwards.

Chapter 30

Peg finished the evening with her parents at *Rusty's,* sitting outside overlooking the inland Port waterway; swallowing raw oysters covered with horseradish-laden, cocktail sauce and chewing steamed clams dipped in melted butter. Lester ordered for everyone and enjoyed himself as he watched his wife peel shrimp like a surgeon, feeling satisfied and full of alcohol. Lester planned to drive the Cutlass home.

The Twilight Zone-like experience for Peg seemed to be a start to being a family again even though it might have an out-of-this-world ending. *This could never be normal*, Peg thought, but they could share some love before Lester died. He was never going to get treatment for his prostate because he would not go through with the biopsy. His doctor said the cancer was probably growing very slowly if at all. Ultimately, Lester did not want any kind of operation that might destroy his manhood or chemotherapy that would ruin his hair. The radiation therapy that might help him was in another state. He figured living another five or ten or fifteen years would be good enough. They finished talking after dinner and it was time to part. Peg walked her parents to the Cutlass and said goodbyes with long hugs. Hazel did not let go of her like she had in the past.

As Peg walked home, she pondered the idea of Frottage and why a man would choose that behavior over intercourse. She understood two men doing it to each other, either penis to penis or penis to buttocks as an alternative to anal intercourse, but how did a heterosexual male get stuck on rubbing their penis on the backside of a girl or woman. *Was it about total control and non-intimacy? No kissing or breast feeling? Well maybe if they were standing up but that was different and could be sexy as a lead-up to intercourse*, she thought. It was too confusing for her right now to figure out.

Did she feel relieved that she was not penetrated but used as a rubbing area for sperm to be ejaculated on? She was not sure what to think. *When it happened with Dragmar it felt pretty bad, but as a kid, I wouldn't know any better was I sleeping every time it happened? Probably not,* she assumed. She had memories of having her back rubbed as she fell asleep and then uncomfortableness and pressure on her back while in semi-consciousness.

What were the chances of the same weird sex act happening to her as an adult? Maybe it was more popular than she knew because of prison. *Is that why Dragmar joined the Frottage club? He must have been a victim,* she decided. It turned her stomach, digesting over a wonderful dinner, into a sour ache. When she arrived home, Peg got in her bed immediately and pulled the covers over her head. *I think I'll sleep on my back from now on*, she implored to herself. As she tried to slow down her breathing, she felt conflicting relief from learning she was not penetrated but her backside was used as a sliding board for cum. *It's disgusting but not invasive*, she tried to settle on, but the memories flooded her consciousness, first the back rubbed as her sleeping shirt got higher, and no underwear to remove thanks to her mother, then a voice urging her to sleep and the deep breathing with kisses on her neck and then the pressure at the base of her spine and buttocks. No wonder she was full of anxiety, trying to normalize that behavior would have ripped through her psyche. *How long was this monster around?*

She was relieved Lester killed him as the tears rolled down her face under the covers. The ordeal seemed unimaginable. She figured her mother got herself lost in meth and coke to pay for her irresponsibility. Somehow, they stayed together as partners in crime. Amazingly, they still had love in their eyes for each other that she could see and feel at dinner.

The questions were flying through her semi-consciousness. Why now were they willing to tell her? Was it her insistence to talk to Dad or just because she finally graduated and got a teaching job? Did the mayor reach out to Lester about her being assaulted by Dragmar and has Lester paid his dues to the Calvanese family?

Finally, she drifted into the ocean of dreams and trips to the tides of her youth as a joyful nine-year-old drifting on her back, waiting for a perfect wave to take her into a deep sleep.

In those final moments of consciousness, for the first time, she thought of her father as an imperfect hero protecting his daughter. It might be hard to try to get more information out of him, but she would have to be patient. Maybe spending more time with him might give him the courage to explain further. He was not fully aware of her anxiety problem. She could discuss that with him which might lead to further conversation. But then it dawned on her, that she needed a family perspective of her situation. Phillip had mentioned that in their talks, but she never understood what he meant. She always assumed her parents had been worthless, especially her mother, and Peg had to fend for herself for the last eighteen or so years. But what if her theory had been wrong and her mom had been victimized or traumatized by this event, just as much as she had? Sure, maybe she had been involved with another man, but what happened? She realized that she knew or had cared very little about her mother's past. Hazel had been a Catholic school kid who went hippie in her high school years, but so had thousands of kids in the sixties. She had discounted her mother as a person for so long, she wondered, could she have a serious conversation with her? Hazel had never shown anger at Peg over the years, just distance. She seemed to acquiesce to the lack of their relationship. Peg had assumed her mother did not care, but maybe it was a self-enforced acceptance of a situation like a prison sentence for her crime of carelessness.

Suddenly her consciousness felt overwhelmed and the warmth of being in bed calmed her to let go. Before she knew it, she went sound asleep and woke up refreshed. She swung her feet off the bed and grabbed her phone and a text from Dragmar appeared.

"I wanted to see you yesterday, but I missed catching you at your apartment. Sorry, but I need to go away for a bit. I will have a new number that will say, Alejandro. I will text you soon when I am safe. I am finished with being Dragmar!"

Chapter 31

Cheverly Santiago pulled into a gated house in the suburban town of Winter Park, just north of Orlando. She was always amazed at the properties that the DEA and FBI had under their control, most being seized in arrests of individuals involved in drug-related crimes as well as extortion, blackmail, fraud, and other corruption felonies. Thanks to Title IX of the Organized Crime Control Act of 1970, the Racketeer Influenced and Corrupt Organizations Act, or RICO, gave the FBI and the DEA legal means to create a large property portfolio. These "safe house" locations were juggled around the country to ensure their anonymity and were usually in non-descript middle-class neighborhoods. Eventually most were sold at auction and replaced by another in the same area. This one was especially nice with a secure wall that enhanced security. The joint task force of the DEA and FBI used it exclusively for Central Florida. The monies collected in the ongoing sales from the property portfolio were used to buy many things, including military equipment to fight organized crime and terrorism and to hire their own "swat-type" police force to provide the manpower. During J. Edgar Hoover's reign as FBI Director, agents either had an accounting degree or were a graduate of law school. *Times were different in the twenty-first century*, Chevy thought.

She knew there were abuses in the system, but she also knew how horrible the crime organizations were. It was a war that somebody had to fight, and she was glad to be with what she considered the good guys. And she was confident that Brooklyn O'Malley was the head of the good guys. He was clean as a whistle financially and confidently used his power to control crime. His latest scheme seemed political the first time Chevy heard it but after digesting it she admired the brilliance of it. Somebody like herself with impeccable values had to be in charge otherwise it would become as corrupt as the politicians it was trying to remove from power.

Her goal was to put herself "out of business" within a decade or pass the fight along to a worthy agent like herself. Those were her orders from Brooks.

She sat in the car trying to make sense of the unusual conversation with Alejandro. He was quiet for most of the ride to Winter Park. Chevy suspected it was girl trouble. It seemed obvious because of the scowl on his normally smiling face. She felt confident that she could make him talk about it as she drove directly west on Route 528, "Tell me about this woman you're so interested in," were the first words spoken.

Alejandro was jarred by the question, but quickly awoke from his hibernation and took her up on the offer to talk about Peg. "If you want to know, her name is Peg Patterson, she's twenty-eight and a fourth-grade teacher. From the first time I saw her, I could see deeply into her eyes and feel the frown on her face. She was the most enchanting woman I've ever met who was trying to look awful. We now have a connection from our souls, and I need to show her that I'm a good man."

"What did you do Dragmar…something stupid?" Chevy said forcefully.

He admired this woman for being bold even though he was put off by the question. He straightened up his posture and wanted to explain his dilemma, "First of all, I'm done with Dragmar. My name is Alejandro Majada."

"That's fair…Alejandro, it is, but you need a nickname like…maybe…Dro!"

He laughed as Chevy smiled. There was quiet for a minute until he finally confessed. "Dro…that's funny Chevy. I guess that's between

180

you and me. I can feel that." He adjusted his collar and felt his unshaven face, like he did when he was in prison getting ready to defend himself. It was like an animal showing his bluster and creating a bigger view of himself, "Yeah I did something stupid. You know my history. We had a moment together that could have been special, but I lost my way. I apologized to her...even with her friends there and the mayor. She accepted it and said it would take time before we could see each other again. I accepted that and promised I would wait. I texted her once a week for a month before she answered. Now we're communicating...that's a start, but I wanted to see her before I left town."

Once again Chevy was impressed by this young man and his sincerity. He had learned from his therapy; she supposed and could become someone special. But she knew the stigma attached to a sex offender. She wondered why people sometimes had less anger towards murderers, arsonists, drug dealers, and thieves than sex offenders. She drew the line at rapists. *They should rot in hell!* That was an absolute for her, but teenage and twenty-something sex molesters, who were victims themselves, she saw that as different. These days in Florida there were enough strip clubs where thousands of young men, Alejandro's age, got off by grinding with a dancer in the back room – legally. Chevy had seen enough of it while making drug arrests in those places in the past decade.

Alejandro could make something of himself with the right treatment, she felt. Some in society seem to adore young drug dealers who turn into rich music producers or entertainers who use every illegal drug created and then become sober heroes – it was a weird world, she surmised as it hit her finally what Alejandro revealed. Like a bowling pin struggling to stand up after being hit.

"Did you say, 'the mayor' was at this woman's apartment?" She was stunned by the information as she tried to stay cool.

"Yes, he was there after I apologized for a short time while Peg answered me. Then I left him with the two other men. I had no choice, Chevy. It was the only chance I had to apologize. Otherwise, she would have never seen me again." Alejandro tried to explain rationally.

"The mayor knows you assaulted that girl?" Chevy turned to him with an incredulous stare.

"I don't think he knows any particulars of what happened between us. Peg would be too embarrassed I imagine." His hands pushed back his overflowing hair as he stayed calm.

"Jackie Calvanese knows your face...holy shit Dro!" She turned her eyes back to the road ahead.

"We did meet each other, but why is that such a big deal?" Alejandro wondered.

"Because Peg gave the mayor her dress after that night to run a DNA test on your SPERM!" Chevy finally increased the volume of her voice as she turned to him dispersing her message with authority, especially on the word "SPERM", like it was an ejaculation.

"Why would she do that?" Shocked by the news, Alejandro finally showed some despair.

"Because you assaulted her, and she was pissed about it!" Chevy poured on the reality, "You're lucky she didn't call the police first," she finished with an amazed look on her face as she turned to see traffic forming ahead.

"How do you know all this?" Alejandro found his footing to continue the cross-examination.

"That's why we had to get you out of there Dro," shaking her head as she accelerated through the electronic toll booth lane, "Jackie knows who you are and who you're not! You were busted and fortunately, he didn't hurt you." Chevy tried to calm down as she paused for a minute. The silence was helpful as the traffic cleared ahead. "We got wind of a DNA test that matched your prison records. We found out that Jackie had a chemist friend in the FBI who ran it through the system. Luckily, we flagged it and found the leak without it getting back to Jackie." Calm was back in her voice as she turned with a slight smile on her face.

"I'm speechless…Peg didn't know what she was doing." Alejandro tried to make sense of it. "She didn't know Jackie was connected to all of it." He reasoned.

"Wow…empathy for Peg, most guys would be raging mad at her…you must like her." Chevy was impressed and smiled with an unexpected relief in her stomach. *She was right about him being worth saving.*

"You're right, she was pissed, but it's a brilliant move. Running a test to see if it happened before, what victim thinks like that?" Thinking like a lawyer, Alejandro was pleased at the logic of it all. "Someone who cares about me because we had a connection," he felt assured. "I think she figured out that Jackie's involved in something. I just want a chance to explain it all to her," he pleaded.

"Well forget that for now," Chevy said loudly to bring him back to reality. "We have a meeting with the FBI guy overseeing all this in an hour. I'm guessing you're getting out of this state for a while."

They pulled up the circular driveway in front of the three-story mansion of a house and followed agents into a back parlor used as an office. They were offered water, coffee, or tea. They both asked for some tea and waited. Suddenly, Chevy started to feel the enormity of the project that was just beginning for her. She had waited her whole life to be this important, but her stomach had butterflies of anxiety. It was something she was not used to having. Never did she feel doubt about her abilities, but Brooklyn had picked her to succeed. He had seen it in her, but the assurance was scary. Had she blustered her way into this situation?

Acting Director Brooklyn O'Malley came flying into the room with his briefcase. The chef followed with the tea. "Can you bring me a cup, so I can join them," Brooks told the chef. He motioned for everyone to sit down as he settled in behind his desk and pulled out a folder from his briefcase. "Everybody is safe. I can see…nice job Agent Santiago!" he stood and shook her hand with vigor. "And nice to see you again, Alejandro," as he turned to the young man, who had physically matured into a handsome man with strong shoulders and arms. Prison had sculpted his body and tempered his mind, he supposed.

"Director O'Malley, we need to update you on the situation." Brooks nodded to Chevy to continue, "Alejandro and I had a conversation on the way here and it is clear that the mayor knows his real identity as Alejandro and his alias as Dragmar and has met him in person."

"Sir if I can explain…" Alejandro added, "We did meet but he may not remember me it was just for a few minutes…either way I have gathered quite a bit of evidence on his empire," he finished.

"I'm trying to imagine the scenario where you and Jackie Calvanese met, and he figured out you were there to fuck him over and he let you go unharmed. That would make quite a story." Brooks offered.

184

"Well, it involved a girl that I care for and two other people." Alejandro tried to counter.

"Of course, a girl is involved…let me guess, she's the same girl that turned in her dress that you ejaculated on and found by an FBI chemist." Brooks stared pensively at Alejandro.

"That is correct sir, but I had to apologize to her and that was the only way I could do it…in front of her friends Joshua and Phillip. I guess it made her feel more secure."

Chevy shifted in her chair, trying to think of something to say, but decided to let Alejandro sink his ship.

"Well Alejandro, I'll have to remember that scene when I write my first romance novel. That is quite gallant behavior. Did you ever think at that point that you were putting yourself and this whole operation in grave danger?" Brooks acted as though he had asked that question a thousand times to undercover criminals or agents.

"I felt sir it was the right thing to do under the circumstances and we have started to text each other sir." He reasoned, hoping to convince Brooks of his good intentions.

Brooks turned to Chevy abruptly, "Agent Santiago, where did you find this young man when you brought him in?"

"Sir, he was in front of her apartment waiting for her to return."

"I wanted to let her know I was leaving town for a while, sir!" Alejandro pleaded.

"Alejandro…when you go to sleep tonight because this has been a harrowing experience for you, can you get on your knees and pray to the Lord and thank him for saving you from being the stupidest mother-fucker in human history?" Brooks's eyes lit up and his reconstructive voice almost came to a halt.

"Yes sir...I see your point and I apologize for ruining the investigation. Thank you for all of your help, sir." Alejandro appeared stoic, but tears flowed down his cheeks without end. He chose to ignore his emotions at that moment. He knew there would be time to grieve at the probable prospect of losing Peg, but now he was trying to show respect to a man who had believed in him. The disappointment was almost too much to bear, but he was determined not to break down in front of Brooklyn O'Malley.

"Sir...if I may say that um...Alejandro has turned in some amazing information on the Calvanese network that will help us with the project. It may turn out better in the long run that we know that he knows and vice-versa. It may help some areas."

Brooks paused and looked directly at Chevy and felt impressed by her thinking. *She's brilliant*, he thought. Without direct communication they could send signals to Jackie in what direction to go or what we support and what was overboard. As a boating enthusiast, Jackie would understand the metaphor, Brooks smiled to himself. The woman might be the key to being another level of contact. He needed to find out who she was and how they could get her on board somehow. "I see your point, Chevy. It may help us move on from this shitstorm. We need a plan for Alejandro's safety, and I want him to stay connected with Peg Patterson. I want all the intel on her, her family, and friends."

"Thank you, sir...that would be...a miracle!" Alejandro said joyfully.

Chapter 32

Brooks dismissed Alejandro and called the staff to set him up in a suite upstairs. He wanted him to rest up for a couple of days while he and Chevy worked out the strategy to keep him connected to Peg Patterson.

"Who were these two friends Joshua and Phillip in Peg's apartment when Alejandro displayed his gallant behavior," Brooks asked Chevy as he sat down at the kitchen's exquisite marble counter in the safe house mansion. Chevy was making tea on the stove as she looked in several of the cabinets for some tea packets. "I think they are next to the fridge in the cabinet." He could use soothing tea after the dry moisture of the plane ride and his vocal use while talking to Alejandro. Over the years, Brooks had learned to keep his voice at a low volume to keep from irritating his rebuilt vocal box. At times, he would lose control of his emotions and the volume would increase exponentially. Luckily, this latest outburst was short and effective.

Chevy waited patiently for the teapot to steam as she prepared two cups with tea bags. She had heard Brooks's question but needed some tea before she spouted off the answer. Her head was spinning from the last two hours with Alejandro. Plus, she was not sure why it mattered who the friends were. She assumed Brooks was just interested in connecting to Peg. It would not be easy in her experience. Nobody at age twenty-eight, wants any part of dealing with any three-letter government enforcement agency. Finally, she poured out the tea and luckily found a lemon in the fridge. She cut it up and squeezed it in her tea, looking for a nod from Brooks if he wanted lemon. He shook his head as he patiently waited for her attention to his question.

"Do want some honey in your tea they have some home-grown stuff." Chevy stalled, waiting for his nod yes. She poured honey into his tea to sweeten him up.

She took a stool at the counter next to Brooks and blew on her tea, dying for one sip of the hot pleasure for her throat. After she survived the sip and felt it warm up her chest, she turned to Brooks. "Joshua is a teacher friend she met in July at a professional training in Cocoa. He is twenty-four from Lynchburg, Virginia, and teaches fourth grade as well at Merritt Island Elementary. They're friends and he is dating a server/café-owner woman, the same age as him, they both met at *Coconuts on the Beach* in Cocoa Beach. Her name is Becky and has become good friends with Peg.

Brooks processed the information without looking at Chevy while he sipped on the tea and enjoyed the honey soothing the feeling of his throat. He had done a million of these breakdowns of situations that could produce evidence or a lead and rarely did they pull up anything worthwhile. When she was done, he had forgotten the name of the second friend but wanted to move on to building a strategy to involve Peg and the mayor's connection. Finally, she started describing the second friend, Phillip, after she had taken a long sip of her tea. After the first two sentences, Brooks almost fell off the stool.

"Phillip is in his sixties, whom Peg met last Spring at a bar and they became friends. He lives in Cape Atlantic part-time and is a writer from Maryland. Peg sees him as a…"

"Whoa…what was that?"

"Phillip is in his…"

"Wait…a writer from Maryland?" he tried to stop and control his emotions and lower his volume of response…*could this be possible?*

Chevy stopped and saw something in Brooklyn's eyes like a light bulb had gone off.

188

"Do you have his last name?"

"Yea somewhere…why? Who is he?"

"He could be one of my best friends!"

Chevy jumped off her comfortable stool and away from her hot tea, then ran into the living room to get her briefcase and folder of notes. She found it quickly and bolted back to her spot of pleasure, "Phillip Finelli."

"Jesus, Mary, and Joseph…you must be shitting me! We just got very lucky!" Brooks smiled and leaned over and kissed Chevy on the lips and grabbed her cheeks, "Nice job sweetheart," in a rare unprofessional move.

Chevy loved it thoroughly; would take more from her Boss anytime he wanted. Suddenly her body was warm and toasty. "Who is this, Phillip Finelli?"

"Are you a sports fan?" Brooks tried to keep his volume low as his voice still felt soothed by the tea and sweetened by the honey.

"Sure…but more into soccer and basketball." Chevy was confused by the question.

"But you remember the DC half-brothers Guy Finelli, the football star, and Alex Santucci, the baseball hero a decade ago?"

"Of course, I have! Wait…he's the father of both of them? Wow, that family must be loaded," Chevy was starting to see the pieces of the situation coming together. "What's he doing in Cape Atlantic?"

"It's a long story…but he loves it down there. He bought a condo in '05 because of baseball returning to DC and discovered some cousins in Satellite Beach. It became a perfect place to write and swim in the ocean. Two things he loves. He put out four books in the last decade."

"So how do you know him?" Chevy was seeking the depth of the connection.

"We grew up together in Parkwood, a subdivision built after WWII that is both in Bethesda and Kensington, Maryland just outside of DC. Playing sports and chasing girls at Catholic school dances took up most of our time." Brooks said cheerfully.

"I'll bet you were good at both of those?" She imagined that scene in the sixties and seventies. Free love, unlimited sex, great music, war protesting, Civil rights fights, Earth Day, and Women's liberation. She wondered how good she would look wearing a mini-skirt, with a halter top – braless. Her body tingled with excitement at the thought. Sometimes she thought she was born thirty years too late but then she remembered most working women were still typists back then.

"If we ever get to a bar sometime, I'll answer that loaded question after a few drinks."

"I'm going to need a bar after we figure out this situation Brooks," Chevy said with hopeful eyes.

Brooks raised his teacup to touch with Chevy's. With a nod, they both agreed to the future celebration. As he sat down, he realized how much he loved interacting with Chevy. She would be quite a catch if he was a young man unattached. But besides being married to his job, his second wife had adjusted to the strains of his career and was looking forward to having him around more often after he retired.

Chevy had a kid, but no love interest, and was committed to her career as well. For the next decade, this project would most likely be her next affair.

Chapter 33

Peg stood in front of her students getting them settled in after the weekend. These three days of school before Thanksgiving were a total waste of time for learning in school, she remembered as a kid. She was looking forward to the break and a Thanksgiving meal for the first time in years. For the past decade, she would spend the holiday on the beach alone without much of an appetite. After a late night out on Wednesday, usually at a bar, she would get to the beach after a light lunch and sun for a while and then walk north to the Port, then turn around and stroll the three miles south to the Cocoa Beach Pier which took up most of the afternoon. She would then walk the eight-hundred-foot pier through various venues and find a spot at the huge circular bar with an amazing roof anchoring the end of the Pier, sitting out above the ocean drinking inexpensive margaritas during happy hour. Finally, after a few to drown out her anxieties, she would navigate herself off the crowded, touristy Pier, just after sunset, and walk back up the beach in the dusk, playing barefoot with the water and thinking of being in a family that should be eating turkey. At the Lincoln Street walkover, she would walk grudgingly, fighting aloneness to her apartment and crash in her bed. Most of the time, she was lucky to get a phone call from Lester or Hazel during the Thanksgiving weekend. Usually checking in from someplace off the Gulf coast with her mom barely intelligible and her father short with words. But this year would be different, they had all committed to a dinner at the trailer home. It had been years since Hazel had managed a cooked meal for her. Peg imagined it would come from the Diner, even though she remembered her mom cooking at times when she was young. A hot meal was on the table most nights before the murder.

"Here's the deal guys and gals…if we work hard today and half of Tuesday or by lunch tomorrow, I promise we'll have fun Tuesday afternoon and the half-day Wednesday. Then by noon Wednesday, you'll be home and can look forward to Thanksgiving on Thursday."

Lots of clapping and hoots came from her thirty-five kids. Even the uncooperative kids in the back seats, whom she referred to Joshua as her "fantastic four", seemed to sit up a little and liked what they heard. She passed out a worksheet went to the board and listed everything to get done by tomorrow at noon. "Here is what we have to accomplish by lunch tomorrow to enjoy the afternoon and Wednesday morning."

There were moans and groans but mostly it was the sound of the worksheets being opened and read. "Miss Patterson, are you going to bring in some pies from *Publix*... and cookies?" asked one of her girl students.

"Hmmm…that's not a bad idea. At the end of today, if we are making good progress, I'll get some ideas from everyone on what they would like to do during Tuesday afternoon and Wednesday morning."

The chatter was positive as the kids got to work. What she did not tell them was that she had received special permission from her principal and the parents to have an afternoon beach on Tuesday afternoon and Wednesday morning, depending on the weather. All thirty-five kid's parents answered her e-mail positively. *Probably a first in school history*, she imagined. Only three blocks away, the beach was not the place that most fourth graders found earth-shattering like she did as a kid. She wanted to share her excitement about the surf with them. Tuesday afternoon would be low tide and Wednesday morning would be high tide. She was hoping to show them both and explain about gravity and the power of the ocean. At least that was how she worded it in her e-mail to the parents.

Several parents volunteered to chaperone the event, three fathers, two mothers, and one older brother home from college. Temperatures would be in the high seventies with low-wind. Perfect beach weather for late November. The men were hoping Miss Patterson would be sunning in a bikini at Cape Atlantic Beach as the rumor mill reported from the kids.

She quickly sent an e-mail chain to just the six volunteers to help out with equipment for some games and snacks for the beach. They quickly figured out their assignments.

Now, it was up to the students to finish their work by Tuesday's lunch. Peg was very happy with her success so far with the fourth graders during the school year and in her first year of teaching. The boys had surprised her the most with so many being good students. Only two of the boys seemed to fit in her worthless category and they were showing some life lately. Three girls were troublemakers in her class and two of them were as bad as the worthless boys. Her theory was being tested by this result and right now she had little answer for it. Only one of the troublemakers showed promise and occasional interest as she tried hard to pull her away from the other two. Not that the "fantastic four" got along with each other. The bad girls were the bullies of the class and tried their hardest to keep the worthless boys from failing.

Overall, out of thirty-five kids (nine over the County standards), thirty were doing well. Peg as a first-year teacher at Thanksgiving break was happy with it but by Easter, it would not be acceptable. All of her students had to be functional students as nine-year-olds, according to Peg's logic and creed of learning. Becoming ten and reaching puberty was a mountain to climb, she thought. Losing interest in school would be a disaster, she believed strongly.

Tuesday afternoon on the beach was like a religious experience for Peg. The parents were in full control of the kids, and they were all having a ball at low tide. All thirty-five of her kids bought into the day-and-a-half goal of challenging work and finished their assignments. She was pleasantly surprised and cataloged the idea to use in her future lesson plans.

When they first arrived at the beach, she walked them down to the edge of the incoming waves, turned around with her feet in the water, and gave them a quick lecture about the beach. The erosion and the restoration, the tides incoming and outgoing, the different paths of the sun during the year, the sunrise and the sunsets, the full moon rising once a month, the direction of the wind, and how storms formed quickly depending on the clouds. Then she instructed the volunteers to take over and found a spot for her beach blanket and watched. She enjoyed the energy of the kids at the ocean – all of them nine years old, free for a couple of hours. It was a learning experience for her. The "Fantastic Four" showed personality for the first time. It gave her ideas for the future.

The older brother home from college came by her blanket more than anyone to see if she needed a drink or a snack or maybe if she might take her shirt off and reveal a bikini top. She did have a bikini top under her see-through top, but it would only come off if she had to rescue a kid in the water. She did remove her jacket to help him see through the see-through top. He was the kind of boy that she would have wasted her time with regularly when she was college age, but not now out of college, teaching, and older. Currently, he seemed so young to her and cute. But cute to her was not sexy anymore. Now wisdom, depth, and being a listener was sexy and food for her soul

The alone time on the beach allowed her to think about Thursday with her parents and how she would approach it with her endless questions about her past and the murder specifically. She had talked on the phone with Hazel and Lester several times each, alone, trying to build some rapport. It would be hard, but necessary, to get all the facts out for the family to repair itself.

Wednesday night, she would get together with Joshua and Becky to celebrate making it to this point in the school year. She was looking forward to it at a local Cape Atlantic bar to which they could walk.

Becky was having Joshua over for Thanksgiving, his first away from his family.

She missed Alejandro being away, but she had been very busy with work, so it was not that painful. The mystery of him leaving was bothering her though and she started to feel her anxiety creep back into her mind. Phillip had reached out to her and wanted to discuss something important after the Thanksgiving weekend. It would be good to talk to Phillip about anything, she thought.

She was being successful in her work and building friendships, while she was trying to restore something more than nothing in her family, but there was a hole in her life. Alejandro had opened something in her, she never knew she could feel. Though it was for a fleeting moment, it was special, but she wanted the chance to chase it and make sure the hole had a bottom. She believed that was how love was built. First, you open your heart to someone which creates a hole in your soul that can only be filled by the love that you create with that person otherwise, it generates heartache.

She was willing to wait for him to respond while she settled things with her family, but she was not willing to be overridden with anxiety again as she had been for the last eighteen years. Her eyes closed for a moment, to feel the sun on her face, the wind in her hair, and smell the salt from the ocean. In the distance, she could hear the sound of happy young voices of the best age in the world. At the last age, she felt free and secure. For a moment she heard a prayer in her head – "My God…let there be love in my life."

Chapter 34

Just Glide Inn was a block north of Lincoln Street with a bar facing A1A with open windows on this balmy Wednesday evening in late November. Becky had arrived early to meet the always-on-time Peg and talk about her interest in the mayor.

"Guess who came to my Café the last three Saturdays?"

Peg looked at Becky and saw the excitement in her eyes. She knew it was something naughty, "Oh god...not Jackie?"

"Yep, the mayor likes my Café. He stayed for an hour last week and was nice to my parents. They think he's the top." Becky was dressing a bit older these days and less slutty. Peg thought it was because of dating Joshua.

"You have a crush on the mayor?'

"Well, so do you Peg!' Becky said with charm and a smile.

"I think I'm actually past it, Becky, to be honest," Peg stated with a calmness she was just realizing about the mayor. He had been a beacon of hope for her in the past and was always looking out for her it seemed.

"Anyway...nothing happened with you two...right?"

"Nope, just hugs and kisses on the cheek. I think he looked out for me and didn't cross that line. I think he would have if I pushed it though." Peg said with authority, looking straight at Becky hoping she heard the warning.

"Thanks that's good to know. I think he would be helpful to know for business and such."

"No doubt sister." Peg took a chug on her Stella draft and was looking forward to finishing quite a few tonight. "He's a powerful man Becky with lots of money in his family... But maybe he could help you expand your café to other locations in the County." Peg reassessed.

Becky beamed with a smile and relief that Peg was being supportive. Something was inviting about her smile that Peg loved to be around. She knew Jackie would find it impossible to resist. "Thanks, Peg for introducing him to me. It could change my life. I mean you've already changed my life, being my friend." Her eyes were getting misty as she got quiet for a moment. "I never met any girl that thinks like you do. You have taught me so much in so little time." Now the tears were flowing as Peg took her hand, feeling such unexpected love from her friend.

"Becky, I've never had a friend…to be honest. Not someone I could talk to. I just want you to be careful with Jackie. And of course, there's Joshua."

"Don't worry about that Peg. I would never hurt him. I like him and right now we're good for each other. Knowing the mayor is something different."

"I hear you sister…just keep your eyes open."

"Noted!" Becky jumped off her stool and warmly hugged Peg. They finished their embrace with a quick kiss on the lips. Becky ordered another round with the bartender and announced, "We'll be back in a few minutes," as she winked at the man. She took Peg's hand and dragged her to the back exit of the Just Glide Inn. "Let's get stoned, we need to start the holidays off right!"

Peg followed along, looking forward to the distraction. It had been years since she had smoked weed. Why not? She thought.

Becky pulled out her vapor unit, not much bigger than a *Bic* lighter, and pushed a couple of buttons, and like magic, she blew out smokeless smoke. Peg held down a button that was the heating element and took in two different full tokes. They felt surprisingly smokeless as she exhaled.

Becky did another toke pushed a couple of buttons and put it in her purse. "Are you good?" Peg nodded, "Let's get back in and start the second round."

About ten feet away from their spots at the bar, Peg felt something. By the time she sat down and drank half of her second Stella draft, her body was tingling. Her mind felt relieved and relaxed. Becky was trading laughs with the bartender she had winked at and ordered some nachos. Good idea, Peg thought, suddenly feeling hungry and happy. She grabbed Becky's arm to get her attention and looked deeply into her eyes, "I love you so much Becky, I wish we could make out right here!"

Becky almost spit out her beer as she reached out behind Peg's head to caress her hair, "You are so stoned, my dear friend! When was the last time you got high?"

Peg laughed, "It's been a long time…but you do have some great lips!"

"We have to find you a great kisser, where's this guy of yours?"

"That's a long story…" Peg lamented.

"Okay, we'll work on getting you a cute kisser that can do other male things like fucking! We could make out some, but you might try to finger me or something gross like that!" Becky laughed while she took another chug of beer

"No, I don't think so…but I might feel your titties, they look so cute!" Peg smiled as she pointed at Becky's chest.

"You can touch them anytime you want but stay away from my pussy!" Becky said with delight.

Peg started laughing and started to lose her balance on her stool. Becky quickly came to the rescue, "Maybe I should tape you to the stool. My god, you are so stoned!"

"Well, whose fault is that?" Peg retorted as she got herself balanced again.

"I'll take credit!" Becky said proudly.

Joshua walked in the door behind the two of them and saw the balancing act going on with his two friends. *Wow, they're drunk already!*

"Hey girls, do we need some babysitting? You guys are having fun already."

"That's what you get for being late," Peg said nicely.

"You want to get a table…I ordered some nachos."

"Nope I'll pull up a stool between my two luvs and try to catch up…or should I say catch you two the next time you lose your balance."

"He's become such a comedian since I first met him…but I like it!" Peg patted Joshua on the back. "Becky…get the bartender over here!"

Three beers were ordered followed by a deep pile of nachos. Joshua raised his mug and said, "Let's toast to our friendships and love to all of us!"

"That's so sweet," Peg felt Joshua's sincerity and kissed him on the cheek.

"Watch out for her Joshua, she's looking for a kissing partner," Becky stated her accusation with the cutest smile and reached across to Peg's face to touch her cheek.

"Sorry Becky, but Peg could make out with me anytime she wants. She taught me how to use my tongue. I owe her that!"

"You would too…my dear little Christian boyfriend!"

"Okay you two, I promise not to make out with either of you…for now at least!" Peg exploded with laughter after her pronouncement. She dug into the mountain of nachos hovering in front of her and stopped talking for a while.

"What did you do to her?" Joshua laughed at Becky.

"Got her stoned out back while we were waiting for you!" Becky pointed at Joshua.

"Looks like she needed it." They high-fived and started in on the nachos.

Finally, Peg cleaned off her fingers after five minutes of devouring nachos, "I hope my mom makes nachos tomorrow for Thanksgiving. I'm looking forward to it." Her friends gave her a thumbs up and Becky ordered another round of beers.

After a couple of great hours of stories and laughter, eventually, they all stumbled back down A1A a few blocks to Peg's apartment where she crashed on the couch and pointed to the bedroom for her friends to sleep. After midnight, kissing or fingering did not happen at all during the short night before dawn.

Part IV
Replenishment

Chapter 35

Becky was the first one to reach consciousness after her phone awoke her at her usual six a.m. She made it to the bathroom and purged herself of any poison left in her stomach. It was part of a morning routine that included a quick shower, peeing, and brushing her teeth. She was barely a hundred pounds compared to Peg's still thin one-hundred fifteen, but it kept her petite while eating at will during the day. Peg heard the retching sounds from the couch as she had suspected during the months, they had been friends. Luckily, Peg had not gone through that phase as a teenager and hoped that it was something Becky would learn to avoid in the future. She noted it as something to mention to her if it ever seemed the right time.

Peg finally opened her eyes and sat up, as she assessed the damage to her body from the night's activities. Amazingly, she felt great and decided to make coffee and enjoy a walk on the beach before heading to her parents. Her intake of alcohol since the Spring had been down to around ten percent of her normal intake for the last decade. Pouring down eight drafts of beer felt more like getting an oil change than having engine damage to her body. It wiped out any presence of anxiety in her mind for at least the morning. The surprise was the effect of the pot taking on her that she did not expect. She knew the THC content in marijuana was high these days, but she was shocked that two hits almost wiped her out. Overall, she liked being able to act a little crazy with her friends for the evening, something she did in the past, anonymously, in forgettable bars.

Becky blew Peg a kiss as she headed for the door to open her café. She would work until ten this morning and then hopefully nap with her parents before Joshua joined them for Thanksgiving dinner. Both Becky and Peg knew he would be asleep until at least ten a.m. His resume of all-night drinking was incomplete, and he was a sound sleeper.

Once Peg made it to the beach after a couple of cups of coffee, the sun was just peeking out with some rays, but not yet peaking as a sphere over the horizon. The picturesque sky never got old for her to witness in the morning, but as she looked to the west, she saw some ominous clouds moving towards the Space Coast in a couple of hours. It would give her time for a long walk to the Port and back.

Sand replenishment, during the last year, had extended the beach into the ocean another fifty yards or so, creating a barrier to the natural high tide moving deep over the beach. The replenishment had stopped the ocean from creating a perfectly level area of sand to walk on during several hours of low tide that was almost a hundred yards wide. Now the low tide had to be at its peak to have that platform of sand to walk on. Peg found it very annoying and was hopeful future storms would extend the pristine walking surface again.

Replenishment was a key cycle in life, but it came with change, she was learning. Today would be a big chance for that to continue to happen with her family. The question in her mind was, would it be like the beach replenishment; an artificial addition of natural material that interrupted the natural cycle of the tides or would it become a perfectly wide surface again to feel free to roam endlessly? She realized the answer quickly. The rare times of her unspoiled childhood would never return but her family could be replenished to enjoy, infinitely, whatever shape it took.

Peg picked up a bottle of *Grand Marnier* liqueur, a twelve-pack of *Blue Moon,* and three pies from the local *Publix.* Her mom would love the orange cognac and save the bottle as a candle holder and her dad would quietly love the taste of a decent beer for a day. As for the pies, she could never bake anything for less than six dollars that tasted as good as these freshly made desserts. The cherry pie was to die for, the lemon meringue was her dad's favorite, and the apple pie was just plain American.

Joshua rolled out of bed after ten a.m., just as Peg was returning from her shopping and beach walk. He looked awful and drank a glass of water before heading out. She kissed him on his forehead and left him at the kitchen table, "Sorry luv, but I have to shower and get ready to go to my parents. Let yourself out when you are ready...no hurry." He nodded his head and waved at her.

Peg sometimes needed a long, hot shower to feel reborn occasionally. This was one of those mornings. Luckily, hot water was never a problem for her apartment even though she used cold water at the end of showers during the hottest days of the year most of the time. She huddled under the shower head like a kitten getting their head scratched but wanting their tummy and back rubbed simultaneously. She wanted her body to feel alive. As a natural impulse, she slid her hand down to her pubic hair and started to explore it like someone was touching her for the first time. It wanted to find a foundry of ripe fruit that made a fantasy unnecessary. She reached climax within two minutes and let out a roar like a lion. After she finished, she laughed to herself, wondering if Joshua was still there, and heard her rumblings. Luckily, she did not care and enjoyed the rest of her shower.

She wore some shorts and a maroon-colored blouse with a gold necklace that looked comfortable but elegant. Her hair was curled and had grown some to lay a few inches down her shoulders with some lipstick that matched her blouse. On the twenty-five-minute drive over, she rehearsed quiet reactions to what could be some of her mom's questions or stories about her friends. She wanted to be a hundred percent positive on this visit and hoped that during the in-between or half-times of the football games, there would be time to talk as a family. She packed a little bag in case she wanted to stay over for the night.

Her Dad would be in front of the sixty-five inches he bought for Hazel at noon watching somebody playing in the Motor City followed in the late afternoon by another metropolis playing Darth Vader. She was not a big football fan, but she hated any Texas team. Now apparently there was an evening game as well, that she heard about in the teacher's lounge at work and would have to contend with football late into the evening. Hopefully, Lester's favorite team from DC would be in one of those games. She looked forward to having the day to watch football with her dad especially if the DC team played. He knew a lot about football and loved to banter with her during the games, she remembered.

She pulled up to their home in the trailer park with a first-class garage for the '69 Cutlass. Her Dad's custom van was sitting in the driveway parked to the side so she could pull up next to him without pulling into the garage. It felt comforting to be home.

Peg grabbed her pies and walked inside to find her mom decked out in a custom-fitted apron without a bra that made her look sexy as she checked Turkey already in the oven. The scent of sex seemed to be in the air competing with the dinner smells. It made her laugh inside and glad there was happiness in the home.

"Oh, Peg...you look so pretty! Come here, my sweet girl..." Hazel reached out for a hug with her apron dress and stirrer in her hand. Peg was happy to oblige as she laid down the pies and squeezed her mom to feel her chest and bones once again. Three times in the last month was more than the last eighteen years, but she was finally enjoying it. "Go keep your dad company for a while, I got some things to finish…and I'm fine. I'll call you over if I need some help." Peg did not protest because she was convinced that Hazel was happy for once in her kitchen and her free-flowing apron dress.

Lester jumped out of his recliner and hugged Peg like he was seeing a friend lost at sea. He held on for much too long, but Peg was comfortable with feeling him breathing and holding her close. "I hope you don't mind the ballgames on all day, I don't need the sound on if we want to play some music or have a conversation. We have Pittsburgh at Detroit right now and Kansas City at Dallas at 4 p.m. But the special game will be DC in New York. When I was growing up that was my team and still is. Will you stay for that game?"

"Absolutely Dad, I'm ready to stay over, if necessary, especially if you have more beer. I brought a twelve-pack of Blue Moon for you"

"Nice Peg…I don't get to drink a wheat ale too often. Don't worry I'm stocked with Stella's for you to drink!"

Peg pulled up a chair next to the recliner and grabbed her dad's hand, "Sounds like a deal Dad," she leaned over and kissed him. His eyes were watering as he grabbed his beer for a distraction. "Give me your assessment of Pittsburgh and Detroit. Is Pittsburgh favored?" Peg asked.

Lester cleared his throat sat up in his recliner and took a long swig of his beer as Peg let go of his hand, "Oh yes Peg, they're pretty talented this year, especially on defense, but the Lions always play tough on Turkey Day. You know this is the original game consistently on Thanksgiving since 1934…it was usually against the Bears or the Packers at the old Tiger stadium – of course outdoors! These indoor games take a little away from the tradition."

"You're right Dad…football should be outside especially when it's snowing. No doubt that's the coolest thing ever!" Peg smiled like a beacon from a lighthouse catching her dad's attention as it cycled in the air. Lester felt her brightness and landed his hand on the top of Peg's as a tear flowed down his face. For a moment he thought he was in heaven.

Chapter 36

"I hear there's a snowstorm hitting the mid-Atlantic and the Northeast," Hazel announced as she brought appetizers and beers in front of Peg and Lester. Her hair was up in a French bun showing her aging neckline and face. It was an unusual style for Hazel, one that Peg had not seen since her childhood. There was something distinguished about it though, Peg observed, remembering youthful pictures of her mom wearing her hair up that made her look like a movie star.

"What was that, Hazel?" asked Lester as he adjusted the volume down on the television.

"I saw it on the weather channel, a storm coming up the coast, they say six to twelve inches by tonight." Hazel was pleased to have all the attention.

"On Thanksgiving! Well, there you go Peg, you got your snow game tonight!"

"Don't they have a covered stadium?" Peg responded.

"Nope…they play at the Meadowlands in New Jersey just west of New York City." Hazel quickly added as she winked at Peg. "Lester when you get a chance, I need help changing out of this thing so I can sit down with you two. Almost everything is ready to go, and the Turkey will be done around three."

"Sure sweetheart!" Lester jumped at the chance to get Hazel undressed.

Peg smiled at her parent's playfulness as she pulled out her phone to check her messages. There was one text to open. "I would be glad to come by around five-thirty from my cousins' in Satellite Beach. Just send me the address and save me some pie!" Phillip wrote.

Peg felt excitement reading Phillip's message. It was a surprise she had set up for her father. He would go crazy to meet the father of a former football MVP for Washington who retired after winning his third straight championship in 2020. Guy Finelli was only twenty-eight, Peg thought, but for no apparent reason, she found Phillip, his father, more interesting looking. It made her wonder about her fascination with Alejandro being her age. Was she getting sucked back into love without maturity? At least for now, she did not have to worry about it. She felt fine not hearing from him for the second week in a row. Somehow, she felt confident it would work out for the best, which was a new construct for her.

After he closed the door to their bedroom on the opposite side of the trailer from the television area, Lester approached Hazel, who had turned around and was unpinning her hair bun while still keeping it off her neck. Lester took a moment to kiss her bare neck and massage her shoulders before unzipping the apron dress. He slipped off the shoulders and moved his hands over her back and around her tummy, which was still tight. It was always a pleasure to have her naked in his arms as Hazel let the dress fall to the floor. He held her from behind for a moment thinking about the morning love making as he caressed her breasts. It would be a couple of days for his member to respond again but it was still exciting to touch her all over. Hazel laughed as Lester tickled her ears and jaw line with kisses grabbed her bra and handed it to Lester. He reluctantly placed her sagging but full breasts in the 32C bra and hooked it from behind for her, "I guess we have to put them away for a while." She turned around with her breasts looking lovely, sitting up high in the supportive bra, and kissed him as she managed to put on her blouse and jeans without any further diversions from Lester.

"That sounds great Phillip. Thanks so much…here is the address…" Peg texted back as Lester headed from the bedroom back to his chair. Kick-off was just happening as Hazel came out of the bedroom to sit with her family. Her hair was down and curly around her silver-white blouse and dark jeans. Somehow, she pulled off a sexy look for appearing almost eighty, Peg thought. Hazel managed to sit on the arm of Lester's chair and hang next to him like a cat stretching out on the arm of a couch. God forbid if she had taken care of herself, Peg wondered, *her flexibility was amazing.*

"I can't believe my two girls are here with me for Thanksgiving," Lester blurted out as he reached out again to Peg on his left and kissed Hazel on his right.

"And watching football!" Peg responded with a laugh.

"I'm not sure this has ever happened Lester, you must be in heaven, my dear!"

"It sure feels like it, Hazel." He looked at his wife seriously as she touched his face.

"Maybe this would be a good time to tell Peg the whole story…like we talked about?" Hazel looked back with softness but with strong intent.

"I guess there's no right time." Lester relented.

Peg knew something was on the agenda but did not want anything to ruin the first family dinner in years, so she took control like she was in front of her fourth graders. "Hey, you two, let's enjoy the moment and dinner first before we talk. There's no hurry. I'll be here all day…OK?"

"You're right dear," Hazel sat up and came over to Peg to kiss her. "Come in the kitchen and help me do the sweet potatoes in the oven. You know with putting the marsh mallows on top!"

"That's so yummy Mom…Dad, I'll just be a few minutes. Do you need another beer?"

"Sounds good Peg…Detroit is ready to play today it looks like!" Lester reported with a smile at Peg.

"That's a relief…otherwise Pittsburgh might roll over them," Peg answered like she knew what she was talking about, and it felt good.

Once in the kitchen, Hazel asked to go outside for a smoke and Peg joined her. Luckily it was seventy-five degrees and sunny, not like the northeast's impending snowstorm. Hazel got her serious eyes on after a few deep inhales, "your dad told me about your conversation on the beach. I'm so glad he told you, but I was wondering how you were doing with it?"

"Mom, it's a relief…but it's a lot to process." Peg tried to explain.

"I'm sure it's a nightmare to try to understand Peg, but we were wrong to wait for so long. I hope at some point you can forgive us," Hazel said with the strength of nicotine running through her bloodstream, "frankly I wouldn't be able to if I were you, but you're a tough gal and smarter than both of us combined." Hazel said with confidence.

Peg stood silent trying to process the compliment from her mom. But she had been certain there was more to the story and was thrilled that Mom wanted to talk about it. "Mom…we're together, that's what counts. Let's talk more after dinner." Hazel nodded as she finished her cigarette like a vacuum cleaner.

After they completed their task in the kitchen, Peg grabbed two beers and sat next to her dad again. "So, what'd I miss?"

"Detroit scored on their first drive…seventy-five yards in twelve plays. It was a masterpiece. Pittsburgh had to punt. So, the Lions are on the move again. They can run the ball, unlike the Lions since Barry Sanders. You know… they have only won one playoff game since 1955! In sixty-seven years…that's amazing. And people still fill that stadium. This coach has built them from scratch defensively, and now they control the game with their run game and defense." Lester said with authority.

Peg handed him another beer and tried to think of something to add but could only produce a question, which was just as good, "Where'd they get this coach from?"
"He was a former Tight End for years, a position of strength and athleticism, so he can relate to players on the line as well as skill positions. He has coached for a while in the league and knows how to develop guys in the trenches."

"Isn't this game hard to get ready for in three days instead of seven?" Peg tried to impress her dad.

"You're right Peg…almost impossible against Pittsburgh, but so far so good. They have to run the ball and eat up time on the clock. You know…limit Pittsburgh's possessions."

"So, a great defense depends on a solid running game?"

"Exactly Peg!"

"How come everybody loves to pass the ball so much?"

"Because everybody loves to watch offense, and the rules make it hard to play great defense," Lester answered like a professor.

"I guess you need a balanced attack…you're saying…some passing, but don't forget to pound the rock!" Peg remembered that from somewhere as she was slinging clichés to keep up the conversation.

Hazel walked in and curled up on the chair again, wondering who this daughter of hers was talking football with Lester. He never looked so happy. She stayed quiet and enjoyed the sweet sound of family in her home. It was not a surprise to her that Peg was so smart and adaptable. She never felt prouder as a mother.

"Did you see that Peg…that's the counter-trey from the eighties when the Skins won three *Superbowls*." The replay from multiple angles showed the two linemen pulling left while three others blocked to the right leaving a massive whole for the running back to explode for thirty-two yards. "See the man-in-motion lead the blocking before the lineman pulls. It's amazing when it works out."

Peg for the first time watched a replay intently and saw exactly what her dad was saying. Until this moment, football had always been like watching cars crossing an intersection randomly following lights, sometimes going straight or turning. But this was truthfully a ballet, with dancers doing their routines as a unit, except in football it was two sets of dancers, the offense and the defense working against each other. The offense tried to do their routine as a unit or "a play" while the defense ran their routine or "a scheme" hoping to get in the way. Now she understood why someone would get so excited about "a good play" because it was so unlikely with competing routines in the same space. It would be like getting through all the lights on A1A on the way to work or at least a few of them in a row, remembering how good that felt driving in her car.

The timing of the play was magnificent, she thought. "Wow that was something!" she shouted out. "What are they going to do next Dad?" she asked.

"I would guess play-action and maybe hit a crossing pattern," her father responded as the ball was snapped. It looked like the same play to the right, but the quarterback faked it and fired the ball across the middle to a wide-open receiver who snagged it for another long gain.

Peg lifted her beer to tap to Lester, "great call dad!" Peg was impressed.

"Not really Peg...Football is a game of misdirection. The defense is always aggressive, so you have to show one thing and do another, but everyone has to be on the same page to pull it off. I guess it's like life. Things are always coming at you --- bills, disease, emotions, rules, and more. Some things you can manage straight on and some things you have to outwit." Lester smiled.

"I guess you're pretty good at the misdirection thing?" Peg said playfully.

Lester laughed, "you're right Peg, but sometimes you have to face up to things and I'm glad you gave me a chance to do that before it was too late." Lester shook his head in disgust.

"Hey dad, we're watching football here. Let's analyze things on a full stomach and more beer!"

"I'll take another one if you're offering?"

"Let's see if they can score in the red zone first." Peg threw out another cliché she knew would amaze Lester. "What do you call here, dad?" Peg asked Lester as he leaned forward loving the challenge.

"I would delay the back out of the backfield, especially if they blitz. See the safety coming up?" Lester pointed at the screen.

Peg intently watched and there it was, wide open over the middle, the back blocked and blocked again and then slipped out from the big bodies into the clear with only the quarterback watching him. "Throw it!" Lester yelled, the football escaped the hand of the quarterback and just over the arms of the lineman into the hands of the back, who was wide open and scampering into the end zone. She was shocked at the beauty of it and felt hooked to watch more. *This is fun,* she thought, as she ran to the kitchen for more beer. Her mother was full of smiles enjoying the pleasant family scene, missing from her life for eighteen years.

Dinner was served at the small dining room table for four just outside the kitchen. Peg could not remember ever having a fourth person at the Thanksgiving table. She hoped it would happen someday. Hazel and Lester helped with serving all the food and made sure Peg never got up. She had never been so hungry. The smells of the kitchen and her emotions of enjoyment had heightened her taste buds. Her plate was so full that it took her ten minutes of eating to make it look manageable. She kept an eye on the game, watching the ballet and hoping to see another great play. Why was it so much fun to watch the game with her dad, she questioned herself.

"You two remind me of when you were young. Peg you would sit with your dad for hours watching games together on Sundays. I guess you don't remember that. Sometimes you would do your homework or read a book, but if your dad said, "Did you see that?" you would look up and watch it on replay or listen to his explanation. It was so cute!" Hazel reported, seemingly [AF1] just as Peg was wondering.

Wow, Peg thought, *can this all be true or some kind of sick joke?* It felt so familiar but so far away that she had no memory of it. She had

216

to take Hazel's word for it. Was she a closet football fan all these years and did not realize it until now? Lester was right about misdirection, she shook her head and laughed to herself.

"Did you see that play, Peg?" Lester said on cue.

Chapter 37

Dessert was put off until half-time of the four-p.m. game. It would give Peg about two hours to open a little room in her stomach. She wanted to take off her jeans because her waist felt so huge. She imagined it was like being pregnant, but worse.

Her parents combined ate about half of what she swallowed. Too bad she did not have Becky's "stick her finger down her throat" talent to make some room in her stomach for dessert. But it was all worth it, she surmised if the beer kept flowing down her mouth.

It was helpful to keep moving around by washing dishes and putting things away while her mom took smoke and carried leftovers to some less fortunate folks in Trailer Park. By 5:30, the kitchen was clean, her parents were cuddled up watching the game and Peg felt more human again. She even buckled her jeans back up.

The ever-on-time person, Phillip, would be here any second. She sipped on a beer in the kitchen waiting for Phillip's knock. Within a minute, she heard the knock, "I'll get it, Mom and Dad!" She shouted to her parents.

Phillip had a twelve-pack of Stella in his left hand and a bottle of Merlot in his right and kissed Peg before he stepped inside. "Happy Thanksgiving Peg! This is so nice of you to have me over."

"Welcome Phillip...it's a big surprise for my dad especially." She whispered as she grabbed his arm and led him inside to the kitchen. "Thanks for the beer. Do you want a glass of wine?"

"Maybe later...let's see your parents."

"Hey Mom and dad…this is a friend of mine who has a place in Cape Atlantic. I mentioned him before…Phillip Finelli."

Both Lester and Hazel hurried to their feet. Hazel adjusted her blouse and hair while Lester stared with his mouth open. "Lester Patterson…nice to meet you Phillip…this is my wife, Hazel. Peg mentioned you had met and were friendly."

"Yes…that's true. Peg is a special person. I'm sure you folks are proud of her. Please sit down, I just thought I would stop by and meet you two on my way back from Satellite Beach, where I have cousins. They filled me up pretty well with Turkey."

"Well, you have to stay for dessert at halftime…" Hazel reached out and intertwined his arm with hers like securing a dance partner as she guided him to a chair near Lester. "Please sit down and I'll get you something to drink."

"Mom stay there, I'll crack open the Merlot he brought…and dad do you need another beer?" Peg took over as hostess.

Hazel kept her arm inside Phillip's while Peg secured drinks. She had not been around a man with shoulders and forearms like Phillip's in a while. Lester was slight and only five foot, nine inches. At six foot, three inches, and two hundred and ten pounds of strength, Hazel knew this was a man she could tangle with in her prime. Something stirred inside her that she had not let happen in eighteen years unless she was high of course. She had been off uppers for two weeks but smoking twice as much and drinking lots of coffee. She was still proud of it as a start to good health.

"I'm sure you get bothered all the time Phillip, but I've been a Washington fan since the sixties. Here in Florida, we had no teams except Miami until the Bucs in '76 and they were terrible. I loved Joe

Gibbs and almost gave up hope until your boy started playing in 2015 and the rest is history. Your son was the greatest player since Sammy Baugh. What an athlete! I'm glad he got out young and that he's doing what he's doing now. Tough kid though! He could have played in any generation." Lester paused for a moment trying not to dominate the conversation, but he could not help himself. He had so many questions in his head to ask Phillip. One was about the national news in 2014 when Phillip's son Guy and girlfriend Anna, an FBI agent who was nine months pregnant with his baby, were attacked by drug soldiers from Baltimore which led to her bloody death and the miraculous birth of his granddaughter, Annie. "How's that granddaughter of yours, she must be around eight?"

"Yes, that's right. She's great and lives right next to us with her cousins and my other son, Alex. Her dad, stepmother, and baby brother all have a house next to us as well. We call it the Parkwood Enclave. She's quite an athlete and brilliant as well. She loves Pistol Pete and plays basketball like him with her twin cousins Hill and Lil. They're all in fourth grade together."

Peg returned with the wine for Phillip and a beer for Lester. "Did I hear fourth grade mentioned? They're my favorites, Phillip. I didn't know you had three grandchildren in fourth grade." She sat across from Phillip, on Lester's left. She looked at her mom, who was beaming as she held on to Phillip like she was a groupie.

Peg laughed as Hazel mouthed, "I can't believe it!"

"Thank you both for letting me interrupt Thanksgiving to visit. I am so honored." Phillip spoke while looking up at Hazel and reaching across to Lester to shake his hand. Hazel gave him a full hug and kiss on the cheek as she finally left his side and sat in between Lester and Peg somehow using her feline talents again.

Phillip re-directed things to football, "Apparently Detroit whooped up on Pittsburgh and KC are ahead of the Cowgirls."

Lester laughed in the middle of a sip and almost spit out his beer,

"Dang that's exactly what I call them. Wouldn't that be something if they lost and DC won tonight?"

"Nothing would make me happier…except eating some of those pies that Peg said she brought." Phillip smiled.

"We still have until halftime. I'm still so full! I need to keep moving." Peg reported as she rose with a grunt.

"Wait Peg, I'll grab a smoke and stroll with you outside." Hazel followed her daughter like a girlfriend needing to talk about a boy she just met.

Lester talked football with Phillip for the next hour like he had found a long, lost friend. They quickly got into the subjects of music, parenting, politics, and aches and pains. Lester realized that his attitude towards health and living out his life was far different than Phillip's. Even with a five-year age gap and the difference in wealth, Lester realized he lacked a plan and the vigor to enjoy his last five, ten, or twenty years left to exist in this world.

Peg had found a friend who could bridge the communication gap between her and her parents. Hazel found him irresistible and trustworthy. Lester discovered a wealth of knowledge in Phillip. Friends would be shocked that Lester and Hazel met someone so famous. At some point after dessert, Hazel and Lester had a moment in the kitchen where they shared eye contact with no one watching them and they both just whispered, "Wow," to each other and then laughed like seven-year-old- old kids.

Peg wanted him around when they talked to help her clarify things instead of getting frustrated refereeing if it came to that. She wanted a chance to love her parents again, not burden herself with hate for what they did to her as parents.

Chapter 38

All four had TV trays in front of them cluttered with pies, plates, and drinks, as they huddled together watching the blizzard of a game in the Meadowlands just outside of New York City. The three pies had been attacked for almost four hours as had the wine and beer. Hazel and Peg had already switched to coffee.

The game could not have been more fun to watch. Phillip told stories about playing slow-motion football in various snowstorms over the years as a young kid, a youth counselor, and then with his boys and family. He was a prolific storyteller and a great listener. Hazel and Lester could hear and feel it.

Peg believed Phillip to be an Empath. It was something she had thought of about herself. It was a personality type that fit her sensitivity to things and seeking replenishment in nature. It could cause great problems for someone like her, stuck in her emotional development for years.

She realized that Phillip had figured out the downsides through his training as a therapist and now as an elderly and wise writer and grandfather. He had a great sensitivity to feeling people's emotions and developed great intuitions about them. Like herself, he liked alone time and found sanctuary in nature. Overall, he had a big heart and liked to give to others.

With Washington assuming a big lead in the second half, the snow game became a pleasant backdrop for Peg to ask a few questions. As she turned down the volume, she faced her parents and asked them for their attention, "Remember earlier mom and Dad, you said there were things to tell me. This will be a suitable time to talk about them. I think you both can trust Phillip and he can help us if we need it…what do you think?

"I think you're speaking the truth my dear girl, "Hazel spoke up with attentive eyes.

"You're right Peg, as long as Phillip doesn't feel uncomfortable about it," Lester said seriously.

"I'm honored to be here for your family Peg." Phillip spoke with encouragement, "Someone just needs to start."

"I guess that's my cue…" Hazel stood up and walked around for a moment. She grabbed pillows off the couch and piled them up in front of the three chairs with her back to the snowstorm on the sixty-five-inch television screen. "It was a tough time for me Peg, but I offer no excuses. For many years I could flirt with guys and never need to be with them but then your dad was gone for a while and things changed. This handsome guy showed up and I just fell for him. He was a drifter who worked for the Calvanese people that winter and then started to show up at some of the bars and the outdoor concerts. People were always partying, but it was a new century and people had kids and so forth. Most of our friends moved on and grew up, I guess."

Hazel was looking down at her hands and not keeping eye contact. Lester was holding hands with Peg. Phillip could see that Hazel was struggling with tears running down her face. He grabbed tissues and got on his knees and handed them to Hazel. She straightened up wiped her eyes and took his left hand. With his right arm, he wrapped his sturdy forearm behind her neck and laid his reassuring fingers on her right shoulder. She could feel a supportive headrest that relaxed her neck. His energy flowed through her chest and arms. She wondered how to speak what she never could say. Admit to her part in making her husband a murderer and a protector of her secret. Hazel for the first time after a day of togetherness with these three bodies around her, felt the courage to go on – *though it would not be easy.*

Chapter 39

The carnage left by the story was intense. With the snowstorm continuing in the late-night game that was all but over and mesmerizing in its beauty. From the distance and comfort of a trailer-park, living room in Florida, there was no feeling of pain from the participants. But the numbness was present in the four participants huddled together watching. Hazel was curled up in the *Lazy-Boy* chair with Lester staring at the screen and hearing the silence of the storm. Peg was lying with her head in Phillip's lap holding on to his thighs hoping the pain would all go away soon. Feeling nauseated, she was ready for relief and ran to the bathroom praying to expunge this ache in her body. It came naturally and after ten minutes she felt human again. As she brushed her teeth with an unwrapped toothbrush left in her spot years ago, she looked in the mirror and tried to piece together the nightmare she just heard from her mother.

"I was there, Peg… the whole time. I caught him with you the night before and confronted him. He backhanded me and strangled me to within an inch of my life. I couldn't scream for help, so I just lay there. He made me drink water that he must have drugged with valium that knocked me out until noon of the next day. I couldn't leave the room and could hardly breathe because I had broken ribs and an injured larynx. You went to school by yourself because he said I went to work early. He took the drug X and forced me to have intercourse with him, multiple times. It was too painful to manage, and I passed out. Afterward, he put me in the bathtub and washed me to clean up the evidence of himself. He told me that he wanted one more night with you and then he would leave town. If I didn't cooperate, he would kill both of us. I fell back asleep until the evening when I woke up in the dark. My mouth was gagged and my hands and feet were tied up under the covers in the bed. I felt like I would die there before anybody found me. Then a burst of noise came from down the hallway, and I could hear something being dragged past my door. I thought he killed you and would finish me off before his escape and maybe even burn the house down. Then the door burst open, and your father rescued me."

Peg spit out the mouthful of toothpaste, trying to get the taste of the past out of her mouth with several rinses. Then she splashed her face with cold water, but she wanted to undress and take a cold shower to numb her body. So, she did.

She wore her mom's skimpy robe that barely covered her ass, but she did not care. The kitchen had a kettle for tea that she used as a kid that always sat in the oven with water in it. Within minutes it was whistling. Peg stood over it the whole time with her wet hair dripping down her neck. The numbness stretched from her head to her toes. She hoped the hot tea would reignite her body temperature from the inside out. The sound of the kettle broke the silence in the house as Peg waited for a few seconds for the vapor to flow loudly from the kettle. Quietly with her tea mug steaming, she headed back to the floor in front of her parents using Phillip as a backstop to sip her tea. The hotness of the green tea seemed to settle her stomach while the warmth of Phillip's body heat penetrated her back. She took both of his comforting arms and pulled them around her so she could feel encased by love. After ten minutes of sipping her tea and watching her parents, she felt some hope. After putting her tea down, she sat up on her knees and put her arms around her parents huddled in the chair. All she heard was mumbled sounds of "We're so sorry Peg," and "We love you so much." She could feel the sobbing from their bodies. In the distance, she heard the door close. The Empath's job was done.

Peg rolled over under the covers of her full-size bed where she last slept as a senior in high school. She pleasantly awoke from dreams so erotic, maybe from her nakedness or as relief from the stress of the night, that she naturally found her labia and nipples and played with herself recreating the fantasy in her dream. It felt so warm and comfortable that she went on and on. After multiple releases, she went back to sleep for a short while. Finally, she awoke and stood naked in front of the full-length mirror in her room. The sun's rays came through the half-opened blinds of the short, east-facing windows near the top of the wall that created a glow in the mirror, surrounding the edges of her full nudeness. For the first time that she could remember, she loved what she saw – a fully developed woman. Now with a pretty smile that replaced her sullen mask just eight months before. She found her bikini and threw on shorts and a colorful top. It would be a beach day!

Chapter 40

It was just before midnight when Phillip arrived at the safe house in Winterhaven. Brooklyn O'Malley had spent Thanksgiving with Paco Lawrence's family in Hunters Creek southwest of the Orlando airport and just north of Kissimmee. It was a high-end neighborhood with a concentration of Puerto Rican population, ever-growing in central Florida since Hurricane Maria devastated the Island of Puerto Rico in 2017. Besides Brooks, Paco's guests included Cheverly Santiago and her son, and Alejandro Majada. It was a Puerto Rican meal with Pavochon or Turkey roasted with Mofongo stuffing, Arroz con Gandules, Tostones and Tembleque, and a green bean casserole. Brooks had flown out of DC before the snowstorm and had a great Puerto Rican Thanksgiving dinner with temperatures in the mid-seventies before meeting with Phillip at the safe house.

"This is a nice surprise to get you down to Florida and get a call to meet, but I'm guessing you're not on vacation, consider the late-night meeting idea," Phillip stated quizzically with a smile.

"Well, it's nice to get an excuse to see you anyway…but I'll get to the point," Brooks said with a tired voice. With his re-built voice box, he only had so many sounds to utter in a day and he was already borrowing on tomorrow's. "I've come a long way to ask you to help rebuild the country." He said without a smile.

"Is that still possible?" Phillip answered quickly with a laugh, wondering where this conversation was going. He had so much history with Brooks as a teenager through his mid-twenties, and then they lost touch for almost thirty years. When his sons became famous, they reconnected a decade ago. Then Brooks quietly took care of his son Guy's big problem. As a high school senior football star with a past drug history, Guy got caught up in a Baltimore drug lord network that Brooks had worked decades to take down. The rest was a story for the ages.

"I will never doubt that as long as I'm alive. No Sir!" He said with an inch of strength. "I believe a force in the universe has placed you and me in the right places at the right moments late in our lives," he paused to wet his vocal cords with water and asked Phillip a key question, "you are friends with a young lady named Peg Patterson?"

"Wow the FBI knows about little old Lincoln Street and young Peg? Why would they care about three blocks of a street in the tiny two square miles of the Cape Atlantic?"

"They don't… but the DEA down here does and because the next potential Governor of Florida is the mayor and he's known Peg Patterson since she was a teenager."

"Jackie Calvanese…you must be kidding! That's like multiplying the miracle of Sarah Palin winning the Governorship of Alaska times fifty."

"Exactly, but the difference is that he has the money and the moxie to pull it off on the scale of a population like Florida and their thirty electoral votes," Brooks said quietly his voice almost giving up on him.

"Let me guess Brooks, it goes something like this; Jackie runs for a state office in 2024 as State Senator of Brevard County. He wins big and makes some noise about Florida's problems in the papers and social media. Then runs for Governor in 2026 and turns the state forever BLUE, because he cements the ex-felon and Puerto Rican vote. This helps the country because the DEMS win the Presidency and put the country back together when Florida is easily in their column in '28 and '32." Phillip sat down feeling exhausted from his rant of verbal consciousness. After a few deep breaths trying to figure out this puzzle, he came up with a key question. "Exactly…how does this help Florida?

I mean Jackie, from what I hear, is probably as corrupt as all the Florida politicians put together."

"That's where I think you're wrong. Jackie is not corrupt about taking advantage of the government system for himself. He doesn't need the money or power for himself or his organization. He is smart enough to divest himself of his organization. His five sons are already running it without him. He will control great wealth when his father dies through trust and can fund any campaign he wants. The organization is in control of all the vices throughout central Florida and the real-estate empire that Francis Calvanese built. Jackie truly believes he must take care of the lower and middle classes, especially by improving the education system." Brooks paused and drank some more water.

They both enjoyed the silence as Phillip felt lucky to be sitting with his old friend, but his heart needed some medication to control his angina. He took a little tin box out of his pocket to find a pill or two. He swallowed them with some water, hoping to gain relief in a minute or two.

"Are you alright?" Brooks asked with concern.

"Heart disease, the beta blocker medicine, and other shit keeps my heart below eight-five or so beats per minute. Sometimes it hurts when I get hyped up."

"What the fuck! How long has this been going on?"

"This century!"

"No heart surgery?"

"Not yet, just the wonders of chemistry!"

230

"You always loved chemicals, especially that Frat house you lived at, it was like a pot factory in some of those bedrooms. Remember that night we got stuck in Phil's room, the tall blocking back guy, and did about fifteen bong hits of hash and some other shit." Brooks tried to hold his throat from exploding with laughter because it would hurt too much as he watched Phillip lay down on the couch with laughter. "I remember that guy that lived at the end of the hall near the telephone in the room, what was his name?"

"Roger," Phillip answered

"He was so fucked up telling this story and hogging the bong at the same time. It seemed like an hour that he kept doing bong hits and complaining about the phone ringing. What was the story?"

"Fucking Roger was one of those Baltimore guys from Dundalk, kind of a southern hippie type, looked like he was in the *Allman Brothers Band.*

"Yea, that's him," Brooks exclaimed.

"Anyway, he starts going on about the phone ringing in the hallway all the time, just across from his room. It drives him crazy that nobody answers it…blah, blah, blah and that he never gets phone calls from anybody…blah, blah, blah, so that's why he NEVER answers it. It rings and rings and rings. So, he takes this humongous bong hit and starts coughing like he's going to die. Finally, somebody gives him a cold beer to drink which he takes and chugs the entire can. So, then he passes the bong along and gets up on his knees, and bellows out, "But I still answer the fucking phone TEN TIMES more than anybody else!" Phillip was holding his chest trying to catch his breath because he was laughing so hard.

Brooks was smiling and enjoying himself with tears rolling down his eyes. He learned to never laugh hard anymore but wanted to remember more about that evening. "Didn't we go to Fraternity row to the lacrosse team house for a party after that?"

"All the Baltimore guys in the house knew the lacrosse team so we went over there for a party with the Tri-Delta girls. They handed out 714s to everyone. It wasn't that crowded but lots of girls." Phillip remembered.

"We met Kathy and Donna, who got so fucked up, that we had to hold them up to walk the hundred yards to their Sorority house. Those Quaaludes were like being drunk without the heavy drinking feel, but those girls could not handle it. Remember they took us out the next week to save their lives?" Brooks asked.

"They were the prettiest girls I ever remember knowing. I was too scared to ask Donna out, but we had a class or two together in the next year and she asked me to escort her to some sorority function. She liked me and loved to talk to me and walk on campus, but she had a rich boyfriend at home. Nice kid from Jersey... just out of my league." Phillip admitted.

"Maybe in a different league but you hang out in the stratosphere now. You were always like that with girls, cautious and nice. You had that Leah girlfriend in the mid-seventies that was gorgeous. What happened to her?"

"That's a long story for a different time."

"I hear you...Kathy and I went out a few times, but it didn' work out. She wasn't thrilled about dating a Catholic guy going to Georgetown being from Long Island and Jewish herself."

"Man…I forgot about all that shit. We couldn't get away with that today with *Snapchat* and *Instagram*." Phillip explained.

"Well, they do…but it's more about alcohol and stimulants. Only those running for office have to worry, I guess." Brooks reported, "Man we must do this again…soon! Such memories. No wonder your son was such a pothead," Brooks said with a controlled laugh, "boy we did some stupid shit."

"Yep…who thought we would ever be talking about repairing the country." Phillip relented, "where were we before I had to take some pills?" he questioned with a laugh.

Brooks smiled and finally continued, "Jackie will be elected State Senator for District 14 in 2024 and then run for Governor in 2026. By then he will have a state-wide network of staff and volunteers set up to run his campaign. Soon his construction empire will invest heavily in an upscale condominium development with set-asides for the lower and middle class to transform Cape Atlantic in the next few years. He will run as a middle-class businessperson ready to work for the people of Florida by improving the health care and education systems and taking care of the environment in the State. Corruption on the State level will get nowhere with Jackie." Brooks rose and went to the kitchen and poured out some scotch for himself and Phillip. He needed to numb his throat and finish talking soon. "We have been watching Jackie for years ascending in his father's network of businesses. He has all the signs of acting like a great patriot and a leader for the underprivileged. Think of Kennedy's wealth and his son's politics, this is the central Florida version of the Kennedy's."

"Your speech has left me speechless Brooks," Phillip said with a smile as he clicked glasses with Brooks before he sipped his drink, "which I guess is how YOU feel at the end of each day!"

"Thanks for the empathy!" They clicked glasses again.

"Well for the moment, let us say your crazy idea about Jackie Calvanese is true. What are going to do to make sure it goes in the right direction." Phillip said emphatically.

"Nothing… the FBI cannot be involved with influencing a politician."

"So, what do you want me to do?"

"Your son was a courageous Patriot in helping us take down a criminal network in Baltimore and he and his brother will help transform the city with their future foundation. I am positive you are a Patriot as well and you will help your country when necessary."

"In other words, become the go-between you and Jackie through Peg."
"Not exactly but close. My voice is getting tired, my good friend, someone will contact you from the DEA. I think you will like her!"

"Sounds interesting...I understand."

They hugged and Brooks whispered in his ear, "Did you see that fucking snowstorm game. Remember when we played in that stuff?"

"DC pulled it out, my boys were texting me like crazy. They know about slo-mo football!"

Brooks nodded and gave a thumbs-up.

Phillip finished his drink and headed outside in his *Under Armor* shorts and tops. *You got to love the temperature after midnight in this state*, he thought. When he got to his car his phone buzzed with a text from a restricted number, "A woman named Chevy Santiago will contact you. Be well, my friend!"

Chapter 41

Friday morning, Chevy Santiago was driving, crossing the Indian and Banana rivers to get to Cape Atlantic. It never got old for her to go over the rising bridges, appreciate the glistening water of the wide rivers, and become in awe at the colossal cruise ships in Port Atlantic as A1A curved south to parallel the Space Coast for forty miles to its end at Sebastian Inlet. She would find her meeting place with Phillip in the first mile that she had suggested even though she forgot to grab a coffee on the way. Maybe they could go someplace he knew to sit down and get her caffeine, she thought. Luckily, she had low blood pressure because she lived on the stuff. She turned right on Central Avenue across from the *McDonald's,* where she could have filled up with some brew because she was not fussy, but she did not want to be late for her first meeting with Phillip because he was reportedly always on time. She passed the new Hotel behind the *Radisson* towards the Banana River. They were building everywhere on this side of Cape Atlantic, she noticed. They were just a half-mile south of the condo that Alejandro had lived in as she pulled into the Manatee Sanctuary Park. This ten-acre park straddling the river had a half-mile paved walking trail with ten exercise stations, a kid's playground, a covered pavilion with a kitchen, picnic tables, and a lovely covered riverside boardwalk to see the Manatees cozy up to the shore for the warm waters and to feed off the sea grass, especially in the winter months. Chevy was pleasantly surprised when she left her car and started walking around the trail. There were several other hardy souls at this early hour withstanding the sixty-degree weather, cold by Florida standards. She loved smelling the salted air as she almost finished a mile when she noticed a man in a DC baseball cap joining her as she came around for a third lap.

"Slow down Wonder Woman if you want me to stay up with you..." came from a deep voice and a smiling face.

"So sorry Phillip…I'm getting some exercise in after eating like an el Caballo yesterday. Nice meeting you. I've heard a lot about you. Congratulations on such a wonderful family and you're writing. I have read your first two books; you know Brooks is a big fan and I like sports."

"Thank you so much…so what did you think?"

They were finally walking together at the same pace. He was much taller than she had imagined and looked great in shorts at sixty-eight. Both he and Brooks must have been studs in high school and college, she fantasized. Chevy knew she needed to break out of her convent life and find a man soon. It was almost hopeless with a growing son and an all-encompassing career. Now with this project for the next decade well…one day at a time she thought to herself. First, maybe that cup of coffee, and then she finally remembered the question, "To be honest Phillip, let's get some coffee!"

"Great idea…we can kill two birds with one stone. Let's go down to the Café Harmony, a new spot about a mile and a half from here. We could walk and talk on the way."

Chevy was a little confused about the two birds and asked, "What's the second bird?"

"Well, I was going to explain that…you know…on the way."

"Ok I trust you," she smiled and grabbed his arm, which surprised her.

He looked at her with warm eyes and asked again, "So what do you think?"

"Oh, about the books," Chevy was confused that she was acting so dizzy, "sorry my brain is missing some caffeine...to be truthful about the books," she paused again and snuggled in a little closer, "I loved them. I read them twice and cried each time. They were nothing like I expected, even though Brooks said they were great. They're going to make great movies."

Phillip was excited by Chevy's support and her physicalness. He should get home soon, he surmised. "Thank you for that. I'm so glad about your reaction. We must be in harmony because that's what I do when I re-read them."

"The family stuff and the description of the games are phenomenal...like you were right there. How did you do that?"

"Years of wasting time talking to myself I guess!" They both laughed.

Chevy felt so much emotion that she could not let go of him. "I'm sorry can we sit down a minute." They found a bench right behind them and Phillip sat down first while Chevy stood above him for a second. She shocked herself by saying, "I need this right now can you hold me for a while?"

Phillip reached his hands up and helped Chevy descend on his lap and curl up like a baby. With her head on his chest, she started sobbing as he wrapped his strong arms around her and held her strongly After ten minutes, she slowed down and wiped her face with her hands Then Phillip used his shirt to dry her eyes and told her to blow her nose They giggled like kids.

Finally, she hopped off his lap and sat next to him catching her breath and shaking her head while Phillip rubbed her back. "Wow, that was the weirdest thing I've ever done. I'm so sorry and embarrassed."

"I thought it was human and I'm glad I could help. I've done a lot weirder shit than that in my life…so I think you're in good shape. Do you feel better?"

"A lot better…sorry about your shirt!" She smiled like the young girl she once was but suddenly felt alive. "That was like an exorcism or some crazy internal tornado that passed through me. You must think I'm crazy."

"A little bit but very sexy. What happens to your husband?"

"He thought he could do better."

"Well, that was a mistake. You're quite a package for someone a lot younger than me…unfortunately!" They both laughed and hugged again. "Let's hit the road and get you some coffee." They held hands out of the park and walked out Thurm Avenue to A1A. Finally, they let go and walked apart, realizing they would be friends for life.

"Tell me why we're walking a mile and a half to get coffee?" Chevy said quizzically as they passed *Southern Charm Café,* a great breakfast and lunch spot.

Phillip starts the story with Becky, Peg's new friend, and how she fits into the situation with the mayor and his future. He thought seeing her at the Café would give Chevy a feel for her energy and personality from an anonymous perspective. If Peg came in, Phillip would introduce Chevy as his literary agent who worked out of Lakeland, Florida which could be true, because he did have an agency at one time work on one of his books out of Lakeland Florida, but not currently. Either way, it was a brilliant cover for Chevy to be around Phillip. She could use her middle and birth name, Maria Gonzalez. Chevy was feeling happy and hooked Phillip's arm for a minute to confirm their plan. They were all set to enter the Café Harmony and finally get Chevy coffee.

On the Friday morning after Turkey Day, the Café was sparsely populated. They ordered from Becky Baker's parents and found a seat near the bulletin boards away from the front door. Chevy got up and paced in front of the shelves looking at the books. Finally, her coffee was ready and brought to the table by Becky, excited to meet new interesting customers. She welcomed them with a big smile and a quick look over to see if they were a couple on vacation, friends, or business folks, but did not ask. She left quickly to get back to the kitchen not realizing she had met Phillip before.

"O god that is better than sex Phillip!" Chevy muttered as she sipped the Latte.

"It's been a long time for you...I'm guessing?" Phillip laughed.

"Typical male response." Chevy teased, "There are some things better than sex, like food and drink."

"If you say so. I mean... I'm Italian so understand how food can send you to great places, but great sex is in another category." Phillip responded.

"There you go...great sex...can be few and far between, Men are generally horrible at sex with women," Chevy uttered.

"I would agree with that...from my experience working with couples a long time ago. I would hope things have moved along since then..."

"Well, it didn't for me…my husband was my first and worst. The guys since have been in the middle somewhere. And I don't see women as an alternative."

"Gotcha."

"You must have a superpower or something. In the past hour, I have attached myself to you and cried my eyes out and now I'm talking about my sexual partners!" Chevy took another sip and made happy noises.

"I guess we like each other. That's a good start if we're going to work on this project together. Trust will be important."

"You're a very wise person. No wonder Brooks likes you." Chevy said softly over her coffee cup which was semi-attached to her chin as she blew over it and sipped every five seconds.

"Hey, the apple turnovers here are amazing. We should get a couple."

"Can you order me a regular coffee along with it? I can't run out of caffeine at this point."

Phillip rose and headed to the counter. Just as he got there, he saw Peg come in the door. She ran towards him and hugged his body like a firefighter jumping down a pole and hanging on for the ride. "I was hoping to see you here, but this is amazing. We must talk about last night. What a day. I woke up at three a.m. thinking about it. I have a lot to reflect on, but I feel great and connected with my parents."

"I am so happy Peg…listen I'm here with my friend, ordering some turnovers and coffee. What can I get you so you can join us."

"Oh sure…a Latte and a turnover for sure. I'm not ready to diet quite yet after yesterday my stomach is so stretched out, it's yelling at me." Peg looked a bit sullen after hearing that she would have to share Phillip this morning after seeing him alone, but she tried to not show it.

"So, tell me about your friend."

"Maria Gonzalez was my agent on my first two books, I told her about my idea for the novel we talked about. I've written some chapters on it. So, this is great for her to meet you."

Suddenly Peg felt important again and was excited to meet Maria. Phillip did the introductions as they all sat at the table waiting for their orders. Phillip purposely asked questions of Peg to get her talking to avoid learning about Chevy too much. Finally, Becky Baker came with the turnovers and coffee. She was so excited to see Peg.

"Becky, you remember Phillip, and this is his friend, Maria, can you sit with us?"

"Of course, Phillip, I'm so sorry. Sometimes I run around here without my head on straight. Give me a minute and I'll join you guys…nice to meet you, Maria." She went to the counter to talk to her parents and returned quickly with a coffee for herself.
Chevy looked at Phillip to take the lead in the discussion. It would be a delicate operation that she had to keep out of direct contact. Being undercover was not illegal, but the circumstances were questionable legally. She would be screwed if anybody she did not trust got wind of it.

"Wow…this is so neat to have you here. Thanks for coming to my little Café."

"It was one of the reasons Maria came to visit me honestly. She loves new coffee shops. I told her my friend Peg said it was the best on the Space Coast."

"He wasn't lying Becky. I am so impressed by your place. Do you have expansion plans?" Chevy tried to pry a bit.

Becky looked at Peg and hesitated, "Well honestly our friend the mayor is interested in getting investors to look at the possibility. I have my hands full running this one, but he's quite a special guy."

"That's what we hear." Chevy echoed.

"Peg, what do you think?" Phillip followed up.

"You know I love the mayor, but I told Becky to be careful getting over-involved with him. He's such a busy guy, I'm sure we're little fishes in his world." Peg explained.

"I don't think so, Peg. He cares about you, like a daughter and he wants to help me out, I think, because of that." Becky added.

"And you're a lot cuter than me, Becky!" Peg laughed.

"I don't know about that…you're both beautiful women," Chevy added.

"Thank you, Maria, after last night it makes sense why Jackie has always looked after me." She eyed Phillip, who nodded.

"Well, I must get back to the kitchen, folks. Let me know if I can get you something else and stay as long as you like. Again, nice seeing you all." Becky waived and kissed Peg on the cheek as she hustled into the kitchen. *What nice upscale people that my friend Peg knows*, she thought, *and how lucky I am to have found her*.

Chapter 42

After another hour of talking, Peg finally said her goodbyes to Phillip and Chevy and headed to her apartment to get ready for a beach day. She talked mostly about the breakthrough with her family without mentioning too many of the details about the stranger, Chevy, whom she thought was Maria the literary agent. She was disappointed to not ask Chevy any questions about her work but was happy that Phillip mentioned their writing project together. She did say, "Let me know if I can help," once which Peg felt was encouraging. It was nice to talk about Alejandro with them, Peg lamented, they both believed there was hope in seeing him soon. Peg felt warm inside after all the attention and was certain they could both be mentors for her in the future. Getting all this attention from older adults and friends, that cared about her after all these years on her own, gave her extreme relief from her normal elevated levels of anxiety. Along with getting replenishment from the beach and attaining teaching status with her favorites – nine-year-olds, things were looking up even with her romantic life up in the air.

Phillip and Chevy headed back to the Manatee Park for their cars. It was already up to seventy-two and sunny with minimal wind. Another perfect day on the Space Coast.

"Well, that was interesting." Chevy started.

"Becky is moving quickly into the mistress role to get her business expanded. She doesn't know all that yet, but Peg does." Phillip stated.

"I'd say things are off to a good start. This may give Peg protection from getting too close to the mayor." Chevy looked at Phillip for assurance. She understood his fondness for Peg.

"Becky is a little tougher and cares about making money which makes her perfect to manage that role. Peg is coming out of tough times and needs some stability and maybe some romance. By the way, what's with Alejandro." Phillip explored

"I was just thinking about that. I'm comfortable with arranging a date if she wants, but it can't be here." Chevy said emphatically.

"I'll see what I can find out and call you," Phillip answered.

They walked on A1A across from the big ice cream cone place and made it to the park. It was a little bit more crowded but still had benches available.

"Can I ask you a favor?" Chevy asked like a teenager.

"Sure." Phillip smiled at her.

"Can we sit on the bench again and maybe you just hold me again for a few minutes before I go." Chevy was disappointed in how needy she felt, but finding Phillip was giving her hope and relief from the total lack of affection in her life. In many ways he was channeling her fondness for Brooks through Phillip. Somehow it felt completely safe.

Phillip shook his head yes and took her hand to find an open bench. It looked out over the river where the Manatees like to play. This time she laid her head on his left shoulder with his big arm around her. She closed her eyes and just listened to his heart beating, feeling his love permeate her soul. She remembered sitting on her grandpa's lap for hours as a kid while he told stories about the homeland. He would put one of his rough hands through her long black hair and use the other to express himself to others. It was a land of affection that she inhabited when he was around. Being the youngest of six she received extraordinarily little attention or affection from her parents. She kept boys away through high school and most of college, as she was determined to get ahead in life. The first young man that swept her off her feet, she married during law school. And regretted after she was pregnant. The Spanish she learned from her grandpa helped her ascend quickly at the DEA in Florida. She missed him every day.

Finally, she felt refreshed and lifted her head and spoke to Phillip. "Are you sure you want to do this Phillip? I promise I won't be a basket case every time we get together."

Phillip looked at her with soft eyes not wanting to interfere with Chevy's thought as she wiped her eyes and straightened her outfit while sitting up. She looked away from Phillip towards the river and watched the birds playing with the water. "Are there Manatees out there?"

"It's a sanctuary…in case they need a place to warm up and feed without fear."

"How do they know that?"

"Probably through generations before and learning the smell and feel of the place."

"A sanctuary…thanks Phillip for being one today. Your smell and touch made me feel safe. It has been a while since I felt safe being that close to another human being. My kid is too old to snuggle anymore!" Chevy laughed.

"I understand completely. I hope you're, okay?"

"I feel great! The coffee helped as well." She stood up and laughed. "I'll set up times and places for Alejandro and Peg to get together."

"He should text her directly, I think. I will need to talk to her sometime about the whole situation without giving it all away."

"Great idea…she kissed him on the cheek and headed to her car.

Chapter 43

Sunday Brunch at the Port Atlantic Grill restaurant was decent food but when the Royal Caribbean's Oasis of the Seas was docked fifty yards away somehow it tasted even better. Now fourteen years old, the first of the Oasis class cruise ships, still within a meter of being the longest in the world, was an impressive sight to witness. Peg and Phillip sat on the same side of their outdoor table to gaze at the twenty-two stories high and three football fields long city on the sea. Phillip hoped the view would help Peg understand the enormity of the plan to save the state of Florida that he was about to reveal. The Thanksgiving weekend had already given Peg too much to swallow in addition to the food, drinks, and desserts. Digesting how she might help the country shift Florida into a blue state might be overwhelming for her, but Phillip thought if she decided to see Alejandro socially, it was important that she be fully informed of what was going on around her. Her parents had let her wander for eighteen years without important knowledge in her life, she deserved better and the full story, Phillip believed.

"How are the crab cakes?" Phillip asked as he worked on his Eggs Benedict.

"Not the best, but I don't like crab cakes that much," Peg admitted

"That's exactly how I feel…crab meat is so good by itself, why mix it with filler and other shit?" Phillip added. "So why did you get it?"

"I do like tartar sauce, and I thought I should try it because everybody is always saying blah, blah has the best crab cakes. I should know better... Anyway, I've eaten so much this weekend. I could go without finishing this today. I'll work on the fruit." She smiled like a kid getting away with only eating the dessert.

"Listen I have something to talk to you about that is extremely complicated. So, if you need another Mimosa let it rip." Phillip warned.

"That bad?" Peg turned sullen.

"Pretty crazy but exciting, so not bad...just complicated...first of all if you want to see Alejandro that can be arranged." Phillip offered to break the news of the plan.

"What?" she was not expecting to hear that from Phillip.

"It's a long story, but I have been contacted by someone working with him to let you know this and some other stuff. You should try to trust me and save us both a lot of explaining. I know that's a pretty lame reason, but for now, it would be better for you to know the least about the source if you can handle the mystery of it." Phillip finished waiting for the tidal wave of emotion, but instead, Peg was playful but inquisitive.

"Well, I do trust you...so give me the basics and I'll yell at you later." Peg laughed nervously.

"How did someone contact you about Alejandro?"

"They know that I know you and they don't want to be involved directly."

"Deniability...I get it. Should this be part of the novel?"

"I imagine so, but it might not be realistic!" Phillip laughed breaking the tension. He was pleased that so far Peg was calm about things.

"My life's been unrealistic so far…some real history could change all that." Peg grinned.

"Well, that's a good place to start…a little history." Phillip started to explain the Calvanese organization built by Jackie's father Francis and the beginnings of Cape and Port Atlantic. He explained Jackie's involvement since his dad's retirement in real estate, construction, and vices that are now totally run by his five sons. He explained Anmar's and Dragmar's roles and evolution as informants. Then he paused and let the information soak in before he went on. He waited out the silence and the staring from Peg, who was in a daze of deep thought.

"I need another drink," Peg said with serious softness as her face went sullen. She rose and went to the brunch table poured herself a full mimosa and came back with it half-finished. She settled in and made eye contact with Phillip, wondering what happened to her last day of fun before work on Monday morning. Trying to assess the situation she asked, "So overall Jackie's a pretty important bad guy?"

"Yes and no. Look Peg I know this is a shock, but I had to tell you the whole story if you're seeing Alejandro in the future. Certain people believe Jackie has the right moral compass to be a leader to represent the lower- and middle-class citizens ignored by Florida's corrupt leadership." He looked at her face to see if he should go on. She finally nodded so he continued. "For years there has been a lack of resources for education and health care. Environmental concerns are paramount for this state. Jackie has enough wealth to fund his campaign and they believe he is incorruptible at the state level."

"Didn't we just have a governor that fit that profile who is now a U.S. Senator?"

"Good point Peg, but you know Jackie is a different animal and not a conservative crazy person who let eight hundred thousand Floridians go without Medicaid for no good reason. Should I go on?"

"Yeah, I know…I was just being argumentative, but we are talking about Jackie the mayor. I mean we are at ground zero of this thing. I know he has the ambition for higher office but what are we talking about here?"

"He's going to run for State Senator in '24 and Governor in '26 mainly on his dime."

"I knew he had money but that loaded…really?" Peg finally was coming to grips with the idea of Jackie's wealth. She looked directly at Phillip with big eyes and a gaping mouth.

"Without a doubt."

"I know his father is on his deathbed…but Jackie seems too interested in regular people to be a bigwig and lives modestly." Peg had many thoughts in her head trying to make sense of it all. "Why do they want me involved?"

"Because he sees you as a daughter. Years back, his father gave him the directive to watch out for you because of your father's work for him. Over the years you have become special to him." Phillip said delicately.

"The pieces to the puzzle are starting to fit together. So, he must know everything that my family went through?" Peg relented

"I would assume."

"Can we finish this with a walk on the beach? My mind needs some replenishment."

They finished at the Grill and walked a mile to the beach through Brevard County Park. Peg expressed her idea to see Alejandro next weekend at the *House of Blues* near *Disneyworld*. It had great music with a second floor that had a long bar overlooking the stage and some quiet spots. There were always lots of people around and places to mingle but was not as packed during the week when a well-known group performed.

Once they got inside Brevard County Park, they followed the pathway, enjoying the quiet while witnessing tens of cats enjoying the coolness under the vegetation. Finally, they reached the dunes to traverse the sand. The wind on the beach was coming from the north but as they walked south it softly enveloped them and pushed them along as they walked near the surf.

"Phillip, how long have you known about all this stuff?" Peg suddenly spiked with anxiety wondering if their whole relationship had been a set-up for this moment.

"Since I left your parent's place on Thanksgiving night. I went to visit an old friend near Orlando who is important in one of those three-letter government agencies who called me out of the blue. It was quite a shock. It was a complete coincidence that I had met you, and he had just found out from his people with eyes on Jackie and so forth."

Peg looked at his eyes trying to assess his honesty. Too many things were coincidental which concerned her, but he had been so supportive, she did not care. She wanted to be on the ride wherever it went. Her anxiety blew away a bit, but still in front of her as her consciousness felt clear of it for now, "I guess I believe you. It all seems like a pretty crazy idea, but if we're in it together." Peg reached out for his hand.

"My friend is an American hero who continues to help our country heal. He saved my son and my granddaughter and helped them get revenge. He asked me to help, and I am honored to do what I can. I hope you will too." Phillip looked ahead with tears in his eyes. Peg felt his energy pulsate through her hand and into her neck and warm her body. It was pure love that could not be faked. She felt it in her bones.

They walked a bit before she asked, "What should I do?"

"Besides figuring out your feelings for Alejandro, there are three fronts with Jackie. Continue to be involved with him as much as you have and keep up conversations that involve the future. As a teacher, it would be natural for you to keep education a problem area in your head. Things that seem to work, things that are lacking etcetera, etcetera. Second, stay on the Becky Baker story. I know you guys are friends and I don't want that relationship to be hurt in any way but keep a dialogue going about what's happening with Jackie. Details could be important to know later by higher-ups. Thirdly, get to know Jackie's oldest son, Paul, who oversees the brothers. He is thirty-one, a lawyer, brilliant, and a quiet leader. Paul is Harvard-educated and works all the time. He loves the water like his father but is all business. No known relationships currently. Jackie's boys are a mystery to the higher-ups. If you could break that glass, it would be very helpful."

"He has five sons, right?" Peg inquired.

"Yes…I don't know the names, but one's a CPA and the other three directly run the construction business."

"Paul, Matthew, Mark, Luke, and John…" Peg recalled like it was a rock group she followed with a big smile, suddenly excited that she could contribute information.

Phillip was caught off-guard, but quickly figured out the riddle, "Ahhh the New Testament writers…of course!"

"Jackie is quietly religious and mentioned his boys quite a bit, but never what they did. It was usually a graduation or a birthday, an occasional wedding. I know he gets excited about his grandkids though." Peg added.

"A real family man huh? How about his wife? Does he ever mention her?

"Never!" Peg said with authority. "Hey…maybe we can get an invite to their Christmas party, I hear it's quite a rumble."

"Perfect for you and Becky to go and mingle," Phillip advised. "I have to keep my distance for now from Jackie.

"Sounds good…I'll work on it. Should Becky know anything?" Peg asked already sensing the answer.

"That is a Big NO…maybe down the road if it is warranted but it would be too risky now. She has a lot to achieve with Jackie first. We don't want her distracted. Most of this plan needs to grow organically…on its own. We will be the gardeners keeping it watered and fertilized when necessary." Phillip stated metaphorically.

"I like that. I always wanted to be a gardener." Peg seemed pleased as she held her sandals in her hand and dug her toes into the sand as she walked. Organically was the way to go, she agreed.

Chapter 44

Peg checked into the *Hilton* Orlando at Lake Buena Vista for the weekend after work on Friday afternoon. She decided to splurge with her credit card because she could pay it off every month with her full-time teaching salary and no more school tuition. It was walking distance to the *House of Blues* in the evening or an Uber home, outlet shopping on Saturday for the latest fashion in clothes or shoes and swimsuits, and some cocktails at the pool. She even got late checkout on Sunday in the weekend deal. No matter what happened with Alejandro tonight, she would have an enjoyable time this visit. She was hoping Becky and Joshua might join her Saturday afternoon and evening to check out *Disneyworld* or the other nightlife in the area.

She had two double beds in the room on the eighth floor and loved her view. After a shower, she snuggled under the great-smelling sheets and landed her wet head on the fluffy pillows for a nap. It was so extravagant, she thought. She had bought a new blouse for the night to go with her most expensive designer jeans and heels. She could not wait to show it off to Alejandro. The situation between them felt like an all-in or leave-the-table bet and right now she was all-in. She expected the date to be completely comfortable or amazingly awkward. They would have tons to talk about or zero to say. Most importantly she was hoping for an animal attraction to Alejandro or an avalanche of anxiety that turned to anger. There would be no middle ground, she assumed, at least on her end. She wanted to get on with the relationship as a part of her life or go it alone romantically with support from her friends and family. It was clear to her now what was important to her in a relationship, and it would be an organic experience finding it with Alejandro or not. Was she being confident in her decision-making or just foolishly naïve about the process? It did not seem to matter, she realized, it was what she wanted.

It was a good deal hotter and humidter than being on the Space Coast, she noticed. No breezes in the prevailing darkness, as she started to walk out of the hotel. Plenty of lights on the sidewalks and the highways to make her feel safe as her red blouse made her feel sexy with several buttons undone. She was wearing an unusual amount of gold chains around her neck that she played with continuously. Her breasts were unencumbered but comfortable against her loose-fitting blouse. Her jeans were up against her skin tightly. She had done trimming of her bush but left most of it natural which felt nice without underwear. The tightness of her jeans made her feel athletic in her stride on the sidewalk, as she strode confidently to meet someone who could make her happy – at least for the night.

The crowd outside the *House of Blues* was full of energy with outside cocktail areas to get drinks and mingle. She made plans with Alejandro to meet at the upstairs bar at 8 pm, so they could have an hour to talk before the first band played. Being a bit early, she headed inside to get a drink and wander around. It had been over six years since she had been inside. It was a cool place, she remembered, with enough spots and levels to get around the crowds, but intimate enough to see the stage from anywhere. There were higher priced areas with tables, but most folks stood around the wooden counters on each level unless they wanted to get tangled up in the main floor area where people would be packed watching and cheering their favorite band. Tonight, it would not be packed and used as a dance floor. She headed upstairs and looked for a couple of stools in front of the bar as she ordered a gin and tonic. As she settled in, the background music was gentle like a breeze on the beach. The outfitted cowboys with their styled hats seemed to be most present with pretty ladies in outfits like hers catching their eyes as they passed in front of her. The log cabin, type-counter of wood, about twenty feet ahead of her overlooking the stage and dance floor, had a row of couples tangled up and talking as they leaned over or against it like characters out of a wild-west movie.

257

Suddenly he found her and sat down without any drama, "I see you're set with a drink; I think I'll join you." Alejandro turned away from Peg and ordered a beer. He looked so handsome dressed up in a country western shirt and jeans but no cowboy hat. "Cheers," he said as he toasted her gin and tonic with his *Dos Equis* in hand.

"I'm glad you made it. You look all dressed up in your country-looking shirt. Pretty cool Alejandro." Peg said with an easy smile. The gin and tonic gave her just the right tension for the moment. "Do I get a hug or a kiss?" She asked inviting appropriate physical contact.

He laughed and leaned in to kiss her on the cheek. "You look like a real fox with that red blouse and gold chains. How did these guys leave a chair open next to you."

"I guess my bitch meter was pretty high," she laughed. "It was not too long, maybe five minutes. I'm sure I would have fought them off until you showed up." Peg continued her cheerful banter.

"Well, thanks for seeing me, Peg. It's great to see you again. How is teaching fourth graders going?" he asked sincerely.

Peg leaned over and kissed him on the lips. She pulled back a couple of inches and said, "It's nice to see you too…" Then she pulled back and ordered another drink as she finished her first one. Alejandro motioned to the bartender to put it on his tab. "I'm doing pretty well… I think... I have thirty-five kids, so it's hard to get to all of them, but I'm battling every day to include all of them in becoming good ten-year-olds next year. That's all I can do."

"That's a good way to look at it, Peg," Alejandro said with his eyes locked on her appealing, tanned face and luscious lips with her black curled hair lying around her shoulders. She had matured in the six months since he had met her and was quite lovely to stare at as a lady

Her chest was arched and inches away from him looking sensual and smelling sensational. He was glad to be turned on and felt comfortable to be sitting with her at this moment and thinking of nothing but her.

In the next hour, they caught up on their lives. Peg shared her re-connection with her parents without revealing the big crime and her new friends. Alejandro recalled books he had read and people that he had met to help him get relocated. He was working to find out what he could about his mother and to see if she was still alive miraculously.

They worked themselves downstairs to the main stage while the first band played and listened for a while from close range. They danced to rocking tunes and got close to a slow dance. They found a corner to kiss for a while. It was passionate, but under control. Peg enjoyed his taste and the feel of his body next to hers. Alejandro kept his hands around her waist not roaming to feel her breasts or her ass covered tightly by a thin layer of jean material.

After another round of drinks, they enjoyed the quietness after the first band ended to talk some more. "That was fun!" Peg hopped on a stool at the bar. "I haven't danced in a while, my moves were a little stiff at first, but then I found a rhythm. What do you think cowboy?" She said quizzically.

"You got good sway going with those hips, Peg. You look luscious in those jeans!" He kissed her gently on the cheek, "Did you see my Peruvian groove going?" He asked boyishly.

"You got natural Latin tempo Alejandro, I'm impressed! Are you ready to go again with the next band?" Peg implored.

"I'm remembering some of my routines…I think!" He laughed aloud.

They bantered for another half hour and then hit the dance floor again. Finally, around midnight they each drank a bottle of water and headed outside. "I'm staying at the Hilton up the Avenue; Come see my room and we'll hang out a bit." Peg proposed.

"We need to order some food, I'm starved, Peg." Alejandro pleaded.

"They have room service, it'll be great!" Peg exclaimed like a kid on vacation.

"I'm paying for it though," Alejandro added.

"Sure, Alejandro, you can leave me some dough!" She pushed him playfully as they held hands on their walk up the Avenue away from the crowds. *The city sky is still pretty, even with the Avenue lights and concrete everywhere,* Peg thought. For tonight, at least, she enjoyed being a fish out of water or a gal away from the shore.

Alejandro checked his phone and found an open restaurant serving Pollo a la Brasa or Peruvian chicken and sides. He called and ordered in Spanish for pick-up. They happily made a short detour to secure the meal.

Spending four hours together seemed like a lifetime after their interrupted date months ago. They were comfortable talking and joking like on a typical millennial date. They picked up a bottle of wine as they finally entered her room on the eighth floor. Alejandro was impressed by such a classy place. He would have never dreamed of being in a place like this with a woman like Peg, eight months ago while still in prison. His journey to get to this point had pitfalls, but most of it he viewed as an education. He had been assured by the DEA that his services could be used for the rest of his life if he wanted employment. Whatever he decided, enjoying the moment with Peg was first in his mind as they set up the food and drink for a little romantic party.

"You know Peg, I can't remember much growing up, but the smell of this chicken reminds me of my mom. She cooked with all these spices in our underground rat hole in Baltimore."

"She must have been amazing. Do you know where she is?"

"No…I hope she's alive and well. The agency I work for has been hoping to find evidence of her in the country. She could have gone back to Peru or another other city in the United States. I pray every day I hear from her or something about her. I trust one man to find her for me. He is the only one who I believe will keep his word. I wish I could tell you more about him."

"I understand…that must be incredibly hard to deal with," Peg said slowly.

"Having freedom is so beautiful compared to the rest of my life. Being with my mom again would be icing on the cake. She deserves to be in a place like this at least for a night."

"I hope so too." Peg kissed him gently between bites of chicken. "Can I tell you something? Is it something serious?"

"Sure Peg…anything...as long as I can keep eating" he smiled.

She nodded and took a deep breath. "Alejandro…we were both abused in the same way as kids…It's called Frottage and that's why I reacted so violently to our episode on the beach." Peg stared at his eyes. "Do you know what I'm talking about?"

"I know what it is. How did you know that happened to me?"

"It's okay that I know…just accept it for now. I just want you to know that it happened to me when I was almost ten and caused a drastic change in our family."

Alejandro was in silence trying to imagine what to say. He had trouble admitting to being a victim because he did not want to use that as an excuse for his behavior. His counselors would always tell him otherwise, but he never accepted it as a reason for what he had done to females in his past. How did she know? Wonderment permeated his thoughts. "I guess the mayor told you something."

"Please just accept that I know, and I understand what you went through. It was probably a hundred times worse than what I went through, but who knows really? I wish I could tell everything, but I can't right now." Peg pleaded.

"I've changed Peg since we first met, what happened was a regression in my behavior that will never happen again."

"I understand Alejandro. I was assured that you had been through years of therapy and the reason for the regression. It all makes sense. I just had a breakthrough with my parents over Thanksgiving that started to heal eighteen years of pain and distance. Strangely what happened with us started me on that healing process. My anger shook me out of the anxiety that I lived with and used as a shield for years. I wanted to get answers from my parents, and I finally did. My friend Phillip helped me." Peg assured Alejandro with her eyes and the softness of her hands on his face. She kissed him again sat down on the bed and drank wine.

"Wow this is not what I thought would happen tonight, but it does feel good, to be honest." Alejandro looked relieved as he slumped down in his chair. "Eating the chicken, rice, and plantains doesn't hurt the situation." He smiled as he gazed at her, "I understand what you're saying, I guess we are both survivors and healing together. We will always share that history. I'm so glad you connected with your parents."

"Thanks…that was really hard and still somewhat impossible to digest, but it's a miracle to have that kind of breakthrough." Peg let out a big sigh.

"Let's change the subject for a little while…tell me about these three friends you have made since the Spring," Alejandro spoke with excitement.

Peg brightened up like an actor on a stage and talked for a half hour about Phillip, Joshua, and Becky. Alejandro just soaked it all in and poured more wine. When her diatribe was done, she took his hand and turned off the light. "Let's get under the covers the bed is so comfortable with so many pillows." Within thirty seconds they were still clothed but intertwined under the sheets and nestled in the pillows. They giggled as they kissed and tried to be comfortable.

After kissing and holding, their breathing increased. "Peg I'm comfortable just being with you…anything else you have to lead me," Alejandro said softly.

"I think it's time to get rid of these clothes…" she chuckled as she started to unbutton his shirt, suddenly they rolled away from each other to remove their pants and tops. Within seconds, Peg rolled on top of Alejandro under the sheets and took command. She took him inside of her and used her hands on his chest to raise and lower herself on him. He watched her toned body and her chest hang over him as he relished the pleasure of their union as his member felt numb inside of her. There were so many emotions that he had above sexual pleasure now. Everything he hoped for was coming true. As she reached her first climax, her body fell on him, kissing him like she was seeking oxygen. His member grew sensitive and felt strong inside of her without movement. Finally, after a few minutes, she smiled and turned him to be on top of her. He rose slowly over the top of her and stroked her gently at first but suddenly felt pleasure beyond control and went faster and faster. Time seemed meaningless as he let go inside of her. They both breathed hard for thirty seconds and then started a joint giggle again as they turned to their sides to look at each other.

"I guess we needed that?" Peg laughed.

"I think we time-traveled to another dimension?" Alejandro added

"It sure felt like it…but I got one more to go if you want to help." Peg said playfully as she grabbed his hand and gave him directions. She made noises of delight for another five minutes before calling it a night.

Chapter 45

Alejandro had a car pick him up at dawn because he had pressing matters to attend to over the weekend. Peg had waved at him as he left her warm bed, too comfortable enjoying her dreams to open her eyes, and quickly went back to sleep with a smile on her face. They had agreed to talk about things later in the week.

By seven a.m. she awoke and left for a walk. She had never felt better and was looking forward to a day of shopping and hanging out with her friends. Her phone buzzed and she looked to see a text from Phillip, "Francis Calvanese has died, viewing Sunday at 6 pm at the Rockledge County Club, funeral Monday at 10 am at the Catholic Church of our Savior in Cape Atlantic. Call me when you wake up." *Wow*, she thought to herself as she pushed the call button for Phillip, *the journey begins.*

"Hey, big news huh?"

"Peg…I thought you should know and attend." Phillip said without emotion.

"Sure…I wouldn't miss it. I'll get a sub for Monday."

"I have something else for you and Becky and even Joshua if he wants to go… a Christmas party tonight in Orlando for one of the Calvanese's construction companies. Jackie and his sons will be there."

"Even with his father's death?"

"O yes…they have a big bash for the workers and always show up. Could be very serious drinking."

"Can we just show up?"

"No problem it's at the Marriott near the airport in one of the conference rooms next to the pool. Casual dress…any time after 7 pm." Acting unusually distant. "Sorry I'm being so bland, I'm editing some chapters and trying to stay focused, I'm dying to go out for a walk on the beach."

"I get it. We can't always be sharing our souls!" Peg laughed.

"I'll let you know what comes up." She offered.

"How was the Date?"

"Great! We'll see what happens."

"Have fun."

"Get on the beach…soon!" Peg shouted as she ended the call. She continued to the lobby restaurant for breakfast and coffee, then the workout room to do her weights and cardio routine, and then finally exposed her bikini poolside. She had a couple of Richard Ford novels with her to start reading. The series with the Richard Bascombe character. *It's time to real twentieth century literature,* she thought with great expectations.

Without noticing it was one o'clock already. She put down her book and dove in the pool for a couple of laps. Peg was committed to Ocean swimming, but salt-water pools were getting tolerable these days without chlorine. She dried off poolside during a final half-hour of lounge reading and then picked up lunch to go upstairs. *I could get used to this nice hotel thing,* she decided, as she took a nice shower and put on a robe. She ate while looking out at the expansive view from the eighth floor and wondered what she would learn tonight at the party. She assumed Becky and Joshua would be up for it. It felt like nap time instead of hitting the outlets, so she got under the covers and slumbered

Her phone awoke her with several vibrations. Becky was texting her saying they were on their way. She rose with great energy and redness from her morning exposure to the sun without protection. *Oh well, a cold shower and Advil should fix it*, she decided.

After getting herself ready in one of her casual summer dresses with the appropriate underwear, she was in the lobby reading her book and waiting for her entourage to arrive.

"Miss Patterson, Becky and I are here for your pleasure, you look quite the intellectual!" Joshua stated jokingly. They all hugged as she led them on a tour of the amenities of the hotel and finally up to her room. "Wow I've never been in a Hilton before; this is quite nice. Is this our bed? Or is Becky going to shack up with you tonight? Whichever is your pleasure, my dear!"

"Becky, can you shut him up…let's go poolside, get a drink, and discuss our plans for this evening." Peg directed everyone to the door, tickling Joshua from behind.

Becky interlocked her arms with Peg, "Don't worry about Joshua, Peg, he's pretty harmless." She turned to look at him, "Right my dear?" Becky smiled at him.

"Oh of course sweetheart, I'm just enjoying myself with my Space Coast luvs." Joshua put his arms around the waists of his girlfriends, standing in front of him on the elevator.

They settled into poolside chairs and a table with a round of drinks. "So, what do you have for us tonight, Miss Peg Patterson?" Becky inquired.

"You won't believe this…I got an invitation for the three of us to a party at the Marriott near the airport on 528. It's one of the

Calvanese's construction business' Christmas parties. Jackie and his sons are going to be there." Peg sold her enthusiastic idea.

Becky was giddy and hugging Peg while Joshua asked, "Didn't the father pass away on Friday?' Joshua asked with confusion on his face.

"Well, the show must go on...I guess. They take these parties pretty seriously for their employees. Most of them don't get to go to a Marriott for a pool party with food and drink every day." Peg reported.

"It sounds lovely Peg...and Joshua we need a metro-sexual escort to keep those Calvanese men away from us!" Becky laughed playfully.

"How many sons does he have?" Joshua took the bait.

"Paul, Matthew, Mark, Luke, and John...and no girls!" Peg blurted out.

"All biographers of Jesus...that's my kind of family!" Joshua added.

The trio shopped at the outlets for a couple of hours before arriving at the Marriott. Peg successfully added to her impressive collection of shoes, dresses, and professional outfits. She forced Becky to buy some professional clothes with a series of tops, skirts, and jacket along with some dresses. With the recent success of the Café', she enjoyed treating herself. Joshua camped at Brooks Brothers and took home a new jacket, pants, belts, and a couple of shirts with questionable looking socks, that Becky and Peg snickered at, but overall complimented his fashion sense.

When they arrived at the Marriott, the lobby was full of folks leaving or checking in for the week in Orlando. Becky quickly scanned the room and found Jackie sitting in a corner with a crew of men while he talked on the phone. She grabbed Peg and Joshua and headed towards him. Peg and Joshua waited on the outer edge of the group while Becky went straight for Jackie knelt to the side of him and touched his arm. He turned with the phone still in his ear and showed a huge smile. He took her hand while he finished. "Becky how did you find me?" he whispered. "I was just lamenting to my sons about surviving this party." He ended the call and spoke out, "Now I can enjoy myself. Is Peg here and your other friend…Joshua?"

She pointed to them, as Jackie got up and met Peg with a big hug, "I'm so sorry about your dad. We wanted to find you tonight and give you our support and love, Jackie." Peg said heartfully. Joshua and Becky also added their sympathies.

"He's in a better place Peg and I'm relieved, to be honest. We can start celebrating his life tonight. Can you come to the funeral and the house on Monday?"

"Becky and I were planning on it." Peg eyed a stunned Becky to nodded her head.

"Great news…let me introduce you to my sons." Jackie went into a proud soliloquy about each son, what they did, married or single, and how each was so important to him. He alternated with each son with news about Peg, Becky, or Joshua that might connect their interest. His master skills as a politician were in full swing. Finally, he got to Paul, still sitting in his chair looking at his laptop. "And here is the hardest worker in the family and my oldest son Paul, the man is a machine and could use some cute women in his life…" Jackie bent down in a squat to meet Paul's eyes, "Son these are some good friends and constituents of the Cape, Joshua, a teacher at Merritt Elementary, Becky, the proud owner of Harmony Café' at Garfield and A1A, and of course Peg, who's like a daughter to me. You might remember her father, Lester Patterson?" At that information Paul looked alert and stood up and greeted everyone but stayed with Peg a bit longer, checking out her tanned but red face and beautiful dark hair. He wondered if she was part Italian and was immediately enchanted by her toned, healthy body and cute dress.

"Hey everyone…let's head over to the party. Please interact with folks and let them know how much you appreciate their work. Everyone that works for us is a part of the family. Let's treat them like that." Jackie announced. The sons followed orders and led the way. Jackie took Becky's arm as Joshua tagged along. Paul stayed behind for a moment fiddling with his laptop and briefcase. Peg stayed with him which he seemed to appreciate, "I'm so sorry Peg. We have so much going on with Grandpa Francis's passing. Let me leave this at the concierge."

"No hurry, I'm not a big crowd, party-person necessarily." Peg offered

"Great…me neither," he looked up and made eye contact, "and thanks for waiting." Paul had distinct features like a fifties, Italian crooner with wavy black hair and inviting but soft eyes like a Perry Como, the wide shoulders of a Dean Martin, and the youthful handsomeness of a Bobby Darin. He was taller than Peg but short of six feet by a couple of inches. Being social seemed like challenging work for him but he was still good at it. He was most comfortable being busy with his face on a computer, writing, or being on the phone. Work was his favorite environment. His last regular girlfriend was in her first year of law school in New York City. It lasted a year but only because there were usually weeks and sometimes months between dates and sex. They did spend one weekend together in Bermuda early on that gave the relationship hope. He returned to the Space Coast four years ago after two years at a top law firm in NYC to take over operating the Calvanese empire. At thirty-two, he was firmly in charge and lived alone in a two-bedroom, two-story small townhouse near North Atlantic Avenue tucked away on Adams Street in Cape Atlantic. The only friends he cared about were his brothers and loved to play Uncle to several nieces and nephews. He would be the architect of his father's ascendency to the Governor's office. In the Spring, he would kick off his father's State Senate campaign and break ground on construction north of Lincoln Street.

Paul fascinated Peg immediately. She casually hooked her arm into his as he escorted her to the party. They chatted about his family and was surprised by his knowledge of her parents. Recalling Lester's and Hazel's names like he had done their Will last week. Then she realized, *he must know everything about her.*

"These parties are important, but I really can't stand them. Peg, you're a welcomed distraction. My dad has talked of you for years. Now I understand why," he said with a natural charm, "you're teaching at Satellite Beach this year. How cool is that?" Paul said with a surprising passion.

"Thanks…I like it. Being around fourth graders is my favorite thing. I love their enthusiasm and honesty about life. Especially now with all the technology available, they know what's going on." Peg explained.

"I love kids, mainly my nieces and nephews, but I'm not sure about being a father."

"Well, my father was forty-five when I was born so you have quite a few years to consider that option," Peg said with certainty as she realized how turned on, she was, rubbing shoulders with Paul. They separated at the bar and then reunited at the buffet. "God I'm starving!"

He glad-handed with ten workers as he made his way to the poolside that was currently quiet. "Jesus…I always take so much food." Paul laughed, "I noticed the last couple of years I must work harder to keep trim. My mother is such a great cook, I have to stay away from the house sometimes. Eating Italian food is like a drug. I try to stay with fish and vegetables. These parties are always catered to by my mom's business. How can you not over-eat?"

"She runs a catering business?" Peg was interested in this news since Jackie never mentioned his wife.

"Oh yes for years out of the house in the Cape, but now it's in downtown Melbourne in a commercial spot. She still goes down there three times a week or so to keep things in line. Otherwise, she lives for the grandchildren. She's an amazing person, always happy. My father can do no wrong in her eyes." Paul looked at her like he was implying a secret.

"It's easy to feel like that about Jackie." Peg admitted, "Your mom sounds like a pretty amazing woman."

"Maybe you could meet her Monday after the funeral?" Paul asked with a smile.

"I'll be there." Peg gazed at Paul, wanting to kiss him but she knew better. She wondered if she was still horny from last night or just attracted to Paul and his personality. She could feel a vacuum of physical love in his life but not an emptiness of kindness. He seemed special. This could be a dark hole for her to avoid, considering her assignment. Hopefully, she could act like a lady and not fuck him tonight or tomorrow night and wait to meet his mother. She had to find Becky and Joshua and get back her bearings. "I need another drink and see what trouble my friends have discovered. Can I bring you back something?" Peg said with urgency.

272

"A beer would be great…thanks Peg," Paul answered, happy to focus on his mountain of food.

As she escaped and went into the banquet room for a drink, she saw Becky hanging on Jackie and Joshua speaking Spanish with several Puerto Rican workers.

"Where did you go?" Joshua exclaimed as he joined her at the bar as she was ordering.

"Since when do you speak Spanish?" she asked while chuckling.

"Learned it in college and on a Christian thing in Guatemala. It was fun talking with those guys. They think they're in heaven with all the food and drink…hey where's Paul? Are you behaving yourself?"

"Just barely! He's out in the pool area. Get Becky untangled from Jackie and come out to rescue me before I do something stupid. He's an impressive guy am I sure he likes me too."

"Will do…you and Becky are such little whores!" Only Joshua could get away with such a statement, even jokingly, and be right at the same time, Peg allowed. The double standard for women pissed her off a great deal because she loved her sexuality. But in this situation, she had to be careful not to walk into a minefield.

Chapter 46

The only mansion on the beach in Cape Atlantic sat alone on an acre of land just south of the row of condominiums that made up the last mile before the inlet at Port Atlantic. It was built by Francis Calvanese in the late eighties when his wealth reached his first hundred million mark and construction was just beginning on the four projects of condominiums to the north. He had much of that business along with the Port expansion that would help build his second hundred million. The mansion was used as a beach house for his family on the weekends and holidays. When the five boys were growing up, there were parties most weekends with Francis and his wife Gilda always around providing food and drink. They would spend the evening upstairs in their suite watching the waves and listening to the music thumping and the sweet noises of teenage heaven.

Otherwise, Francis and Jackie both had houses south of Lincoln Street that were jointly protected by a privacy fence and blended into the neighborhood. Since Francis had been in a nursing facility for the past year, the beach mansion sat empty except for a few weekends of use by the sons. It was a perfect place for Monday's reception after the funeral of Francis Calvanese and the only home he ever built. No one was turned away from the funeral or the reception. Becky and Peg were greeting people at the door and directing them to refreshments and the family inside. Most residents spent little time eating or drinking but wanted the chance to pay their respects to the mayor for his loss and the loss of a founding father of Cape Atlantic. Francis Calvanese, a World War II veteran, had grown up in Jersey City working below the train tracks at night repairing the idle train cars. He saved enough money to get a structural engineering degree from Rutgers and moved to the City of Cocoa in the early fifties. A dozen years later, his construction company had built many buildings in the rapid expansion in Cocoa Beach and his eyes looked to incorporate Cape Atlantic in the early sixties.

An older generation was well represented amongst the visitors, many remembering the growth of the village into a town of ten thousand and a resort to thousands more.

As the darkness came early on this December Monday, the family of five sons and their parents were left at the grand residence with grandchildren, wives, friends, and newcomers Becky and Peg. Jackie's wife, Bernadette, had the new young women cornered in the kitchen, drinking wine with her as she oversaw her company's workers cleaning up. "I am thrilled you girls could join us today. I wish you could have known Francis. He was always happy to have family and friends around…and to make new friends." As she raised her glass to toast Peg and Becky. "Jackie has his personality and his love of family." She smiled proudly. "But Francis avoided the limelight unlike Jackie," she laughed.

Peg and Becky sat in awe of this powerful woman who could change their lives. A dynamo mother of five, business owner, and caretaker of Jackie and his image as a family head. Without her energy and undeniable support Jackie's ambitions would never succeed.

"Becky, I understand you run the Harmony Café and are thinking of expanding. I have some great locations in mind for that. Jackie loves to invest in great ideas." Bernadette acted naïve and clueless about the motivation for that, Peg figured.

"I'm honored and thanks for your time, Bernadette, the food was out of this world. Do you make the pastries as well?" Becky inquired about her competition.

"Of course, everything comes from our kitchen. You'll have to visit sometime. We could supply you with what you make now or when you expand. It would save you time and money." Bernadette said with authority as Peg disregarded her previous assessment, undervaluing Bernadette's salesmanship.

"We should go together, Becky. It sounds like fun." Peg added, showing support for Bernadette's idea.

Bernadette looked at Peg like her best friend. "Peg I can't believe I never met you. You're even prettier than Jackie told me. He would say that Peg never smiles, she's always nervous about something." Bernadette smiled, "He must have you confused with somebody else." She laughed. "I guess finishing college and getting a job has lightened your load. I know you're a diligent worker Peg. Congratulations!" Bernadette kissed her on the cheek like it was an acceptance of the family. "By the way…" she whispered, "what do you think about Paul?" Bernadette smiled like she had a big fish on her line and was about to reel her in.

"He's delightful," Peg said succinctly waiting for the other shoe to drop.

"Well to be honest girl, I've never seen him more talkative to a woman since college. I know he has a crush on you." Bernadette winked.

"Peg, I told you that. He's quite a catch!" Becky added

"Well…we'll see won't we." Peg followed with a big gulp of wine and was trying to think of a question to change the subject when the subject himself came into the kitchen.

"There you are, Peg. I want to show you the upstairs…if you can entertain Becky for a few more minutes Mom." Paul asked with a dashing reverence for his mother.

"No problem son, Becky and I have a lot to talk about," Bernadette said confidently as the beautiful catch was in the net.

Paul escorted Peg out of the kitchen, into the main foyer, and up the grand staircase.

"Thanks for the rescue. They about had us married in there." Peg reported trying to smile.

"I'm used to that Peg. Every pretty girl Mom sees becomes a candidate for me to marry. I guess being thirty-two and single is uncomfortable for my mom." Paul admitted as he took her to a balcony overlooking the ocean. "I could stay out here for hours. The beach is my best friend. The sound of the ocean, feeling my toes in the sand, smelling the salted air, and swimming in the waves." He said while in a trance gazing at the low tide gaining on the shore.

If he was told to play a song for her, he was hitting the right chords. Being so convincing, she chimed in with her favorite parts of the beach. "I love to walk from Lincoln Street up to the Port and back with the water lapping my feet just enough to be a challenge in low tide."

Paul touched her hand and then interlocked his fingers with her. Was she over Alejandro so soon? She had not decided, but she was presently thrilled to be standing with Paul overlooking the beach. "Let me show you an even better view…" He let go of her hand and guided her to other stairs that went to the roof and a perch ten feet above it, "This is the view of the above condo for the rocket launches from the north. My grandfather made sure none of those buildings were more than five stories high." He said with great honor.

"Let's toast to him Paul," Peg suggested.

He looked at her with his dark eyes and said, "To my grandpa...a great man!"

Peg leaned forward and kissed him quickly as she went for the moment. Paul smiled and waited for the next move. Peg just stared and finally said, "This is something, Paul. Thanks for bringing me up here. We should head downstairs before they send out a search team for us." She laughed with some energy trying to pull herself away from kissing Paul again more intensely.

By ten pm the house had cleared except for the four of them on the first-floor balcony. Jackie was puffing on a cigar with Becky at his side while Paul and Peg listened intently as he told stories about Francis. "He was the most patient man I ever knew. When we had parties here, he and Mom would stay upstairs without interference. If he thought things were a problem, he would turn the light on the balcony in his bedroom, that's when I knew to quiet things down. When the light went out, we were okay!" Jackie blew a big smoke ring towards the sky, "He was the smartest man I ever met...Pop this is for you," he blew a bigger ring of smoke toward the heavens, "May you and Mom rest in peace together."

"That's nice Dad...I remember him smoking cigars. Where did you get that one?" Paul asked knowing Jackie did not smoke.

"These were his last box of Cubans; I got eighteen left. I'll smoke one a year on his birthday until I'm seventy, God willing!"

"No wonder they smell so good Jackie," Becky added.

"Thanks, Becky," he put out the cigar and got up, "let me show you the rooftop deck sweetheart, you'll love it!"

"We saw it earlier Becky, it's amazing!" Peg added.

278

A minute after they left, Paul spoke, "Can I tell you something to keep to yourself, Peg,"

"Sure Paul,"

"We will be announcing in the Spring Jackie's campaign for State Senator for 2024." He said with great excitement.

"I wondered what Jackie would do after being Mayor. That's amazing. Why are you telling me…if you don't mind me asking?" Peg asked gently.

"I want you to be my first volunteer and manage his education platform," Paul said seriously with a hopeful smile at the end.

"Me…Paul I just started teaching, I'm only twenty-eight. I don't know anything about a campaign platform." Peg said with anxiety.

"Peg…you would be perfect, young and in the schools every day connecting with kids and parents. The millennials will love it. You'll have almost six months to produce something. We can work on it together." Paul was closing hard, and it would be perfect for the plan to work. Being a part of the campaign, Phillip will shit when he hears this, she thought.

"I guess it won't work to object any further," she looked at him with soft eyes and a pensive smile.

"We'll make a great team!" Paul said with certainty.

Chapter 47

By mid-week Peg realized she was over Alejandro. She drank her coffee watching the sunrise and surprisingly felt good with a sense of relief. There was a touch of sadness with the normal regrets and apprehensions but was happy with it. She had learned so much about herself and her past, being with him was the beginning of escaping her world of anxiety. Trying to set aside meeting Paul, Peg knew when Alejandro left that morning, she was not sad to see him go but also did not think it was over. She was not longing for him anymore on Saturday. She enjoyed her time alone exercising, reading, and suntanning, then hanging with her friends was exciting and funny, but then connecting with Paul at the party was the cliffhanger she never expected. Before the weekend, she could only think about the future with Alejandro or longing for someone to love her, never pondering that Paul could be the piece to the puzzle that produced a future to love. The six years of having a crush on the mayor was funneled into a chance to be part of his family for real with Paul. *What can I do other than fall in love*, she thought. It was all right in front of her to play her part.

Alejandro called on Wednesday and quickly relieved Peg of the burden of telling him the news, "I have a strong lead on my mother. She's alive in Southern California. I will drive out there and find a way to rescue her. I'm leaving tonight. I don't know what to say. Friday night was the greatest night of my life, but my future is unclear. You must go on with your life and I will save my mother. I will contact you when can. The message will be from "House of Blues."

"I understand, be well Alejandro., Your mother is lucky to have you." She said when the conversation ended, she was sad but recognized the need for him to reconnect with his family. She had been there.

Phillip was back home in the DC area, and Chevy needed to tal to Brooks in person. At the same time, Chevy was reporting to Brook about the contacts Peg had made and the death of Francis Calvanese. She wanted Phillip to meet with Peg before she got lost in the family web of the Calvanese's. They knew Paul and Peg had spent lots of time together and Becky was already working with Bernadette on the Harmony Café's expansion. "It's like they know our interest by sweeping up Peg and Becky into the family. The pipeline could not be better, but we must make sure we don't lose Peg as our informant," Chevy pointed out to Brooks.

"We need to get her up here to explain the hierarchy and the plan behind what Phillip told her. Plus, she needs to see Phillip, I imagine, if what you're saying is true about the son Paul."

"Of course, it's true sir. We've had the mansion wired for years."

"Good to know. You could fly her up here Friday after work. We can have a plane at Patrick's Air Force Base ready and I'll get Phillip to Beltsville." Brooks suggested.

"How do I get her to Patrick's" Chevy questioned.

"It's on her way home… make up something about drafting the book and meeting at a parking lot on the beachfront park. We can have a car there ready to meet you about three-thirty you'll have to disclose the information once she's on the Base." Brooks ordered stirring up gravel in his voice.

"Got it sir…see you Friday. Have some food and scotch ice." Chevy suggested with a laugh.

It was an awkward conversation, but Peg agreed to meet Chevy, or who she thought was Maria Gonzalez, the literary agent, on Friday afternoon. She was assured that she would be able to meet her friends that night. Chevy told her Phillip was coming down for the meeting. She eventually got excited.

They left their cars in the parking lot and entered the car together. "This is first class, Maria, this must be important."

"Yes, it is Peg. We want to get your opinion on several characters that Phillip has created for the novel. He has laid out an idea for the story so far, but it might be too personal for you." Chevy was trying to engage Peg to keep her from noticing the entrance to the Air Force Base which was larger than Cape Atlantic and employed ten-thousand people. Besides the massive airfield and hangars, it had many houses for Air Force personnel and a full eighteen-hole golf course designed by Robert Trent Jones Sr. The base was just south of Cocoa Beach and just north of Satellite Beach as the Banana River bordered its west side with the A1A Highway on the East. An array of beach parks paralleled the Base for easy access to the Ocean. After 9/11, the A1A was closed for years until concrete barriers were built on the East side.

Several times over the years, Peg had driven past the air base seeing Air Force One parked about a half-mile from the highway. It still looked huge, she remembered, as she finally noticed their location. "I've always wanted to visit the restaurants in here. I hear they're fantastic." Peg was confused but played along.

"Peg, I have something important to tell you." Chevy paused for a moment as they got closer to the air hanger and the jet they were taking north to DC. "My name is Cheverly Santiago and I'm with the DEA. I want you to fly with me to DC and meet the coordinator of this project that your friend Phillip told you about."

Peg just stared for a moment and thought of something to say "Really?" Was all she could muster.

"I know it's shocking but after the weekend of meeting with Jackie's family, we thought it was important to fill you in totally on our plan. We were trying to protect you from knowing too much, but you may get in too deep without a strong tether to us. You don't have to come but I suggest it and you'll get to see Phillip alone to talk if you like."

"So, you know about my meeting with Paul and the reception at the mansion and what we talked about."

"That's our job to keep you safe and to keep tabs on the Calvanese organization."

"Is Becky safe?"

"Completely! We can't bring her in on this. It will be your job to oversee what she is doing and what she learns."

"What's your name again…I was just learning Maria Gonzalez and now I have to forget it?"

"Cheverly Santiago…but call me Chevy…like the car."

"I guess I'm not meeting my friends tonight?"

"Probably not…but we could get back by midnight or so if you want."

"That's fine. I call them to bail… I would love to see DC at night!"

"We can arrange that!" Chevy smiled

283

The jet paralleled the coast and the sunset to the west as it flew North. There was just enough daylight to see the DMV area start to glow in the moonlight. After they landed at Andrews Air Force Base, east of DC, they rode through serious but moving traffic on the I-495 Beltway to Beltsville. They reached the small FBI warehouse in the rolling hills of the massive Beltsville Agricultural Center in complete darkness. They stepped inside and made it to a conference room with their phone light on, providing light as they entered the door. Phillip was the first face she recognized. They hugged and he introduced her to Brooklyn O'Malley and another man that she knew. "This is Anmar Douglass, the A1A Pawn Shop owner, he does intel for us." Peg's mouth stayed open as she shook the drug dealer's hand. She immediately recalled the first meeting with Phillip at the Chicken Shack and her explaining to him about the drug problem on Lincoln Street, *boy Is this an ironic turnaround?*

"Thank you, Miss Patterson, for the last-minute trip up here for this briefing. We appreciate you volunteering to help your country and I thought it was necessary to make it a formality." Brooks spoke with his scorch-sounding throat box. "We have food and drink that will be served as we talk. I am Brooklyn O'Malley, acting director of the FBI, but please call me Brooks behind closed doors." He smiled as he paused for a moment. "Phillip and I have been friends since middle school years."

Chevy took over and spent time talking about their plan to oversee Jackie's ascendency to the Governorship of Florida and how this would help the country. Brooks then explained that all of this was from a distance or from the point of view of overseeing possible criminal behavior. "Once I was informed by Chevy about the progress you made this weekend with the Calvanese family, it became clear we had to inform you of what you were getting yourself into. We know you trust Phillip, but you are both private citizens and can stop informing us at any time, but none of this can be shared...ever!"

"I think I understand sir, but all of this is a shock to the system. Things are moving extremely fast. Are you concerned that Becky and I are getting sucked into a criminal enterprise?"

"No, we don't believe that. Jackie and Paul are not involved in any criminal behavior personally."

"Do you think they know what you're up to?"

"That's a good question. They knew about Dragmar because of your connection to him, but they don't have any reason to believe you, Phillip, or Becky know anything about us. Right now, they only have an FBI chemist, a close friend of Jackie's, who revealed Dragmar's undercover status after examining your dress and his DNA. That's why we had to remove him from the Space Coast." Brooks explained.

"O shit...I guess that fucked up everything." Peg's stomach fluttered at the thought of that situation being known.

"No Peg, if I may call you that?" she nodded as Brooks continued, "It gave us the idea to go ahead with the plan because Jackie would know that we knew about his empire and that he was being watched."

"Like the 'Deep State' that some people have been complaining about." Peg offered.

"To be honest Peg, after the re-election, I realized that's what we needed, exactly what they feared. Almost like a white-collar Navy Seal team to go into a political situation under darkness and make some changes without anyone knowing. That's what you are a part of Peg." Brooks's eyes became like iron embers too hot to stare at for long.

Peg felt an adrenalin rush, she always thought she could be a Navy Seal. At the beach, she played in the surf at times sneaking onto the beach like on a Seal mission. Finally, she added, "They have no idea of my role, and they barely know Phillip. So that's not an issue; Becky knows nothing." Peg explained with authority. "As I told Phillip, I'm in and now after this past week I'm really in." She said with emphasis like she was taking charge. *Boy, that felt good*, she thought. "Are you concerned about my attraction to Paul?" She asked.

"We think that's a plus actually," Chevy spoke up. "Especially if it's natural and honest. Overall, the best thing for us to do is supervision and no intervention. Through you, we gain influence on policy about education reform. We think Jackie will expand health insurance for almost a million citizens and support much-needed environmental policy changes. The question will be what he does about state corruption in Tallahassee if he ever gets there. By then, he may lose effectiveness or supervision of the situation and we may have to figure out how to intervene."

"You mean threaten him with prosecution for running a criminal enterprise?" Peg asked.

"Chevy will be in charge at that point. It will be her decision. We all lose if it ever comes to that. Right now, we need to focus on getting him elected to the state senate. Let us know how we can support you with writing policy information or anything else. We would love to hear about the structure of the campaign organization once it gets up and running. I guess this will depend on what happens between you and Paul." Brooks tried to speak softly with his rough-sounding voice.

"Either way I plan on being a part of it. I have a good feeling about Paul. Both he and Jackie are brilliant and well-read. For me, could be a good Christmas." Peg smiled and exhaled through her mouth "Boy…I could use a drink if you have anything."

"I told Brooks to have scotch and ice." Chevy grabbed her hand.

"That'll work!" Peg raised their hands in the air. She felt the woman's power in the room.

Paco Lawrence arrived late as the food was served and drinks were consumed. Soon Paco, Anmar, Chevy, and Brooks went into another room to discuss cleaning up Jackie's ties to any drugs or vices on the Space Coast. Anmar Douglas, agreed, he would be the scapegoat if necessary. He could then be lost in Federal prison and relocated with a new identity.

Barry from the Chicken Shack and running the legal Casino Boat and illegal gambling would be another target if needed, but not brought in on the plan. He had too much criminal history to worry about becoming a rat. He could be brought into custody if possible.

They discussed Peg's father as a scapegoat for the three murders that they knew of in the past thirty years involving the Calvanese organization. His prostate cancer could make him available to confess to anything, if necessary, though it was hoped to be a last-option situation.

Paco would continue to be the conduit from Anmar and Peg for information to Chevy because, by the 2024 election, Brooks would no longer be in charge. A loop through Phillip would be his only connection.

Phillip and Peg stayed at the table in the conference room and picked at the food as they drank scotch. "Well, that was quite a weekend for you?"

"My life has changed drastically in one week, Phillip!"

"What happened with Alejandro?"

"It was a great night. We made love at my hotel, and he left in the morning. It was therapeutic for me but right away it didn't feel like a forever thing. He's too young and unstable for me. I was surprised to come to that conclusion so quickly, but happy about it at the same time."

"And then?"

"And then I met Paul Calvanese...and it was magical. I felt like myself. I wasn't trying to impress him, but I was trying to learn about him. For being a busy guy with zero social life, he's very laid back. I could see a future together with him and being free to do my own thing."

"Is he a womanizer like Jackie?"

"He could be, but I doubt it. I don't think he has the time or interest. We'll see, I guess. I know this sounds stupid, but if he treats me well and doesn't embarrass me, I could live with it, if our plan works out."

"It might be good to ask him about it if you get serious with him."

"You mean ask Paul if he wants to fuck another woman if we get married?"

"Something like that." Phillip laughed.

"If we get involved that far, you're right, being direct with him would be the smartest thing to do. I'm not sure I believe in romantic love anymore. I can live on my own if I must, so if I'm going to be with a man and live with him, it needs to be something good for me. Not just being all starry-eyed and foolish." Peg admitted.

"I'm glad you have found your truth, Peg. Breaking through the anxiety that ruled your life has been amazing to watch in the last nine months." Phillip reflected on their history together.

"Thanks, Phillip," she paused with a smile, "Hey…when are you coming down to the Cape?" she inquired.

"After Christmas for a few weeks. Call me if you need me."

"Thanks…this could get crazy when he announces in the Spring."

"It's getting crazy now! Enjoy the romance between now and then."

"Good point…I'll see what I can do!" Peg agreed with a wink.

In June 2023, Jackie stood in front of a crowd of a thousand supporters in Titusville announcing his candidacy for State Senator of District fourteen in Florida. He was extremely polished in outlining his campaign for the election in November 2024, but he was laying the foundation of his run for Governor in 2026. Education, Health Insurance, and the Environment were his three concerns. The crowd loved how he talked about his family turning Cape Atlantic and Port Atlantic into the jewel of the Space Coast and a model for the state of Florida. The new mile-long, Lincoln Boulevard corridor under construction would be finished by the time he announced his run for Governor in two years.

The newly engaged couple of Paul Calvanese and Peg Patterson sat on the stage along with his wife Bernadette and his four other sons Matthew, Mark, Luke, and John with wives, and Jackie's four grandchildren. Peg had finished her first year of teaching at Satellite Beach Elementary as the teacher of the year at the school. Their wedding was scheduled for June 2024 after her second year of teaching. She would then leave her position and work with the campaign full-time and then join Jackie's staff after his election. Jackie would tell her story at every campaign about being homegrown in Brevard County and a proud citizen of Cape Atlantic. He would tout her self-determination in finishing school and defining the nine-year-old as the most critical year of development. Jackie would hammer this point throughout the campaign about making sure that nine-year-old kids would never be forgotten in Florida's education system and become ready to be ten-year-olds that could take on the world. Crowds loved it. *Who didn't like a nine-year-old kid?* Peg proudly said out loud.

Later that night, Jackie took his family out on his forty-six-foot boat to celebrate the election kick-off. Bernadette never did boats, so Becky was at his side most of the evening. Bernadette was her mentor and investor in overseeing four Harmony Café openings in Brevard County and Jackie was her lover. It seemed to work out perfectly. Becky had a beautiful condominium on Merritt Island overlooking the Banana River with Joshua as her roommate and sometimes boyfriend. The arrangement seemed to work for all parties.

Paul and Peg found a corner of the boat drinking champagne. They enjoyed being affectionate with each other and were always surprised how easily they got along, "I guess things will get crazy by this time next year?" Peg asked.

"You're right with the wedding and the election in the Summer and Fall. At least you won't be teaching." He stated.

"I'm glad I'll finish two years of teaching. Everything else will be amazing to be a part of. I didn't even know you at this time last year. I didn't even have a job!'

"I needed to meet you when I did. I hadn't come up for air in four years. Are you surprised how well we get along?"

"Luckily, we're both independent and you're pretty good-looking!" Peg smiled.

"Something tells me you're going to be the star in our family. I think you're just getting started and not thirty yet."

"Thanks, Paul…that's a nice thing to say but we know you're the brains behind the situation." Reinforcing her support of his importance in the family. Peg felt a constant struggle between what was real and what was her job. She felt love for Paul and felt adored by him, but she was also focused on her goal to be a part of change in the state and the country. She would always feel allegiance to the group behind her led by Phillip, Paco, Chevy, and Brooks. Her life had changed so much in sixteen months but staying connected to the beach had been constant. Within a year her little apartment building on Lincoln Street would become a property on the new Lincoln Boulevard and she would move to a house on the crossover to the beach at the end of Lincoln Street. She returned to Paul and thought of her birthday. "Hey, maybe we should go somewhere for my birthday in January, maybe Italy?"

"Wouldn't that be something Peg. I'll work on it." They kissed and finished their drinks on Jackie's boat. The night was young, and the party would go on with Jackie touring every nook of the Banana River with Becky at his side. Peg and Paul joined them as he pointed out every landmark. In the mornings, Jackie would take out his twenty-seven-footer and travel up the Indian River to check out the best fishing spots at least three times a week. He was always alone, with no one to entertain, just himself and the water. He loved to catch and release. It was his favorite sport to hold the fish in his hand and give it back its life. He knew the next level of political opponents in the State of Florida would not be so easy to catch and not such a clever idea to give them life again.

Chapter 48

Peg headed to her office in Titusville after the "rush hour" an inside joke between her and Paul, who spent time in NYC. Leaving at nine-thirty from her ocean- front house, gave her a wonderful ninety minutes on the beach walking and wondering, two of the four virtues she committed to almost three years ago. The other two, work and write, she would get to at her job in State Senator's Jackie Calvanese headquarters.

The mayor had won in a landslide in the Republican-dominated Brevard County with a huge campaign with a small paid staff and thousands of volunteers. The staff would move into his State Senate office and work to run the business of satisfying his constituents. Building the volunteer numbers would be done by Jackie's campaign manager, Paul Calvanese. He was intent on keeping his enthusiastic core of volunteers and growing it state-wide for the new campaign to start in June of 2025 for the Governorship of Florida. Jackie's rhetoric, charisma, and huge victory became a national story on most media outlets. Even most of the right-wing politicians noticed but dismissed any chance he had to win the top prize in the Sunshine State.

Paul Calvanese was enjoying married life after thirty-two years as an unmarried person and was splitting time between his law firm and the campaign headquarters. As usual, he would be at his desk at seven a.m., before "rush hour."

"Hey, sweetheart I'm crossing the Indian River, and its lovely weather in paradise. You must miss those Manhattan morning rush hours. Are you all settled in and busy today?" Peg inquired. "Not too bad Peg. We should meet for lunch or a walk today. Soon it will be so busy, we'll need appointments to see each other." Paul lamented.

"I doubt that…you will never let that happen. I believe this little body of mine has a great deal of gravitation pull. If you're in my orbit, you'll be pulled right in on top of me." Peg joked with her sexiest voice.

"I won't argue with that, my dear. If we're in the house at the same time, I can't keep my hands off you. I thought married folks got tired of each other. That's why I was never interested in long-term relationships. If I knew it could be like this, I would have married you a long time ago." Paul pleaded.

"That's so cute sweetie…but I wasn't ready before I met you." Peg waited a couple of beats. "When should we meet for lunch and a walk today?"

"Around one pm. I'll call you…ok, Sunshine?" Peg liked the nickname that Paul created because of her love of the beach and positive outlook. It seemed ironic to her because three years ago her face wore a permanent frown. Now she was happy, in love, and out to change the country or at least the state.

"I'll be down the street…waiting for your call." She hung up still feeling connected in her soul to Paul. They had their independence as well as together time. So far, Paul has not exhibited a jealous muscle or bone in his muscular frame, and she also did not worry about where he was when they were not together. *How long would this last?* she thought.

The clean-up of Lincoln Street started with the relocation o. Anmar's A1A Pawn Shop a mile down the Highway in Cocoa Beach and the razing of the Neptune Apartment complex. The new Lincoln Boulevard was on-time for a late Springtime completion. It would correspond with the announcement of his Governor Campaign in June Peg was so excited to see her sleepy small town get such a remarkabl makeover.

Becky's little Café was still doing great business and the new locations in Brevard County were coming along in sales. Hiring the personnel and setting up the stores had been an intensive labor of love. Becky was doing very little of working with her parents in the original location. She was "extremely, very-busy", she would lament to Peg, and complain they had not been available for a beach day in several months. Peg made a mental note to demand a date with her first real friend.

Joshua was in his third year of teaching on Merritt Island and was still loving it. His relationship with Becky was weird but functional. They had become good friends and had enough intimacy to keep him happy. During the campaign, he met so many people that his friend network on the Space Coast had soared. He was in charge of getting Peg and Becky together on Fridays after work at Coconuts at least once a month. Now that the campaign was over, he hoped it would be more often. Seeing Peg happy and married gave him goosebumps whenever he thought of her. And when he saw her, he would pinch himself that he was friends with her because she was getting so famous.

Phillip had been away since the beginning of January and would return in late March. Peg was looking forward to talking with him soon now that the campaign was over. It was different than the days of desperately needing his calmness and counsel, but she still could use his insight for the future. Amazingly, her parents had continued to be close with her since the "Reunion-Thanksgiving" in 2022. Her Dad was traveling less often and was keeping Hazel happy and functional. Phillip had helped her change the history of her family from a great tragedy to a fabulous rescue narrative. It just took her family almost twenty years to see it.

Chevy fully took over operations in Central Florida as Brooks O'Malley retired from the FBI. She had met with Peg every month in locations around Titusville and talked on throw-away cell phones whenever necessary. They had molded together, along with Paco, a clear path for Peg's job and offered several white papers for her education campaign platform. Peg studied these papers and anything else to become an expert on how to teach children. Her focus on nine-year-old kids had touched the hearts of voters in Brevard County and she planned to extend that concept to the state-wide campaign. It had been very emotional to leave her position at Satellite Beach Elementary teaching fourth graders. She was named teacher of the year two years in a row at the school and a semi-finalist in the County for her second year.

The media coverage throughout the Orlando Stations on her education work and entering the campaign was a big attraction to viewers. Peg had a good look for television and spoke well to the camera. Her engagement and marriage to Paul Calvanese was like local royalty picking from the commoners of the Space Coast. The Peg Patterson story had a Princess Diana feel to the Central Florida viewership and they were waiting for more. The focus on nine-year-old kids gave the voters something to which they could relate. Everyone raised or knew someone who had raised a nine-year-old and feared the real problems that could happen at that age. It was real meat and potatoes politics with some vegetables thrown in. And in the campaign advertisements that Jackie Calvanese would build upon for the Governor's race, they would blanket Florida with pictures of happy nine-year-old kids, the question would be —- How can we keep this face smiling?

Chapter 49

By the Spring of 2026, the Governor's Primary was over before the election. Jackie Calvanese had spent so much money on the campaign since announcing in May 2025, that all challengers dropped out by the Fall of '25 and joined his campaign or came out for his candidacy. The state-wide democratic leadership knew that a disjointed party would have no chance in the November election to beat the Republican candidate. There were many backroom deals made to make all the candidates unite behind Jackie.

He had visited every county in Florida at least once already, focused on the Fall Election. In many counties, he would show up in his boat at dawn and would tour the waterways of many rural areas sharing coffee as he spoke his message to voters directly. The video of these boat appearances became red meat for the four major media markets in Florida. Soon not a voter in Florida did not know Jackie and his boat and his charismatic personality.

The Florida Convention would officially take the primary vote and select the ballot for the November election of Governor, Lieutenant Governor, Comptroller, and Secretary of State. It was a party to rev up the campaign. Jackie had lobbied hard for it to be in Gainesville in mid-August 2026 just as the students started arriving. The campaign was looking to double their volunteer corps with Gator students.

The St. John's River is three-hundred and ten miles long and flows north from the St. John's Wetlands (west of I-95 and parallel to the end of the Space Coast at Sebastian Inlet), through Jacksonville before it spills in the Atlantic Ocean. The longest river in Florida takes a meandering journey through lakes and desolate rural areas that Jackie loved to learn about in his home state. He took a week to travel in his boat through this maze of lakes and waterways to wind up eventually in the Lochloosa Wildlife Area near the little town of Cross Creek about twenty-five minutes outside of Gainsville. It was in the middle of Alachua County with Gainesville as its' County Seat with a population of close to three hundred thousand, half in Gainesville, and a vast amount of Wildlife areas and greenery.

His entourage would travel the roads through Orlando and find US Route 301 through Ocala to County Road 325, the go-between Orange Lake and Lochloosa Lake. They set up camp before the Convention to party and talk strategy. It was the Calvanese sons and spouses with Jackie and Bernadette. The top dozen campaign staffers were included as were Peg's friends Joshua and Becky. The media was allowed for an afternoon to take their pictures and get the quote of the day from Jackie. The Calvanese campaign was as hot as the Florida summer in the Sunshine State media. Volunteers were already established in Gainesville to sign up volunteers ahead of the convention.

***

Paul and Peg ventured up in his BMW to the camp setup. They would spend the evening outside of Gainesville in a nice Hilton for the week of the convention. Peg was getting major exposure in the media with her education message for the campaign. She visited hundreds of elementary schools throughout the state. Some in the campaign though she should be on the ticket with Jackie as Lieutenant Governor. She thought it was a ridiculous idea. Somewhere she was confident there was a rule in Florida about a daughter-in-law running on the same ticket She was still Peg Patterson in name but married to Paul Calvanese.

"Sweetheart, I hope you have squashed the talk of me running for lieutenant governor with your father, it would be a stupid idea Besides, we need a person of color on the ticket as Lieutenant Governor and another woman as Comptroller or Secretary of State. I would be best as an advisor on Elementary Education."

"Don't worry Peg, you're safe for now from the wolves that love your numbers in the polls. I would love to have you run Education on the state level with a good administrator as your guide. It would take your exposure to the campaign and continue it during the administration. Hopefully, the state senate and representatives go blue if we win big on the governor level. Winning new funding will be key to your success in implementing your policies." He took a moment to ask this question softly, "Honey, I was wondering if you wrote all that stuff, It's pretty brilliant and very detailed for the county and city-level procedures for teaching nine-year-old kids."

Peg looked at him with her serious face but a forgiving face, "I appreciate your surprise at my brilliance sweetheart, but I was a teacher of the year two years in a row, and I know how to write. I admit I got help from Phillip and some of his colleagues on the federal level, but I would be a fool not to." She forced a slight smile at her husband as he drove.

"Anyway…it's brilliant work and I'm glad you have a network of people you can trust with data and information. Science should make a comeback in our state government. We have so much data, especially since the Pandemic in '20 & '21 that kept kids home for so long. There should be useful information on web-based, homeschooling and that should help with slowing down school construction costs substantially in the future. The Republicans would love to hear that stuff. It attends to the homeschoolers and limiting costs folks. I'll bet you with a fifty percent cut in school construction, we could pay for higher wages for teachers, home laptops for every kid connected to our schools, and home day-care assistance for kids at home three days a week. For those over twelve, they could be monitored on Wednesday for a schedule of home tasks like cleaning, laundry, and so forth as a part of the learning curriculum. Then on the other two days, their home laptop would help monitor their progress like we do with our folks working from home."

Paul turned from his serious lawyer face to his calm sweet smile face to hear Peg's response.

"I can see you've done your homework." Peg's smile grew large. She turned herself in the front seat to face Paul and touched him on the shoulder. "Thank you for your input and reading my policy papers." They had become so connected physically. Their bodies constantly satisfied by each other for three years had increased their confidence and creativity. "You're right honey! We increased aid for those things you mentioned and some more things for each county's special needs. Altogether it will save the state money. It will be a big winner for Jackie to propose starting Labor Day and during the debates. The media will eat it up!" Her smile beamed as she had both hands on his bicep and shoulder.

Paul was looking directly ahead with a smile stretching from coast to coast. If he turned to his suddenly charismatic love, he would explode inside and have to pull over. "That is spectacular, my love, now we have to sell it to the campaign and Jackie".

Peg pulled her hands back and sat like a good girl, quietly in her seat with her eyes looking forward with her feet on the BMW floor mats for a few moments, but then confidently said, "That shouldn't be a problem!"

***

A dozen fashionable tents were set up for the sons and wives and top staff members each with comfortable beds and mobile A/C units. Jackie took his wife, all five sons, Peg, Becky, Joshua, and his top staff people out for a spin in the dark on the lake. Jackie found a quiet cove with a beautiful view of the sky. "This is what it's all about folks! The water below us, the open sky above, and the Florida heat upon us. I appreciate the input and all the challenging work by each one of you for the selections for the ticket. Our diversity and talent will sweep up the voters for an uprising in the Sunshine State. There have been sixteen years of oppression of the people in Florida from the middle class down, especially people of color, women, and those working at minimum wage. That will all end in the first session of the 2027 Florida legislature. This Sunshine Uprising will make the economy flourish when we expand Medicaid to all that need health care, the environment will be protected for ocean, rivers, and lakes to be clean and our coastlines to survive, and the education of the nine-year-old kid will be our priority. After my eight years every nine-year-old kid will be ready to graduate with a high school degree that means something. That something will be knowledge and guidance to a good paying job at a minimum of fifteen dollars an hour or more education and training. Hopefully, both. That will be our uprising and lasting legacy."

Jackie kept going in a rare form of super intensity, "You know our eyes have three cones to see light: red, blue, and yellow. And that is for us to see all colors. For too long, the state government of the Great Sunshine State has seen only black and white. As state servants to the people, we need to see them in their entirety, we must see like hummingbirds see, with four cones, three to see a mixture of primary colors, and one to see ultraviolet light. For us as public servants, we need to see that fourth light...hidden in the dark. We need to understand the emotion of the frustration and pain that our citizens carry every day as they walk to the bus stop take a train or walk or bike or drive to work. We need to see folks in their everyday environment and never see just darkness around the primary colors. We can ride our boats, and our BMWs and live in our condos or beach houses because we earned it. But for too long government has been making that lifestyle easier for rich folks and harder for poor folks. That's backward. Businesses don't need all of our help; the government was started for people to fight the rich ruling class. Read your history books. Not to cut taxes for the rich and take away health care from the poor, not to build huge university campus buildings and forget about elementary school children. Not to build high-rises on the beaches to kill our shoreline or drain the Everglades for golf courses. We live in the Sunshine State and should be leading the world in solar energy. Every house should have solar panels. Every building, every school. We don't need to burn coal for electricity. We have the sun to power the uprising needed in this state.

So, every time you see a voter, think of the hummingbird and see what's around that person, become perceptive to their lives, not the other way around. They will hear our message, expand our economy with health care, serve the environment with safe energy, and educate that nine-year-old kid perfectly. Thanks for coming and enjoy the evening. I'll ride us back to the shore."

A roar came from the dozen close family and staff on the boat that echoed in the darkness like a lion responding to a challenge. Jackie smiled and hugged everyone quietly and intently as he walked over to the helm. He started up the boat and headed back to the camp as he enjoyed the isolation of the leadership and heard the joyous energy abound on the deck behind him. His message was for his closest disciples, but in five months it would be a speech for the millions of Floridians on inauguration day.

* * *

Jackie was the last to leave the boat in the darkest of nights. His guests headed to their comfortable tents. He walked hand in hand with Bernadette, who was leaning on his shoulder and saying wonderful things about his talk on the boat. She was so into her husband's world that she could see only strength and feel happiness. She opened the door to their MASH-style tent with a nice area rug on the bottom tarp of the tent. Jackie lit a candle and helped Bernadette get into her nightshirt, an extra-large Yankee pin-stripe uniform that covered her shapely bottom and the middle of her thighs. Jackie slipped out of his shorts and cuddled his wife from behind under the sheets of the mattress. He messaged her

302

back, ass, hamstrings, calves, and feet for fifteen minutes before turning her on her back to work on her chest, stomach, thighs, and shins for another fifteen minutes. He then focused on her pelvis and breasts and licked her vagina and felt her nipples until she released a quiet orgasm. They cuddled for a while, as she kissed him feeling many aftershocks. Finally, she turned on her side away from him and helped him enter her behind and stroke her for thirty minutes slowly but deliberately. She held his hands on her breasts and felt several post orgasms highs that made her body buzz. When she heard Jackie finally released, she felt completely satisfied and drifted off into a coma of sleep.

Jackie stayed still for ten minutes and then slid on his shorts made it back to his boat and poured himself a whiskey. He put his feet up on the deck and looked out over the lake and the moonless sky. He knew all the major star groupings and the brightest ones from millions of light years away. He was always aware of when Venus dominated the sky but allowed Mars, Jupiter, and Saturn to have their turn. It was paradise on earth to view the heavens of the sky at night.

Jackie walked around the boat and thought about the next few days. He raised a toast to his father and mother for their demanding work and leaving him a fortune to win the Governorship. *They would be proud of me and my work so far,* he thought, "But it's just the beginning…Pop's," he spoke to the stars, "the whole state will become the leader in the country of educating kids and taking care of your beaches that you loved so much…God Bless you, Mom and Dad!" He toasted them and finished his whiskey.

After making another drink for himself, he headed down to his deck below and saw her there. Becky had fallen asleep on the bed, fully clothed, waiting for him. He stopped for a moment near her and sipped his whiskey. She heard the ice cubes tingle in the glass as she opened her eyes and smiled. "You were inspirational tonight, Jackie!" she said softly as she got to her knees and put her hands on his back.

Jackie took her hand and let her off the bed, "Let's see the stars and take a little run with the boat."

"Sounds sexy Jackie with you at the helm and me." She smiled as she looked bright-eyed from her nap.

He turned on his small rotor engine used for parking or close quarters and slowly headed into the lake barely making a noise over the insects chirping. They went for a mile or so before he shut down and sat with Becky on the deck. Though Becky had been a part of Jackie and Bernadette's lives for several years, she never had intercourse with him. It was his decision, not hers, but she was okay with it. They were intimate in many ways and shared orgasms countless times. They were affectionate with each other unlike he was with his wife. She made him feel young and alive. Permission had been implied by Bernadette when she offered to help Becky expand her coffee shops throughout the County. That included no intercourse. Becky imagined this had happened before but never asked Jackie about it. At one time she thought Peg had been "a girlfriend" but learned that was not the case. She enjoyed living with Joshua as a cover and as a friend who did have intercourse with her occasionally. Being friends with Peg as she ascended into the Calvanese family and the campaign was exciting. It was a long way from where she was over four years ago. They had been together but never in his boat at night, it seemed off limits like making love in his house with her.

"Becky...you see those stars over there in Orion's Belt?" With his arm around her thin waist, he pointed the other towards the sky Jackie had Becky's full attention. Well, two of those bright ones are amazingly different stars."

She smiled and leaned into Jackie as she stared up at the starry sky.

"The brightest star in the sky is Sirius, like the satellite radio, it's only 8.6 light years away. The other bright one is Betelgeuse, which is the tenth brightest star in the sky. They seem close, don't they?" Jackie smiled at his question and kissed her.

Becky kissed him back fully wanting more but knowing to wait and answer the question. She pulled away for a second and eyed the sky. "They do Jackie. How many light years away is Betelgeuse?"

"643 light-years…meaning that what we're seeing is light a century before Columbus sailed to America as opposed to light from 2016." Jackie looked at Becky's pretty face with affection.

"Holy shit Jackie…that doesn't make sense. Betelgeuse must be a massive star?"

"It just goes to show you that things can seem to come from similar places but are vastly different. We can never be satisfied with what we know. If we win this election, we can't stop listening to the people…especially those far away."

They sat back down on the deck, as Becky started kissing Jackie like she had just felt his gravitational force. She rubbed on his leg with her pelvis as he went under her blouse to feel her breasts. She was on fire as orgasms finally permeated her entire body. She stayed on him forever as his arms rubbed her back up and down. Tears flowed down her face. She finally lifted her head to see Jackie, "I've never been so happy!"

***

Peg turned towards Paul who was lightly sleeping. She lifted her head to meet his lips to kiss him. Slowly he came to life as she rolled on top of him. Soon they were making love with Peg doing the work on top. After they both reached sleepy satisfaction, she rolled off him and heard something coming from the lake. She sat up and walked naked to the door to look outside to see nothing but a peaceful shore and water in total darkness. The camp was silent. Her nudeness caught Paul's attention as she headed back to bed. "You look great even in the darkness honey…" Paul softly mumbled. He sat up to greet his wife as she got back in bed to cuddle with him. "What were you looking at?"

"I thought I heard something coming from the lake." She said quietly as she nestled into his chest.

"You have better hearing than I do and probably a fourth cone of vision that Jackie mentioned. That was so cool." He kissed her generously.

"I wish I had night vision and hearing like a dog. I'll have to work on that," she smiled as she closed her eyes next to his chest.

"Probably Jackie just scooting around the lake and checking out all the little inlets. He doesn't sleep much, and he loves to go out into the darkness."

Chapter 50

Luckily, the warm water helped Becky swim to shore. It had been since being a teenager on a high school swim team that she swam a mile, but now it was her talent at backstroke and floating on the water that was keeping her alive. She had dove off the boat. *The shot must have hit Jackie on the deck and the boat went haywire*, she assumed as her body was buzzing with energy. *I had no choice with the boat going sideways and speeding up*, she relived the horror as she stroked one arm over another. Jackie had just taken over the helm and was turning around the boat to head back when the bullet slumped him forward and pushed the accelerator control without steering. Becky screamed but abandoned ship without a life preserver. She freestyled two hundred yards before stopping to see anything behind and heard the crashing of the boat on some rocks near the shoreline. She continued, hoping to find a shore and the campsite soon to get help and find Jackie and the boat. *Hopefully, the bullet was not life-threatening*, she prayed, as she looked at the sky and saw Sirius and Betelgeuse sparkling overhead to confirm her direction. *It had to be an accident*, she thought, *who would shoot Jackie?*

She cried out.

She made it ashore in fifteen minutes, dripping wet, and went straight to Peg and Paul's tent. Peg got her undressed, dried off, and in a long tee shirt within minutes as she relayed the story to Paul and Peg. Helicopters started combing the perimeter of the lake within thirty minutes. Finally, they saw an explosion and could not get to the boat to save Jackie. The local police would let the boat burn and identify the body in the morning at the hint of light.

The hunters got to the boat, removed the bullet from Jackie's neck poured and untraceable solvent, and remotely started the fire. The evidence would show no signs of entry, blood, or foul play. It would be ruled an accident probably from falling asleep as the speculation would say. The burned body was taken to the coroner.

Following instructions from Paul, Becky changed her clothes quickly and got into bed with Joshua, who slept through everything. She would not be connected in any way with the "accident." She lay there, turned away from Joshua, with her eyes wide open and adrenalin pouring throughout her body. Finally, just before sunrise, she fell asleep for an hour before everyone was awoken to meet around the campfire.

Paul held his mother with his other brothers and Peg to his left as he announced his father's death. Within the hour, media of all types would be there, and he planned to have the camp gone. "Jackie has died in a terrible boat accident." The silence turned into moans. "We must clear out as soon as possible and get to the hotel outside Gainesville. I will address the media at 10 a.m. Please hold your grief and get it together for Jackie to carry this campaign on."

After packing and leaving the tents for the crew to clean up, Peg was on Route 20 driving while Paul worked three cell phones. The convention brokers would work with him on a replacement because Jackie's money was holding the campaign and the state-wide party together. Two hundred million dollars goes a long way.

The Calvanese brothers and Bernadette would be the main force for the new slate of candidates. Paul put his shock and grief aside because he could not imagine another four years of Republican control in his home state. After getting into the hotel and meeting several delegate chairpersons, the idea came to him. It was radical but it could work.

Normally the lieutenant governor candidate would want to run as governor but in this case, he did not fit the charismatic profile of Jackie at all. Colonel Lucian Lamar was part African American and

Seminole Indian and was Baptist, He retired military with a great administrative background as a commanding officer of Fort Bragg which bordered Georgia and Alabama. He was a council member for the City of Tampa for many years. Hardworking and loyal. Jackie picked him because he had the perfect complementary talents to himself. He would be asked to stay on the ticket.

The Comptroller candidate was a former accountant with the Calvanese business in the eighties before he was set up in politics by Francis Calvanese in Orange County. Frederico (known as Rico) Geumsaek was Hispanic, Korean, Catholic, and a Florida native. His connections to the Calvanese were deeply buried as he became involved in Orlando investments on his own and was a state delegate for two terms. He would stay as well.

The Secretary of State was Celeste Williams, half African American and half German American and Jewish. She was a rising star in Florida and would be a replacement candidate if she were not so perfect for the Florida job of Secretary of State. Her credentials as a lawyer were impeccable as both a prosecutor and a private attorney. And spent time at the State Department in the diplomatic corps in several countries in Europe. She spoke English, Spanish, German, and Italian.

It was an all-star line-up to back up the ultimate charismatic candidate in Jackie Calvanese. Paul was certain his idea would check all the boxes and keep the line-up close to being intact. He thought, *this will show we can handle a crisis without missing a beat*

The mood around the hotel was sullen and quiet. He and Peg took hundreds of visitors' condolences in his suite. The other brothers were dispatched to be with their families and the main staff. They would all meet at nine a.m. before the ten-a.m. media event. The first Convention event was set to start Wednesday at noon. The nominations would be Thursday night with the acceptance speeches Friday night. As the last visitors left the room, Paul took Peg into the bedroom.

"Let's talk about replacing my father on the ticket. You're the only one I trust to tell my decision to and get valuable feedback." Paul looked sullen but alert.

"Can I put my two cents in, or have you made up your mind?" Peg said seriously.

"Sure sweetie…I'm all ears!" as Paul forced a smile.

"I think Celeste Williams would be perfect. She is a great campaigner and charismatic." Peg said with a rare enthusiastic tone for the last eight hours.

"I agree Peg. She's perfect…for Secretary of State. But we don't have an ironclad connection to her as Governor. We need a solid no-doubt connection and a runaway winner to sweep both houses of legislators. She might eke out a victory but I'm not here for that. Neither was Jackie… Anybody else?" His emotions were showing life.

"Yes, you…Mr. Calvanese!" She said with a kiss on his lips and a huge smile.

"You know I would be terrible as a campaigner and besides my job is harder to do. Nope, that doesn't work either…anybody else?"

"Nope…I give up…what have you got Columbo?"

"Her name is Peg Patterson Calvanese!" Paul unleashed a smile that brought tears to his eyes as he found a chair in front of the bed. He took out his handkerchief dried his eyes and blew his nose.

Peg stood motionless with her stomach suddenly in her throat. It was the closest to throwing up in years. Her neck felt a pain that went between her shoulders. *Maybe I'm having a heart attack,* she feared. So, she took deep breaths quietly and calmed herself down. Paul seemed unaware of her reaction because he seemed like a man that had done his job and he was relieved. He was certain it would work. Peg was perfect. Her story was out of central casting for Florida. She would win in a landslide. And she was capable and smart. She would need help but that would be no problem. Money was not a problem for any kind of consultant needed. They had a plan that Jackie had laid out. He would help her follow it.

She moved a few steps and found the chair opposite Paul's. Her voice would work but it was all choked up, *I will sound like a moron talking,* she thought. "Paul…I ummm…know…umm….errrrrr. I know…umm….errr. I know you do not…. um….err joke around." Paul got up and brought her water and one for himself. She nodded thanks and gulped it down. "So really…what the fuck are you talking about?"

"Sweetheart…all of this is a shock, but it came to me this morning. You are perfect! You just have to deliver or read a speech and accept the nomination. We will have three weeks to get you ready for eight weeks of campaigning. Which you were going to do anyway!"

"I have two years of being a schoolteacher, otherwise I'm a beach bum for most of my life."

"Floridians love that shit. That's your strength! People will relate to you, and you look great my dear."

"O so my looks will get me over the top?"

"You know what I mean…what do you say? I would not ask you if I thought it would fail." Jackie would be proud. Bernadette will be ecstatic. Every one of my brothers loves you. It would give a whole lift to the campaign."

"Okay, Paul…I'll do it!" She jumped into his arms, fell into the bed, and cuddled for thirty minutes then uttered "Let's get some food and tell everyone."

"That a girl, my sweetheart! You will save my Sunshine State."

Epilogue

Eight months later under a nice big canopy on the beach in front of the Calvanese mansion, Joshua, Becky, and Peg enjoyed a minute of not talking as they noticed the usual train of beachgoers walking from the rocks of the Port to Cocoa Beach Pier or places in-between. The citizens and visitors to the Space Coast were a hundred yards or so away with various state troopers in beach attire scattered around in beach chairs to protect the Governor and her friends with another set of Troopers around the yard of the house for protection. The youngest female Governor in history had survived a campaign, won the hearts of Florida voters, and surged through the Spring legislative session with scores of victories. Finally, a long rest would start with a beach day with her trusted friends.

Being Governor had delayed her return to the beach mansion with her husband until April 2027. Peg Patterson Calvanese finally walked the streets of Cape Atlantic and rededicated North Atlantic Avenue from Lincoln Street to Washington Street as Jackie Calvanese Way. On the same day, she toured many streets and bars to feel reattached to her hometown. Her apartment on Lincoln Street was gone but the walk to the ocean was the same. The Old Beach Highway had more cars traveling very slowly from sightseers and citizens checking out the town. It was hard to get used to the entourage of troopers who tried to stay distant, but her safety was their only concern.

Becky broke the silence first, "Hey Peg…do we have to call you Madam Governor every time we address you?" she laughed.

Joshua defended her friend, "Holy cow Becky, she did the impossible, she deserves a little slack. I think her holiness is fine. Don't you Peg?" He slapped hands with Becky as Peg lifted her sunglasses.

"Do any of you fools have the ability to put a beer in my hands? Then you can call me Peg!" She kept a solemn face as Joshua jumped up and got three cold Stella's from the cooler and popped the tops. Peg took hers and smiled and lifted it in a toast, "to my first two real friends who are both good kissers…!" the beers clicked together, and lips touched all around. "Now this is an official beach day, and my name is Peg Patterson."

***

Soon after the election, Peg received a call from Cheverly Santiago, they met one night in a safe house in Orlando. State Troopers checked the house first and then stayed down the road.

Chevy came in from a back entrance in the darkness. "Congratulations misses Governor Elect Patterson or is it Calvanese?" they hugged for a moment.

"Peg Patterson sounds better, don't you? The campaign just pasted 'Peg Patterson' over 'Jackie' to save a lot of money on posters!" Peg smiled with confidence.

Chevy smiled and got right to business, "Madam, I thought I would give you some chatter about Jackie's death and the chance for investigation."

"Please… Chevy go ahead."

"It's pretty certain there was a bullet through his neck area that went into the lake somewhere from the Satellite data. We got an image of a heated body on the east side of the lake and another on the west side near the rocks. There is also evidence that the body and therefore the boat were torched with a fast-burning solvent, probably acetone or toluene. The Feds will proceed with a full investigation if the State wants them to intervene."

"Do you have any idea who did this?" Peg said in a monotone, emotionless voice.

"We doubt any Republican operative. It would be too obvious to track down with money trails. No drug or casino players would do this. Jackie was their ally. There was no chatter days before or after about death threats. It was there like there was a truce between all the crazies out there for the convention to happen without threats." She finished her words and looked at Peg with laser eyes hoping she might understand the unthinkable suspicion that she would never say out loud.

Peg thought about the hummingbird and its fourth cone to see ultraviolet light and how Jackie spoke of it on the boat to her and eleven others. One of the Apostles was the Judas! She suspected. "Thank you special agent Santiago, I think what's been done is done. I do not see the State wanting any assistance from the FBI on this matter. I do appreciate your help and anything in the future that you think I should know."

"Very well madam Governor-Elect," she smiled and turned off her eyes and looked away. As she got to the door, she turned back to Peg and finished her thought, "The message from Brooks, Phillip, and myself is congratulations on a job well done and we are always just a phone call away." With that, she pulled out a phone from her pocket and handed it to her. "You might want to put this in a safe place just in case you need it."

"Thank you, Chevy,…be safe!" Peg put the phone in her pocket and headed to the front door shaking her head thinking to herself about the twelve apostles on the boat listening to Jackie's last speech and in big letters in her head it came to her…BERNADETTE! She let out a quiet "WOW!"